Years of Grace

Phyllis Crossland

Grace Bramall

Years of Grace

A BIOGRAPHICAL STORY OF LIFE IN RURAL ENGLAND 1893–1973

Phyllis Crossland

The **Hallamshire** Press
1994

*To Mary Emma, a willing worker whose patience, cheerfulness
and loyalty to my mother were an essential part of my early life.*

Copyright © 1985, 1994 Phyllis Crossland

**This edition published by The Hallamshire Press
The Hallamshire Press is an imprint of
Interleaf Productions Limited
Exchange Works
Sidney Street
Sheffield S1 3QF
England**

First published by Bridge Publications, 1985

Typeset by Interleaf Productions Limited
Printed in Great Britain by
The Cromwell Press, Wiltshire

British Library Cataloguing in Publication Data

Crossland, Phyllis
  Years of Grace:Biographical Story of
  Life in a Rural Area of England,
  1850–1973. – New ed
  I. Title   II. Freeman, Bruce
  942.825082092

  ISBN 1-874718-45-8

Contents

Photographs

Acknowledgements

I AM PLEASED to express my thanks to all who assisted in the production of this book. Firstly, I am grateful to my family. The idea for such a book was originally suggested by my daughter Julia who also supplied the title when the writing was finished. Many thanks are due too to my husband for various items in the story material as well as for his moral support, and to my other daughters for their interest and constructive criticism throughout. I am greatly indebted to my sister Betty for her loan of photographs and valuable help with information, especially in the later chapters. For confirmation of family details in the earlier chapters I am grateful to my uncle, Mr George Spenceley, my late aunts, Gladys Hill, Jessie Bramall and Annie Spenceley, also my Purseglove cousins.

Other information, freely given by Mr Norman Vaughton and relatives of the late Stanley Illingsworth and Bill Marsh, was particularly appreciated, bearing in mind that sad memories might have been awakened.

In searching for confirmation of other facts I was willingly assisted by the excellent library services at Penistone, Barnsley, Stocksbridge and Sheffield, whose staff were invariably pleased to help.

My thanks also to Mr Steele of Oxspring School for access to the old log book, to Ray Hearne of the WEA and to the many others whose interest and good wishes contributed in making the work more pleasurable.

Not least, I must say that the initial encouragement I received from the Yorkshire Arts Association was an added incentive to write.

If I have inadvertently omitted to acknowledge any other help that was given in any way, I take this opportunity to do so now.

Phyllis M. Crossland
Trunce Farm, Greenmoor
August 1994

Foreword

The *Years of Grace* were the lifespan of the author's mother, Grace Bramall, née Grace Spenceley.

Great-grandfather James Spenceley was a Swaledale man who came south to find work in the coalmines. Grace herself was born, in 1893, in what Sir Walter Scott in the first words of *Ivanhoe* fittingly calls 'that pleasant district of merry England . . . watered by the river Don'— a district where it has been my privilege to spend most of my life. Her parents, James Jr and Elizabeth, kept the Victoria Tavern at Cranemoor, a steep-streeted village of stone cottages hidden in the valley of the Yorkshire Dove, four miles south-west of Barnsley.

Along with cheerfulness, industriousness and a fund of sound, practical sense, Grace was blessed with an eye and memory for detail shared by her elder daughter, Phyllis Crossland, who here narrates her story. Her earliest recollection was of the mug that she was given, at the age of four, to mark Queen Victoria's Diamond Jubilee.

Grace remembered Cranemoor as a place where the 'bush telegraph' was operated by knocking on party walls, where the local Lady Bountiful, Mrs Neville, bestowed gifts on the not-always-deserving poor and where, when attending balls at the 'big house', men were expected to put on white gloves for fear their hands might soil the ladies' gowns.

When her father became licensee of the 'Travellers Inn', which stood at the junction where a minor road crossed the Sheffield-to-Halifax turnpike, Grace, the fourth of his eleven children, was called on to assist with the cleaning. Each week she scrubbed the stone-flagged taproom floor and then put down fresh sawdust. Each night she emptied out the brass spitoons, so useful to the chewers of 'Thick Twist' and to miners and quarrymen with chest complaints, afterwards polishing the outsides with black lead (the substance used, along with 'elbow grease' to shine black Yorkshire ranges). Blanche, her elder sister, had the pleasanter job of providing the piano accompaniment for those Saturday customers who, when emboldened by drink, would treat the assembled company to a song.

Grace's adult life was destined to be spent within a few miles' radius of her birthplace. When seventeen, full of vitality, with grey eyes, luxuriant dark brown hair, a trim waist and a flair for dressing well, she met handsome, black-haired Ernest Bramall at night school. He was two years her senior. Ten years later (James Spenceley did not believe in encouraging teenage romances) they were married and settled first at Willow Lane and later at Coates Farm which, like many in that upland area, was in the author's words 'essentially a grass farm, geared to the needs of the butchering business'. There two daughters and four sons were born.

Ernest's father, Dyson Bramall (it was a local idiosyncrasy to give a boy his mother's maiden name) was a butcher who sold meat from a horse-drawn cart and also killed pigs for those householders who reared them to supplement the family diet—a ritual here recorded in great detail, from the moment the animal was roped to a 'plonk' to the making of brawn and the curing of hams and flitches.

Dyson's brother, known as 'Bill Brammer' or 'owd Bill', feckless, noisy, drunken but likeable, and a habitué of the 'Travellers Inn', is one of the more-than-lifesize characters with whom the book abounds. Proud of his strength, he once pulled a cart full of coal up the steep road from the River Don to Penistone Workhouse.

Grace died, aged eighty, in 1973, after thirty-three years of widowhood. She had lived through two world wars. To readers of her daughter's generation, the most nostalgic chapters may prove those which describe life at Coates during the second of these.

In December 1940, Grace heard bombs fall during the Sheffield 'blitz', sounding much nearer than twelve miles away, and hoped a stray one would not hit her home. Sometimes waves of German planes droned overhead, their target Liverpool. (It was said, I recall, that on moonlit nights they followed the gleaming metals of a goods line joining the Sheffield-to-Manchester railway at Penistone.)

She schemed to save sugar to make cakes and pies, and to sweeten the blackberries growing in profusion along the country lanes. With shop tomatoes kept 'under the counter' for favoured customers, a neighbour found a ready sale for those cultivated in his greenhouse.

Like her neighbours, Grace put up cheerfully with standing on crowded public transport. (The Yorkshire Traction or 'Tracky' Company, I recall, put the seats round the sides of its single-decker buses to leave more standing room.)

A minor but irritating wartime shortage was that of wallpaper. House-proud Grace, ashamed of the appearance of one of her rooms, took the Traction Company's bus to Penistone and a 'boneshaker' the eight twisting miles on to Holmfirth, having heard that a few rolls could be obtained there. (Perhaps she would have thought it slovenly to use one of the marzipan-like blocks being sold to rub on and freshen old paper.)

How my father would have sympathised with her! He made a comparable wartime Odyssey. When the rollers on my mother's wringer burst, he took them to York for re-covering (two return journeys on a bus and three wartime trains), having seen a notice in a small shop there advertising this service.

Through being in a designated 'green belt', the countryside Grace knew is little changed. The 'Victoria Tavern' has gone, and the school that she attended is to close, but the rest of Cranemoor remains unspoilt. The 'Travellers Inn' still welcomes customers, though the old turnpike road is now the Penistone Bypass.

With its footpaths, lanes and panoramic views, the area is popular with weekend walkers from the neighbouring conurbations. Those of them who read *Years of Grace* will in future see it not merely as attractive scenery, but as the background to characters and events which, had Mrs Crossland not recorded them, would have passed into undeserved oblivion. Readers who lack first-hand experience of it will enjoy making the acquaintance of this little-known corner of Yorkshire.

Margaret Ottley
Hoyland, Barnsley
May 1985

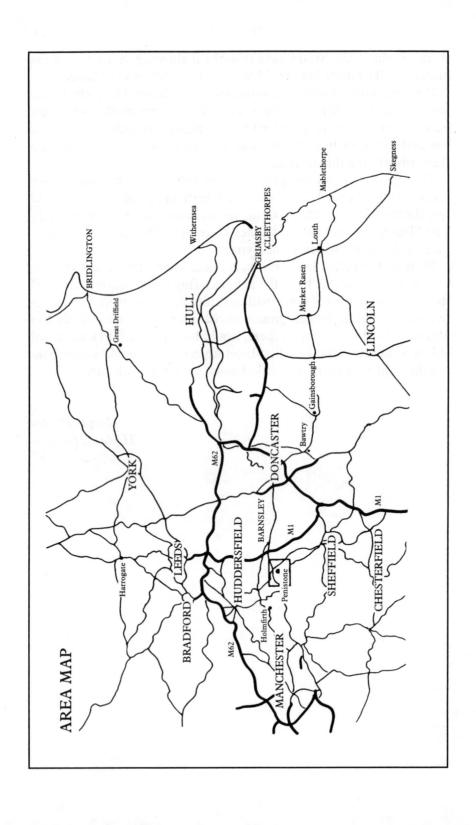

AREA MAP

LOCATION MAP

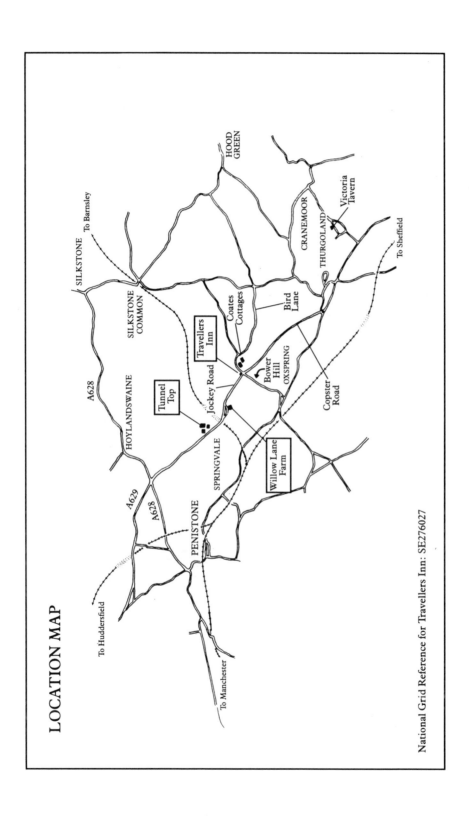

National Grid Reference for Travellers Inn: SE276027

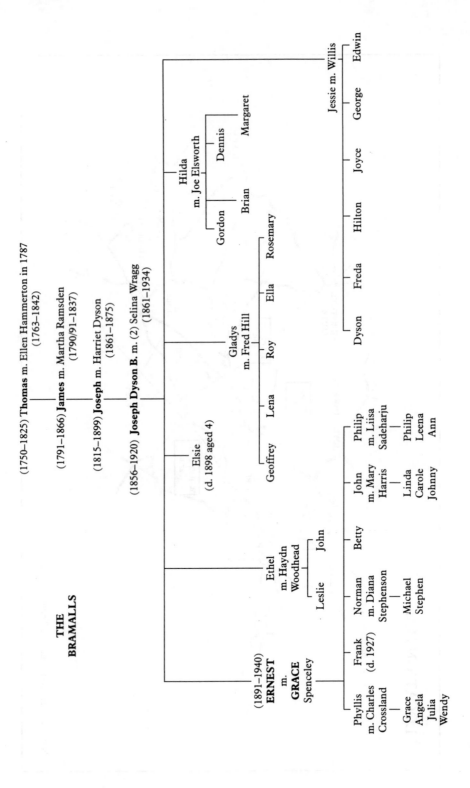

THE
SPENCELEYS

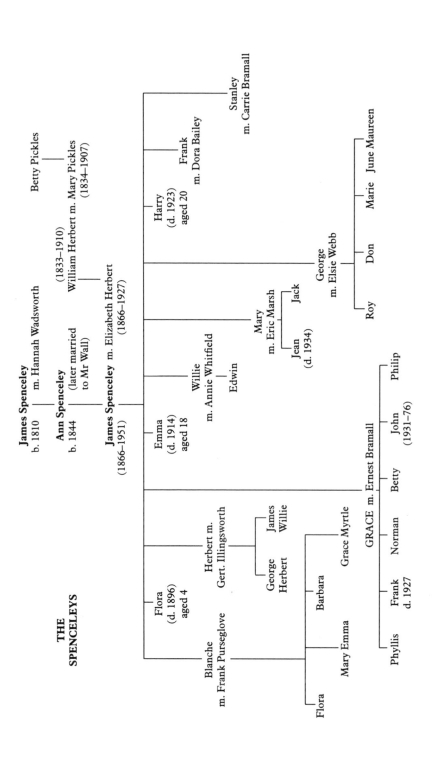

James Spenceley
b. 1810
m. Hannah Wadsworth

Betty Pickles

Ann Spenceley
b. 1844
(later married
to Mr Wall)

(1833–1910)
William Herbert m. Mary Pickles
(1834–1907)

James Spenceley m. Elizabeth Herbert
(1866–1951)   (1866–1927)

Stanley
m. Carrie Bramall

Frank
m. Dora Bailey

Harry
(d. 1923)
aged 20

Marie   June   Maureen

George
m. Elsie Webb

Don

Roy

Mary
m. Eric Marsh

Jack

Jean
(d. 1934)

Willie
m. Annie Whitfield

Edwin

Emma
(d. 1914)
aged 18

Flora
(d. 1896)
aged 4

Herbert m.
Gert. Illingsworth

James
Willie

George
Herbert

GRACE m. Ernest Bramall

Philip

John
(1931–76)

Betty

Norman

Grace Myrtle

Barbara

Blanche
m. Frank Purseglove

Frank
d. 1927

Mary Emma

Flora

Phyllis

CHAPTER 1

Beginning at Cranemoor

'PLEASE TEACHER 'AVE CUMMED,' chirped the gipsy-looking little three-year-old, her round face upturned to the schoolmistress. Her long dark hair hung roughly down her back because it had lost its ribbon. Her dress, reaching almost to her booted feet and concealing the short, sturdy legs, was covered by a frilled pinafore. This had been clean earlier in the day, but had since acquired dust from the lane.

Grace's arrival caused some amusement amongst the older children assembled in school. It was not every day that they were interrupted in their lessons by the premature appearance of a three-year-old anxious to join them. The teacher, no less amused than her scholars, looked down kindly into the young grey eyes confronting her and, to the child's announcement, made reply, 'Yes, I see you have, but does your mother know you've come?' On being told she didn't, Grace was instructed nicely to return home as her mother would be wanting her. She was told with a smile that she could come again to school when her mother said she was old enough.

Grace was the fourth child of James and Elizabeth Spenceley. She was born on the twenty-fifth of March, 1893, at Victoria Tavern in the small village of Cranemoor in the southern part of Yorkshire's old West Riding. Her father had been born in that village too, at a house in Brick Row, just a little further up the Nook from Victoria Tavern. He was the grandson of another James Spenceley who had come down to South Yorkshire from Swaledale in the early part of the nineteenth century to work as a coalminer. Grace's father had been brought up by his grandmother because his mother Ann was unmarried and working away in service at Harrogate. The Spenceley household was quite a large one for, though his grandfather had died two years before he was born, there were several of Ann's brothers and sisters still living with their mother in Brick Row. James was regarded more as a younger brother than a nephew by these uncles and aunts, who usually referred to him as 'our Jimmy'. To the end of his long life James never knew who his father was, and neither did anyone else. At least, no information on the subject was ever forthcoming from anyone.

James showed great promise as a scholar during the few brief years he was allowed education. On one occasion when Mr Renshaw, headmaster at Thurgoland school, was taking his top class for arithmetic, he posed a certain problem which no one was able to solve. Somewhat exasperated, he declared to one big boy, 'Go fetch little Jimmy Spenceley here, he'll do it for you.' The boy hurried off to the lower class and soon returned with young James who, at barely seven years old, proved the master's assumption correct by solving the problem.

During James's childhood there had always been a strong affection between him and his grandmother Hannah. Unhappily for him she died when he was twelve. In the previous year he had to leave school to earn his own living. Though he had loved his learning and taken full advantage of what school had to offer, he accepted as inevitable the fact that this must be cut short. Education then for all working-class children stopped at eleven or twelve, irrespective of their talents and abilities. James, however, did not follow his uncles into the coalmine. At first he worked as errand boy and porter for a grocer called Mr Laycock in the next village of Thurgoland. It was not only groceries that he delivered to customers. Mr Laycock owned a hand-operated sewing machine which he hired out for sixpence a week. One of James's duties was to take this machine to the women who wanted it and collect it again when they had finished with it. Delivery was by means of a hand-cart which James, with some effort, pushed to the various destinations where the machine was needed. Often it was necessary to negotiate a stile, in which case he had to lift the sewing machine over first and then the hand-cart before resuming his journey.

Later on he served his apprenticeship as a wiredrawer, to which work he applied the same diligence and conscientiousness as he had shown during the brief period of his schooldays. When, at the age of twenty-three, he married Elizabeth Herbert, he was a tall, well-built, good-looking young man, upright not only in physique but in character too.

Grace's mother, Elizabeth, was also twenty-three when she married. Fairly tall and of smart, attractive figure, she was a daughter of William and Mary Herbert. Elizabeth was already living at Victoria Tavern because her father was publican there. He was, however, first and foremost a miner, as were most of the male Herberts who were prolific in Cranemoor a century and more ago. William had worked down the pit as a 'trapper' when only eight years old, his job being to open and shut doors to allow for the passage of coal-tubs. Often he sat in darkness because his candle was finished. It would seem he was quite a tough character because, in spite of early deprivations, he well surpassed his allotted three-score years and ten. When he retired from coalmining, he worked as a gardener on the Wortley estate nearby.

William's wife had been born Mary Pickles. As a girl Mary had lived at Low Engine, quite a remote place across some fields from Cranemoor. Her mother Betty had been an incomer to the district from Low Moor, Bradford. Elizabeth Herbert was named after her grandmother and remembered being told that, when she was a young woman, Betty used to milk a cow in Wortley Park. Whether the cow belonged to Betty or whether she was milking it for someone else as part of her duties is not clear. There is a possession of Betty's that is still in the keeping of one of her descendants and still useful, though it must be at least a century and half in age. It is a brass preserving pan which Betty Pickles handed down to her daughter Mary who, in turn, left it to her daughter Elizabeth. In due course it passed to Grace and is now the property of her daughter. Just how many pounds of jam and jelly have been made in it would take some reckoning.

When the Herberts left Victoria Tavern, James and Elizabeth Spenceley became the occupants. During the next nine years while they were living there, six children were born to them, their names being Blanche, Herbert, Flora, Grace, Emma and Willie.

In that year of 1896 when Grace had her early preview of school, everybody in Cranemoor knew everybody else. Most of the houses were by the sides of the long, unmade road which ran downhill the length of the village from Top o' t'Heights to Cranemoor bottom. At Top o' t'Heights the Cranemoor road joined the Sheffield-to-Halifax turnpike road which, at that time and for long years afterwards, was still referred to by that name even though the Turnpike Trusts and tollgates had ceased to exist. Apart from a few farms and smallholdings, the other main centre of population in Cranemoor was the Nook. This was, and still is, a narrow lane forking off from the main village road to bend back again further along to rejoin the road near the top of the hill. Victoria Tavern was situated at the lower end of the Nook. The small school, which at that time accommodated only infant children, was about a hundred yards further downhill, being more or less in the middle of the village. On reaching the age of seven, Cranemoor children had to attend the school at Thurgoland.

Grace's father and mother were always fully occupied by essential duties, the one working long hours at the wire mill during the day and attending to the tavern in the evenings, the other caring for a growing family. Besides looking after her children, Elizabeth had always to be on hand to serve the daytime customers who called for a drink, for at that period inns were open all day. Whilst this daytime trade was not very brisk, it did mean that Grace's mother was tied to the place all the time. The children who were not at school had to amuse themselves by playing with one another round their house or in the lane. It was safe to play in the lane in those days as there was no motorised traffic; only the occasional horse-drawn cart would pass up the Nook at a very slow pace.

The wire mill where James worked as an apprentice, and during the nine or so years afterwards, was Wordsworth's mill or, as some folk called it, the New Mill, there being another, older wire mill not far away upriver. Both mills were situated by the River Don and near to Old Mill Lane at the bottom of Thurgoland. James walked to his work, of course, as did everyone else in the village. There was no transport other than one's own two legs. Wordsworth's mill was only about a mile distant as he could take a short cut over the fields by footpath much of the way. James Spenceley enjoyed working at Wordsworth's but it had one big disadvantage. When there happened to be a spell of dry weather, as usually occurred during summer, there was, as a result, insufficient water flowing downriver to New Mill to keep it working. Consequently, the wiredrawers had to be laid off for a period, so losing pay.

In that same year as Grace had tried to gain admittance into school, her father decided to change employers. He was offered work by another firm of wiredrawers, Winterbottoms of Oxspring. This meant he had a two-mile walk each way, as Oxspring was the other side of Thurgoland at the bottom of the long, steep road known as Thurgoland Bank. Whilst the toil up this hill after a long day's work was rather tiring, James was better off financially at the Oxspring mill. There was always regular work because, being higher up the river than Wordsworth's, it got the water first and, even in a dry spell, this was adequate for work to carry on.

Just as James was changing his work, the happy prospect of better wages was sadly marred by a tragic happening in the family. Grace's little sister Flora, just a year older than her, was taken suddenly ill with diphtheria and died in the space of two or three days. She had appeared quite well one evening, running over the field to meet her father as he returned from work. The next evening she was very ill, unable to find comfort either in her mother's arms or in those of her grandmother. Mary Herbert had always been popular with her grandchildren, and Flora in particular had often persuaded her to stay overnight when she visited them. Now, even her well-loved grandma could do nothing to ease her, much as she tried. To everyone's great sorrow, that cruel disease beat them. Although Elizabeth Spenceley had many more children and many troubles in her life, she never forgot the pain of losing her four-year-old daughter. In after years she would tell her other children about Flora who, in appearance, had been a complete contrast to Grace. Whereas the latter was dark with straight hair, her sister had been fair, her hair light and curly. Apparently the two little girls had got on well together as playmates during the short time they had together, but Grace had only retained a vague mental picture of Flora, as she was only three herself at the time of her sister's death. The little girl was buried in Thurgoland churchyard and it was ironic that her father's first week's wages from Winterbottom's mill were spent in buying her coffin. No doubt Grace missed the companionship of her sister during the months that followed her death. The two older children were already at school and it could have been a feeling of loneliness that prompted her to seek early admission there.

The occasion of that first visit to school had not been remembered by the girl herself. She had heard about it in later years from her mother, who had been given a first-hand account of the incident by the teacher concerned and other children who had witnessed it. Thinking it quite amusing, she retained the little episode in memory and recounted it to her own children in due course.

The first clear recollection Grace had was of an important event that took place when she was four. This was the big celebration staged in the village to commemorate Queen Victoria's Diamond Jubilee. Grace remembered being amongst the crowd of people in a field; she remembered running and playing games, and being given a bun to eat. All the children, including herself, also received a mug with a picture of Queen Victoria on it. This was treasured to begin with but must have met with an accident at some stage, since it didn't remain intact long enough for her children to see it.

The village community of Cranemoor was very closely knit in those days of the nineteenth century. It was reputed to have been such that news of any stranger appearing at one end of the village was quickly communicated to those living at the other end before the person had walked halfway down. Whilst there was possibly some exaggeration in this statement, it was certain that the villagers welcomed news from outside. Some of the women rarely left their homes, especially those who were old or who had young children. The only interest they had apart from working with their own families was what their neighbours' families were doing and any other news they could communicate. It was true that, when strangers did enter the village, their curiosity was aroused, and the feeling was that everybody should be informed. This, however, had to be done without the visitors being aware of what was happening.

In the absence of telephones, by far the quickest and best method of achieving this, especially where the houses were in rows, was by wall-knocking. The first observer of anything untoward would knock on the adjoining wall to her neighbour, who then did likewise to the woman on the other side of her. In this way the need for vigilance was swiftly communicated without the informers being seen from outside. Once the women were alerted, a discreet peep from behind the curtains would enlighten them as to what was afoot.

According to Grace's mother, there was a certain lady whose visits to the village were warmly welcomed by the miners' wives. She was Mrs Neville, a lady of substantial means, and wife of Colonel Neville, a retired military man. They lived in a large house quite near to Cranemoor and were noted throughout the area for their generosity and charitable deeds. Mrs Neville would often bestow gifts of food and clothing on needy families, making visits beforehand to ascertain where her help was most required. Whilst there were several people in Cranemoor who were genuinely poor, there were two or three, however, who imposed on their benefactress's good nature.

One of these women, alerted one day by the wall-knocking, slipped quickly to her window. Drawing her curtain slightly to one side she observed it was Mrs Neville who was approaching, having been sighted as she entered the village. In order to gain a greater degree of sympathy than she actually merited, the woman took quick action to prove her 'poverty'. By the time Mrs Neville entered her house she had taken off her blouse and was seated at the table, sewing box at hand, ostensibly mending the garment. The picture she presented was one of abject poverty as she intended it to do. Her visitor, looking most concerned, exclaimed in a voice expressing pity, 'Is that the only blouse you've got, my good woman?' Whereupon the woman, with downcast eyes, replied meekly, 'Yes it is Ma'am.' 'Well, we shall have to do something about it,' promised the good lady. Needless to say, before many days had passed, her carriage was at the woman's door and a manservant carrying into the

'Is that the only blouse you've got, my good woman?'

house a huge box that contained not only blouses but a large assortment of other garments too, all of good quality and showing little wear.

Mrs Neville held occasional balls at her large house. Showing typical generosity, she extended lavish hospitality at these times to the people from Cranemoor. This included a sumptuous supper, besides the music and dancing. Before his marriage, James Spenceley attended these balls which he would describe, long years afterwards, to his grandchildren. He said the ballroom floor was covered over with holland, a strong material resembling canvas. This was laid down over the carpet to facilitate the dancing. All the gentlemen had to wear white gloves so that their hands wouldn't soil the ladies' dresses.

It would seem these rare occasions were as bright splashes of light in his workaday existence for, when relating about them in his old age, his face would become animated with remembered pleasure. When, at eighty, he heard waltz music coming over the radio, he would hum the tune and move his hands and feet in time to the music. His granddaughter would hear him murmur, half to himself, 'They used to play this at Mrs Neville's ball.' The gleam in his eyes as he listened would suggest he was looking back beyond the cares, worries and work of sixty years to see a young man of twenty, wearing white gloves as he waltzed round a holland-covered floor.

Grace's mother was not allowed to go to those functions of the 1880s. William Herbert was always very strict in the upbring-ing of his children. He held the view that dancing was immoral and his daughters might easily be corrupted if they went to a ball, even though the hostess was such a respectable person as Mrs Neville.

Before Grace Spenceley was five she had her long-standing wish fulfilled by becoming a schoolgirl. She was the only child of her family then to attend the infant school in Cranemoor, since her older sister Blanche and brother Herbert had passed the age of seven and so graduated to the school at Thurgoland. Grace was very fond of going to school, and soon became an apt pupil. Besides learning quickly to read and write, she was evidently eager to absorb other knowledge that her teacher imparted. It is on record that she received a prize for scripture even before her fifth birthday. The *Thurgoland Parish Magazine* for March 1898 includes the information in a brief report of the annual children's entertainment that took place at Cranemoor infant school on Wednesday, January 26th of that year.

Grace's time as a scholar at Cranemoor was, however, of less than a year's duration. Her father had decided to uproot his family from that village and move to Oxspring, some three miles away. James had heard that the Travellers Inn there was needing a new licensee. As this public house was so much nearer to his work than was Victoria Tavern, he applied to the brewery for the tenancy and was pleased to be granted it. This meant that his walking time to and from Winterbottom's mill would be considerably lessened and he could therefore take over the tavern duties from his wife earlier in the evenings. The demands of her growing family made this increasingly necessary. So it was that the move was made.

James and Elizabeth no doubt had mixed feelings as the horse-drawn waggonette carrying their family and possessions moved slowly out of the Nook to lumber heavily up the village road. Grace remembered some of them crying because they were leaving Cranemoor. It seemed to her as if they were journeying to the other end of the country, with little chance of ever seeing the village again. Turning right by Top o' t'Heights onto the turnpike, the journey then took them through Thurgoland. Passing by the church they thought sadly of the one small member of their family they were leaving behind.

The ride in that waggonette was not a very comfortable one, this being due to the rough state of the roads. At the end of their journey Grace's mother showed great annoyance when, on unpacking their possessions, it was discovered that some of her best crockery had been broken by the jolting of the vehicle. It is possible, though not known for certain, that the Queen Victoria Jubilee mugs also came to grief at the same time.

The Spenceley family outside Travellers Inn

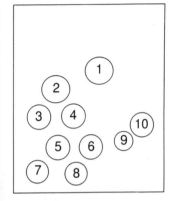

1 *James*
2 *Elizabeth*
3 *Grace*
4 *Marjorie (Madge) Buckle*
5 *Herbert*
6 *Blanche*
7 *Emma*
8 *Willie*
9 *Mary*
10 *Matilda (Tilly) Smith*

CHAPTER 2

Early Days at Travellers Inn

TRAVELLERS INN was to be Grace's home for the next sixteen years. Today it is still a public house, whereas the old Victoria Tavern at Cranemoor has long since been converted into a private dwelling. The outer structure of Travellers Inn is still basically the same as it was at the end of the nineteenth century, but nowadays the walls are white, the natural stonework having been covered over. Some of James's old customers might have to have a closer look today to ascertain that it really was their inn. If they ventured inside, the place would be quite unrecongnisable to them, as during recent years its interior has undergone extensive alterations.

The inn, which became the Spenceley family's new home, is situated about half a mile from Oxspring village on the Barnsley side. It stands at Four Lane Ends, or 'T'Fours' as local folk say, where the

A629 road from Thurgoland to Huddersfield is crossed by the Oxspring-to-Barnsley road. Because of its position at the crossroads, the inn too is often referred to as 'T'Fours'. Nowadays this place where the roads cross is quite a busy one, the Huddersfield road in particular carrying a fair amount of traffic.

At the end of the nineteenth century the scene at Four Lane Ends was vastly different. The roads were only roughly made and the traffic passing along them consisted of carts, waggons and an occasional trap or horse-drawn carriage. There were, of course, people on foot and animals being herded from one farm to another or to market. Across the road from Travellers Inn was a little old whitewashed cottage occupied by a family named Wright. This dwelling was one of the oldest in the area, dating from the seventeenth century at least, but probably earlier. It survived for another forty years after the Spenceleys took over the inn, but is no longer in existence. At the opposite side of the road near the other corner was a shop kept by a Mrs Saunders and her husband Dick. They had a son Walter and daughter Clara. The shop was a small general grocery store that served the needs of people living at Four Lane Ends and in the outlying farms. Adjoining the shop and its living accommodation were two more cottages. All these premises remain, but are greatly changed. Three cottages that were close to the inn on the same side of the road have now disappeared.

Grace continued her education in the village school at Oxspring, walking down Bower Hill each morning with her sister and brother. The country road with fields on either side was quiet and peaceful, so the half-mile walk was pleasant enough. At the bottom of Bower Hill they crossed the bridge over the River Don and then turned right to walk uphill again past the plantation of elm trees, which in spring was alive with the noisy calling of rooks. The last part of their walk took them past the Toll Bar, a small cottage which, in earlier times, had been the tollhouse serving that part of the turnpike road.

Oxspring School was less than twenty years old when Grace Spenceley became one of its pupils. It had been built in 1880 and accommodated all children from the age of five to the age when they left school to begin work, this being about twelve or thirteen at that time.

When Grace first attended the school the infants were taught in a gallery. To reach their places necessitated the ascent of a flight of steps from the yard outside. When settled aloft in the gallery the infants could, by looking down, see the older children in their classes on the floor below. After a time this arrangement was considered unsatisfactory. Following some minor accidents it was realised that a crowd of small children moving up and down a steep flight of stone steps could be

dangerous, especially since the steps had no protection on the outside. If a child was pushed or slipped off into the yard the consequences might be serious. Because of this fear the premises were later
altered so as to dispense with the gallery and steps. A classroom on
the ground floor was then allotted to the infants. The three Spenceley
children soon adjusted to life at their new school and continued to do
well in their lessons.

Elizabeth, their mother, was busier than before. Although her three
eldest children were at school during the day, she had the two youngest
ones, Emma and Willie, to look after at home. Travellers Inn was also
a bigger place than Victoria Tavern. There were more daytime customers calling, as might be expected considering its situation at the
crossroads, and since they called at all hours of the day Elizabeth was
constantly on duty. It was true her husband was home from Winterbottom's much sooner than before and able to take over the tavern
work when he'd had his meal, but there was always plenty of work
involved with the children. Less than a year after the family moved to
Four Lane Ends the next child was born, another girl whom they
named Mary after her grandmother. Willie, who was two when he got
this new sister, had of course been given his grandfather's name. The
girls, Blanche and Emma, were named after their aunts, Elizabeth's
sisters. Grace received her name in a more indirect way. When her
uncle John was a policeman at Golcar near Huddersfield, he was in
lodgings with a family by the name of Weville. They happened to
have a daughter called Grace, which prompted Elizabeth to give her
child the same name.

Apart from the pressures of work, Elizabeth soon began to have
those of worry too. Blanche was very ill with rheumatic fever, which
left her with a weak heart. Although she managed to continue her
schooling, she was never very strong after her illness. Had she been in
good health she would have been assisting her mother by the time
Mary was born, but as it was she could only be asked to do the light-
est of tasks. It was soon realised that some strong, permanent help
was needed at Travellers Inn. Before long this help materialised in
the form of Tilly.

Matilda Smith was engaged by the Spenceleys as a living-in maid.
She was known to everyone as Tilly and, during the next few years,
proved to be an invaluable help to all the family. Tilly was only small
of stature and slightly built, yet luckily possessed the strength and
tireless energy that was needed to enable her to carry out her many
duties. Though engaged initially as a nursemaid, she could well have
been described as a maid of all work, since she willingly undertook

washing, cleaning, cooking or anything else that needed doing. This was just as well because, when Elizabeth was confined with subsequent babies, the whole running of the house fell temporarily onto Tilly's shoulders.

Tilly had dark hair which was plainly dressed, being brushed straight back from her face and fastened up behind her head. She had good features and a pleasant manner in spite of all the work thrust upon her. Though she was busy from dawn to bedtime her tasks were performed with such patience and good humour as greatly endeared her to everyone. She was particularly good in caring for the young children and babies, who looked on her as a second little mother. Tilly was generous almost to a fault. Quite often, when she received her fortnightly wages, she would, at the first opportunity, spend a large part of it on food and clothes for her married sister's children. She held the opinion that they were more in need of it, which could well have been true.

The fact that a maid was employed in the Spenceley household did not mean that Grace was excused household chores. On the contrary, she began washing pots and glasses before she was tall enough to reach the sink, and had to stand on a box to make up for the deficiency in height. She had to assist from an early age because she was always regarded as being the strongest girl in the family. Her sister Emma, who was the next after her in age, was found to have a heart defect even more serious than Blanche's. She could do little of anything that required exertion. Sometimes she attended school, but more often than not had to be absent because she wasn't well. The doctor stressed that she must always take things steady and never hurry in any way. Grace, on the other hand, was seldom away from school, and retained vivid recollections of happenings there throughout her life.

As the nineteenth century drew towards its close, the main news of the day was concerned with the Boer War in South Africa. At Oxspring school the headmaster, Mr Cooper, took keen interest in the progress of the war and was anxious that his older boys did likewise. Grace remembered him having these pupils round his desk each morning to inform them of the latest developments in that far-off part of the British Empire. The relief of Ladysmith at the end of February 1900 caused great excitement amongst the scholars. When, in May, Mafeking was also relieved by the British soldiers, the jubilation was such that a half-day's holiday from school was granted to celebrate the achievement. Grace was too young to be one of the select band gathered around the teacher's desk. In any case, it was only the boys who were summoned to hear about the war. Mr Cooper evidently thought such things as battles and sieges were not meant for girls' ears. War did not concern womenfolk. The only way in which they could be involved was by knitting things for the soldiers.

At the beginning of the following year was the sad event which everyone heard about, girls and boys alike, not only in Oxspring but throughout the land. That was the death of Queen Victoria, the little old woman whose picture was on all those mugs she'd seen that day in the field at Cranemoor.

Grace's closest friend of those early days at Fours was her cousin Marjorie, or Madge as she was usually called. This girl was the same age as Grace. She was the only surviving child of Elizabeth's sister Blanche, who had married Arthur Buckle from Dodworth. They had kept the Horse and Jockey Inn there for a short period but Arthur had died at the early age of twenty-five, within a few months of the death of their two-year-old daughter Lilian Emma. Madge was a mere baby at the time, so could never remember her father or sister. Unfortunately her mother, Blanche, was an epileptic. The fits had begun when she was about fourteen, and became increasingly frequent as she grew older. Although Arthur Buckle had been aware of this he had been so attracted by Blanche's pretty face and agreeable personality that the fits had not deterred him from marrying her. After leaving the Horse and Jockey, Madge and her mother went to live with the grandparents, William and Mary Herbert, who had bought a small house at Copster.

Copster was the mile-long stretch of road between Four Lane Ends and Thurgoland. There were haif a dozen scattered dwellings along its length, four of these being small farms. The Herberts occupied the little cottage nearest to Travellers Inn and it took the children only a matter of minutes to visit each other. More often than not it was Madge who, at holiday times, was to be seen playing with her cousins at the Fours. Apart from the companionship, the atmosphere at her Aunt Lizzie's was less strained than in the house at Copster.

Though the children adored their grandmother Mary Herbert, who was kind, patient and understanding, they were very much in awe of their grandfather. William could not bear to see them having fun, and would frown upon the least signs of any frivolity. This attitude could perhaps have sprung from the deprivations of his childhood, when he was forced to spend much of his time in the darkness of a coalmine. Perhaps he had feelings of jealousy on seeing a new generation having fun, bitterly recalling there hadn't been much laughter in his own childhood. On the other hand, one might have thought it would have pleased him to see how things had improved since he was a boy back in the 1840s. As it was he reprimanded and chastised them severely for the slightest offences, so much so that the children kept out of his way whenever they could.

Madge was fair and pretty like her mother, but luckily was not similarly afflicted with epilepsy. She was healthy and fun-loving, making up for the restrictions imposed on her at Copster by enjoying to the full her time spent at Travellers with cousin Grace. Basically a happy girl in spite of her adverse circumstances, she remained a happy and well-loved person throughout her life. Having a good sense of humour, she would often see the funny side of something regarded by others as dire misfortune.

Years later, Madge would laughingly recall how she started making bread. She was only ten years old when, one Friday morning, her grandmother was seized with such a bad asthma attack as made her incapable of baking. 'You'll have to stay off school today Madge and make the bread,' Mary Herbert gasped out to her grand-daughter. When Madge showed apprehension, saying she wasn't sure how to do it, the older woman said she'd tell her just what to do. After following her grandmother's instructions, and expending much energy in the kneading operation, she was eventually praised for the satisfactory result. It was so satisfactory in fact that her grandmother declared, 'Well, now that you know how to do it, you can bake the bread every Friday, because I think you can do it better than me.' After that day Madge's seat in school was always vacant on Fridays. When the teacher first queried her absence, she had to reply, 'I can't come on Fridays any more—it's baking day.' Probably knowing of the family's predicament, the teacher never pressured Madge into attending on those days.

During their childhood, Grace and her cousin were often dressed alike. Because of this and their being so much together, they were usually mistaken for sisters by casual callers to the inn. In some ways Grace's mother did regard Madge as one of her children. She was sorry that the girl's own mother was incapable of looking after her and felt that, in a small way, she was helping her sister by taking Madge 'under her wing' sometimes.

In the first year of the new century another son was born to the Spenceleys. He was their eighth child and was christened George after his father's uncle, with whom he had lived in Brick Row at Cranemoor. Again Tilly coped cheerfully with the extra work that another new arrival brought.

Despite the growing numbers of her own brood, Aunt Lizzie, as Madge called her, still welcomed her niece into their family circle. On reflection, she might have considered that nine children weren't all that many more than eight if looked at collectively. Yet, with such a family, one could not become complacent. There was often one of them, usually Emma or Blanche, who wasn't well and needed special attention.

Much to everyone's surprise, when she was eight years old it was Grace, the tough one, who succumbed to illness. The dreaded diphtheria raised its evil head again to threaten a second member of the Spenceley family. James and Elizabeth watched with alarm those symptoms they had seen before, the feverishness, pain on swallowing, and swelling at the side of the neck. Anguished memories of their little girl Flora came flooding back to them from five years past. Agonisingly, they wondered whether they were going to lose Grace too. Fearing the worst, they summoned the doctor, who soon confirmed their suspicions.

The redness at the back of Grace's throat, with the tell-tale yellowish-white patches on the tonsils, were sure indicators of the disease. He ordered her to be confined to bed in a room to herself. The child felt very ill for two or three days, but the use of a steam kettle in the bedroom helped her to breathe better. The back of her throat was painted with iodine, not a very pleasant experience to remember. Whether the medical treatment she received was an improvement on that given to her sister five years earlier is not certain. Perhaps the disease attacked her less severely or, being older than her sister had been, she was stronger to withstand the attack. Her normally healthy constitution no doubt gave her a better chance of survival. Whatever the reasons, survive she did, though she had to remain resting in bed for most of a month. Sulphur candles were then burnt in the room to rid it of any lingering germs.

Once recovered from the illness, Grace was the sturdy, energetic and lively girl she had been before. Her mother thankfully realised that there were no lasting ill-effects as sometimes occurred after diphtheria. Reflecting that two of her daughters already had heart trouble, it was gratifying to know that this one hadn't. Moreover, that time in her life when she had diphtheria was the only time in all their years at Travellers Inn when Grace was ill enough to warrant staying in bed.

It seldom happened that any books were bought for the Spenceley children by their parents. There were rather too many children for this to be afforded. The books they did possess were mainly Sunday School prizes. Grace, however, did have one book bought for her by her mother, and this is still intact. It is a *Chatterbox* Annual for 1902. There are over four hundred pages of stories, anecdotes, poems and illustrations in the annual. The hard front cover has a colourful picture of two small children in Victorian dress sailing tiny boats on a small pond. Also on the front cover is printed the price of three shillings, which was a considerable amount to spend then on a child's book. Grace remembered receiving this book after she had had the diphtheria. It seems likely that her mother bought it as a special treat for her to look at during convalescence. Probably the mother's generosity came in part from the thankfulness she felt in knowing she still had this daughter on whom she could spend three shillings.

CHAPTER 3

Schooldays at Oxspring

IN 1902 was the coronation of King Edward the Seventh and Queen Alexandra. All the children who were in attendance at Oxspring School received a book to commemorate the event. This was entitled *King Edward's Realm*. Measuring about seven inches by five, the book has a strong hard back in red. The title on the front, and the small royal design surmounting it, are in gold printing. The information contained in its 224 pages is mainly the story of the British Empire and how the various countries belonging to it came to be under British rule. Grace's book and that of the boy who later became her husband are still in excellent condition after eighty-two years because they have always been carefully looked after.

Grace told her children in later years that King Edward and Queen Alexandra actually passed through the area when she was a pupil at

Oxspring School. Mr Cooper learned of the impending visit well in advance and, being a patriotic man, felt that his scholars and staff should express their loyalty in some way. He thought it fitting that the children should sing a suitable patriotic song for the royal pair as they passed by. His musical abilities, including singing, were quite considerable and, under his direction, the scholars diligently practised the song until they were trained to perfection. The first part of the song was:

> *Hail, hail the happy day that sees*
> *King Edward wear the crown,*
> *Which hath for long long centuries*
> *Spread wide its world renown.*
> *And hail, good queen who to us came*
> *Across the northern seas,*
> *We bless thee and we here proclaim*
> *Our love, O queen, for thee.*

When the big day arrived, the Oxspring scholars, including Grace Spenceley, sang with great zest and enthusiasm but alas, how disappointed were they and their teacher alike that the king and queen passed quickly by without acknowledging or even seeming to notice their effort to please them. Grace said, 'They never slowed down at all, but went past so quick that we didn't even get a proper look at them.'

Joseph Cooper was highly respected by his scholars. Though he was strict, and often wielded a cane to help him maintain order and discipline, he was generally regarded as a fair man and an excellent teacher. His hard work and dedication certainly showed good results as far as Grace and her contemporaries were concerned. The education they received at Oxspring equipped them well for their future as working boys and girls. It provided them with the basic tools that would be needed then and throughout adult life. These were the skills of reading, writing and arithmetic. Once acquired they would enable the children to cope successfully with life outside school when the time came. In schools generally during that period the emphasis was almost entirely on those subjects. Children were not encouraged to show initiative in school by doing their own thing. It was the teacher who ordered what should be taught, because he knew best what the children needed to know for their own benefit later on. It was felt there would be ample opportunity for them to exercise initiative when they left school and had to make their own way in the world. This certainly proved true in Grace's case and, fortunately, she was never found to be lacking in initiative in her later life, even though her time in school was ordered and formal.

Reading was learned mainly by the phonic method. Most of the pupils in Grace's class became good readers, and there was no one who couldn't read at all by the time he or she left school.

Writing was done in the traditional style of her father's schooldays, using loops to join tall letters. Grace maintained this style of writing throughout her life and it always remained beautifully neat, clear and legible. When looking through one of her school exercise books of 1904 to 1905, one gets the impression that more importance was attached to the quality of the writing rather than the quantity. Some of her essays filled only one side of the page, and were never longer than two sides. They did, however, neatly include all the necessary punctuation, as well as correct grammar and spelling. Besides the essays there are pages of copy-writing, exercises in grammar, and pieces of transcription connected with history and geography lessons. The fact that Grace had not been encouraged to write her essays at greater length might have been due to books and paper being in shorter supply to schools in those days. Judging from her writing ability, she was capable of writing more. Many of Grace's essays were on the subject of how she spent Sundays and holidays; others were about famous people or descriptions of foreign lands.

An old arithmetic book that she filled during the same period shows the various kinds of 'sums' that scholars had to do then. Knowledge and application of number tables were essential for the correct working out of these sums, since they involved much multiplying and dividing. Some examples of the arithmetic which Grace Spenceley did in 1904 were:

> Divide £3784 14s 2½d by fifty-nine
> £7285 14s 5½d x 95
> £ 88 18s 9½d x 595
> Reduce 3 years 29 weeks 5 days to hours
> Change 123,785,427 minutes to centuries,
>   years, months, weeks, days, etc.
> How many years of 365 days are there in
>   456,789,012 seconds?
> Change 137,809,241 drams to tons, cwt.,
>   qrs., lb., oz., drs.
> Divide the difference between 238 half-
>   crowns and 190 half-guineas by 17

These were purely mechanical sums which, providing the scholar had a thorough grounding in the four rules of number and the tables involved, could eventually be worked out correctly. Admittedly it took more than a little time to arrive at the answers, considering the only calculators available were the children's own brains. No one could doubt that those young brains got plenty of exercise in their arithmetic lessons. Apart from the mechanical sums, there were problems to be solved too. These included such questions as:

> If £16739 6s 8d was paid for 476 horses, find the cost of one.
> If a well has 750 gallons of water in it and a man fills a bucket 3 times a day for 24 days, and the bucket holds $3^1/_2$ gallons, how much would be left in the well?
> A coal dealer bought a ton of coal at 17s 6d a ton, and sold it at thirteen pence per hundredweight. What did he gain?
> A wheel is 2 yds. 2ft. 2ins. in circumference. How many times will it turn round in a distance of one thousand two hundred and twenty-five yards?
> If a man earns 9d per hour, how much will he earn in $1^1/_2$ months, allowing that he works 9 hours a day, 6 days a week?
> A girl lives 195 yds. 2ft. 6ins. from school, and another 300 yds. from school. How many inches has one to walk more than the other in going to school?
> If one dozen books can be bought for a sovereign, how many books can be bought for £1 8s 4d?
> At £3 17s $10^1/_2$d each, how many suits of clothes can be bought for £206 7s $4^1/_2$d?

To all these problems Grace had obtained the correct answers. In the whole book very few of her sums were wrong.

Mr Cooper taught history and geography to the older scholars. The history lessons were mainly involved with lives of famous people, and events connected with empire building, kings, soldiers and politicians. The transcriptions in Grace's English exercise book included information on the four Georges, Sir Robert Walpole, Lord Clive of India, William Pitt, Charles James Fox, Queen Victoria, and a short account of the fighting against Napoleon in Spain where that famous English soldier, Sir John Moore, was killed. The geography she was doing in her last year at school was of European countries, their seas, rivers and mountains. It was important to know the names of capital cities and what rivers they stood on, if any. She wrote an essay on

'The Playground of Europe', which then meant Switzerland, and another about Rome, 'The Eternal City'. She described 'The Baltic Sea', 'Gibraltar to Naples', and 'Glaciers and Icebergs'. They also had a lesson on Russia. Grace's impression of that country at the beginning of the twentieth century was vastly different from that of the modern scholar, eighty years later. In her 'Essay on Russia' in 1905 she writes:

> *The Russian people are very dirty and noisy, their hair is dirty and shaggy. They are a very ugly race of people. In Russia they are very ignorant and not one child in six goes to school. The Russians are also good-natured and friendly. They live chiefly on cabbage soup and black bread made of rye. St Petersburg was named after Peter the Great, who founded it in 1703.*

The schoolmaster initiated his pupils into the art of map drawing too. The maps were done in pen and ink, since coloured pencils and crayons were not available for them. Grace took pride in her mapping book, showing the various countries of Europe. The maps were neatly done and she kept it, along with other school books, for many years.

It is doubtful whether she and her contemporaries learned much science. The only bit of evidence that she learned any at all is a short description in her writing book of one lesson on 'Gas'. She wrote:

> *On Thursday we had an object lesson on Gas. First of all a boy brought a gas lamp. Then the teacher pulled it to pieces to show us the works of it. The teacher showed us how gas was made. He got some calcium and some water. At the top part of the lamp there is a place to put water in, then there is a perforated tube and at the bottom part of the lamp there is a place for the calcium. The boy lit the lamp (because it is his brother's lamp and he was used to it). It would not go right the first time so he got some soap and placed it on the lamp and it shone a very bright light. Then he got something with a glass in and placed it in front of the light and the light shone brighter still. Gas smells very much. The name of the gas that the teacher made was 'Acetylene Gas'.*

There was one period during the school week that was welcomed as a bit of temporary relaxation from the other lessons. On Friday afternoons, for a time, they were left to do drawing on their own. This took the form of sketching scenes and objects which they copied from printed cards. Sketch books were provided for these drawings, which were done first in pencil and then inked over. Grace's copies of the pictures were very good, looking almost as if they had been printed. Her favourite was a picture of Ann Hathaway's Cottage. It seemed no tuition was given in drawing and they were never free to do their own thing. Painting in school was then unheard of. Grace enjoyed their sketching periods, nevertheless, but the subject she liked better, and at which she always excelled, was needlework. This was perhaps as well in view of all the sewing she would be called upon to do later in her life.

Needlework in school at that time meant sewing garments and household articles by hand. In the lower classes girls were trained to hem and join two pieces of material together with a neat seam. Flat articles were made to begin with, such as mats and covers for sideboards, cushion covers, kettle and iron holders. The skills of making gathers, darts, tucks, pleats, working buttonholes and putting on bindings and facings came a little later. By the time the top class was reached, the girls could incorporate these skills to make a petticoat, apron, nightgown, or even a dress. Those who were really deft with their needles could display their ability by adding embroidery to their garments. Feather-stitching round collars and cuffs of nightdresses called for patience and dexterity if a neat result was to be achieved. The girls became proficient in knitting too, beginning with simple articles such as scarves which were done on two needles. Progression to knitting with four needles produced socks and gloves.

An important part of the needlework scheme was patching and darning. To become adept in this field was essential if the girls were to be efficient housewives in due course. The headmaster's wife, Mrs Cooper, was employed part-time to instruct the girls in sewing and knitting. For the darning lessons she would produce her own family's socks and anything else that needed repairing. When her son happened to need a new pair of socks she would commission one of the older girls to knit them. She thus scored doubly by being paid for her teaching and getting her mending and knitting done free at the same time.

Joseph Cooper's love of music prompted him to organise concerts from time to time to which parents could come and hear their children's singing. One such performance was called 'The Holiday Concert'. Grace Spenceley had a solo part in it because she had a good singing voice. She was the flower girl. There were fourteen main characters in the musical sketch, as it was described. The rest of the children formed a chorus. The play depicts a group of children playing on the village green during their holiday. They are joined by the fairies who, in turn, introduce other characters of varied occupations. These all join the children in their holiday festivities. Grace kept her copy of 'The Holiday Concert'. In addition to all the words, it shows a tonic-solfa version of the music. Against the characters in the book she wrote down the names of the children who represented them. Grace said that everyone enjoyed this concert, children and parents alike. It was cheerful and the chorus music went with a lilt. It certainly left a happy impression on her, because she was singing her solo piece fifty years later as well as some of the other parts, not to mention the lilting chorus. No doubt Mr Cooper gained satisfaction from his efforts on that occasion.

Where poetry was concerned, the headmaster chose certain pieces that he considered suitable for learning. The poems had to be committed to memory and then recited aloud. The most outstanding poem in Grace's memory, one which she could still recite well into her adult life, was 'The Burial of Sir John Moore'. This is a very lengthy poem describing the funeral of that famous soldier after the battle of Corunna in Spain during the Napoleonic wars. Grace got the impression that Joseph Cooper admired Sir John so greatly that he wished to perpetuate his memory through the poem. By having the scholars learn it all by heart, extra weight was given to the history lesson they had that included the exploits of the great hero. The teacher's aim succeeded, at least as far as Grace was concerned, in that she still remembered the doings of Sir John Moore when she had forgotten about Napoleon.

During the opening years of the twentieth century there was no school building between Oxspring and Penistone. Most of the children who lived at Springvale, between the two places, walked the mile to Oxspring. Some of them were really poor. Quite often they were so hungry that if they saw another child begin eating an apple they would keep close to him until it was almost finished, then beg desperately, 'Give us your core.' Since there were usually two or three contenders for the apple core, the lucky recipient lost no time in making short work of it. Crunching ravenously he would devour the last little bit, including the pips and stalk. Not a morsel was left.

The Spenceley children were never reduced to begging for apple cores. Despite the large number of mouths to feed, James and Elizabeth were always able, by hard work and good management, to provide them with the essentials of food and clothing. They achieved this by their own efforts, never asking for any outside financial help. What was also important, they managed without getting into debt. As commonly expressed, 'they managed to keep their heads above t'water'. There were no luxuries of course, and treats in the form of outings were far

'*Give us your core.*'

between. Whilst keeping priorities in mind, any unnecessary expenditure had to be curtailed.

By the time Grace reached her thirteenth birthday her parents took the view that paying for domestic help was an unnecessary expense. They affirmed that their daughter was old enough and well able to take the place of Tilly who had served them faithfully for eight years. James decreed that she must leave school to work at home instead. To this end she was told to ask Mr Cooper for her attendances. The ruling in education then was that a boy or girl could leave school at thirteen providing he or she had made sufficient attendances. Grace was reluctant to ask for hers. She was enjoying her lessons and doing well at school. The prospect of having to leave did not appeal to her. She was also a little afraid of what the teacher's reaction might be. In the event she went home without having broached the subject to him. When her father wanted to know if she had got the attendances she replied to the contrary, upon which he told her firmly, 'Well, if you come home tomorrow without 'em you'll have to go straight back again and get 'em.' Grace knew he meant what he said. Next day she asked for the vital information, much to Mr Cooper's displeasure. She was allowed to leave school, since her attendance had been good and came up to the necessary requirements, but her teacher said it was a great pity that she wasn't permitted to stay on longer. 'It's like nipping you in the bud,' were his words.

Tilly, incidentally, found another situation. Grace and her family continued to see her from time to time as she paid them visits. Having lived with them in close proximity for eight years, she had felt herself to be part of the family, and did not wish to sever connections with it. Years later, when Grace visited Tilly, their former nursemaid was bringing up a son of her own.

Oxspring School served as a place of learning not only from Mondays to Fridays, but also on Sundays. The Spenceleys attended Sunday school both morning and afternoon on that day, walking up and down

Bower Hill twice. This often extended to three times each way, since there was usually a church service in the evening too. This was presided over by someone from Penistone, because the Oxspring Sunday School was affiliated to Penistone Church. From Grace's accounts on 'Sunday', so frequently featured in her writing book, one gets a good idea of the programme they followed in Sunday school. Hymns and prayers were supplemented by readings from the Bible and by information or stories told by the teacher. The children were always given a verse from the Bible to learn by heart for the following Sunday, when they would have to say it individually to the teacher.

During the time Grace attended Oxspring Sunday School three of the teachers were members of the Winterbottom family, owners of the wire mill at which her father worked. They were generally referred to as Mrs Arthur, Miss Kate, and Mr Frank. All appeared to be very dedicated to their Sunday School work and were held in high esteem by the Oxspring people.

Two other teachers who were also genuinely concerned for their scholars' welfare were the Misses Dransfield: Sarah and Gertrude. The latter was affectionately known as 'the little Miss'. These ladies came from a well-known, greatly respected Penistone family. Both sisters gave long and devoted service to Oxspring Sunday School and to the village community in general. They kept in touch with some of their former scholars after they were grown up. In 1902 Miss Gertrude taught, in her Sunday School class, the boy whom Grace Spenceley eventually married. There still exists the small green 'Birthday Book' which was given to him in that year by Miss Gertrude and which bears her signature. On the occasion of his marriage to Grace, more than twenty years later, the 'little Miss' sent the couple a letter of well-wishing for their future. They appreciated the thoughtful gesture so much that the letter was kept, along with their Sunday School prizes.

The Misses Dransfield were not in favour of strong drink. Whenever they could, they tried to steer people away from it. One of the sisters had this objective in mind one day when she approached a droll, elderly man, noted in the village for his fondness of ale. 'Do you think you could give up beer drinking?' she enquired hopefully. 'Water does us a lot more good, you know. It's stronger than beer.' 'Oh, beer's plenty strong enough for me, Miss Dransfield,' came the reply. On another occasion the lady expressed to Grace's mother her grave concern that such good girls as her daughters should be brought up in a public house. Elizabeth had to point out that they could be just as good living in a public house as living anywhere else.

About once a month, following the usual afternoon Sunday School, would be an extra hour or so for parents and other grown-ups to attend. The children could either go home after their Sunday School period or stay behind with the adults for the extra worship and entertainment. This combination of the two formed the P.S.A.—Pleasant Sunday Afternoon. There were visiting speakers and soloists, and usually someone to give a recitation. This was in addition to hymn singing and prayers. They were, on the whole, bright and cheerful occasions. According to Grace's book she enjoyed staying on to the P.S.A.

The highlights of the Sunday School year were the annual School Feast and the Prize-Giving. In 1905 the School Feast took place on the last Tuesday in June. Special hymns had been diligently learned during the preceding weeks. On the actual day the children had to walk a long way, or so it seemed to Grace, to the spot where everyone was congregating. After singing all their hymns and no doubt working up an appetite in the process, tea when it came was welcome and enjoyable. With energy replenished, everyone then went into a field to play games and listen to music from the brass band.

At the Prize-Giving event each scholar was given a book, providing that his attendance and conduct had been good. These were treasured long afterwards, since books of one's own were not easily come by at that time. Grace, her sisters and brothers had always to put brown paper backs on their prize books the very next morning after receiving them, in order to keep them clean and preserve the covers. This effort proved worthwhile for, eighty years later, the Sunday School prizes Grace received are still in very good condition. They include such titles as *Tom Leslie's Secret*, *The Basket of Flowers*, *Cassy* and *The Grey House on the Hill*. The grey house, incidentally, was the workhouse. The stories all have similar themes. The main characters are poor, destitute children, unjustly treated by unscrupulous adults. Yet, through cruelties and hardships, their honesty and sense of what is right prevail, so in the end they triumph over the evil and wrongdoing. Often the poor child is an orphan and an inmate of the workhouse. Sometimes the hero or heroine is at the point of death because of ill-treatment and starvation but, even in such dire straits, the temptation to steal is resisted. These books were not intended to make children laugh. They were aimed at improving moral values. They instilled into receptive minds the Christian ideals that the Sunday School set out to teach. At two of the Prize-Givings Grace Spenceley was awarded, in addition to her book, a bronze medal. These were for her very good attendance and conduct.

The Sunday School had lasting influence on the Spenceley children. Much of what they learned there stayed with them throughout their lives. Considering that there were ten in the family, and obviously they could not always have what they wanted, they never caused their parents any serious behaviour problems. None of them ever fell foul of the law. Whilst this was largely due to the parental influence, it is more than likely that the Sunday School helped to a great degree. Grace often said in her later life that going there stood her in good stead. Her days as a scholar at Oxspring, both on weekdays and on Sundays, were mainly happy ones.

CHAPTER 4

Holiday Occasions

GRACE'S HOLIDAYS from school during the 1904–1905 period were spent largely in nursing babies, taking them for walks, and in helping her mother generally. She also went stone picking in a field at Four Lane Ends. Her father rented the field of grass and had hay made from it in summer. Earlier in the year, before the grass grew long, the children were sent in to pick off all the stones so that they wouldn't obstruct the cutting later on. The stones were afterwards used in road mending.

Holiday outings were much appreciated, probably because they were comparatively rare. While their excursions did not take them very far afield, they were enjoyed as a change from working at home. During their years at Four Lane Ends, the Spenceleys occasionally visited their Aunt Emma at Dodworth near Barnsley. These outings were regarded as real treats, because Aunt Emma was one of the kindest of people and always made them welcome. She was another sister of Grace's mother and Madge's mother, having been Emma Herbert before marriage. She and her sister Blanche had married brothers by the name of Buckle. Aunt Emma Buckle also kept a public house in Dodworth as her sister and brother-in-law had previously done. Her house had the same name as the Spenceleys'—the Travellers Inn.

When the fair came to Dodworth, Grace was allowed to go to her Aunt Emma's for tea and enjoy the fair at the same time. The fair was held annually and was always referred to as 'the Feast' by local people. Dodworth feast was eagerly anticipated for a long time in advance by the Spenceley children, and remembered with pleasure for a long time afterwards. They were strictly limited in the amount of money they could spend at the feast, but just being able to look around, see other people and hear the music made a pleasant change. This, together with tea at Aunt Emma's, was a memorable highlight in their young lives. In her brief account of the holiday week Grace wrote:

> *I went to Dodworth feast on Monday. First of all I*
> *called at my Auntie's, then I went up to the feast till*
> *teatime. I went down to my Auntie Emma's to have my*
> *tea. I enjoyed my tea very much. When I had had my*
> *tea I went in the room and looked at my cousin's Post*
> *Card Album. Then I went up to the feast again. I stayed*
> *at the feast about an hour, then went down to my*
> *Auntie's again. Then we went home.*

Besides Aunt Emma there was another auntie who lived at Dodworth. Actually she was their great-aunt, since she was the aunt of Grace's mother. She was known to the children as Aunt Fielding. It is doubtful whether Grace knew her Christian name, as she was always referred to by her husband's surname. Whilst the Spenceley children sometimes did call on Aunt Fielding when they were in Dodworth, the time spent at her house was considerably less than that spent at Aunt Emma's. The reason was that she was held in some awe by her niece's children, who were expected to sit still when in her house. This was always spick and span, with nothing out of place and not a speck of dust to be seen. Elizabeth had once been heard to remark that it was easy to keep a house tidy and clean if there were no children to upset it. Aunt Fielding had never had any children and was very intolerant of any shortcomings on their part. Grace and Madge always retained the uneasy feeling that she had never quite forgiven them for the time when, hardly old enough to know better, they had stuck jelly babies all over her nice clean wall. Madge had been intrigued by the pretty pattern the jellies were making with their various colours. She could not understand why Aunt Fielding disliked it so much that she took it quickly to pieces, exhorting them at the same time to 'Get off to your Aunt Emma's, you naughty girls; tell her I've had enough of you today.'

On these visits to Dodworth the Spenceleys and cousin Madge rode in Grandad Herbert's trap, pulled by a horse called Doctor, or merely Doc for short. William Herbert had originally obtained the animal from a member of the medical profession, hence its name. The children had to be on their best behaviour when in the trap. Their grandfather would not have tolerated anything less. Sitting sedately for the most part, they had sometimes to change position according to whether they were going uphill or down. When they were travelling uphill, a sharp command to 'sit forrard' would issue from William. On downward gradients the order was 'sit back'. These commands had to be swiftly obeyed, the children moving their bodies so as to balance their weight in the horse's favour.

In August Grace and Madge went to Thurgoland 'feast' which was a similar event to that at Dodworth. They did not need their grandfather's trap to take them there, since Thurgoland was within easy walking distance. The other local fair to which they were allowed, and which was perhaps the most popular over a wider area, was Penistone Feast. The two-mile walk to Penistone took them up the Jockey, that stretch of road leading northwards from Four Lane Ends in the Huddersfield direction. After the first mile or so they turned off the road to the left by Whitefield Farm, then followed the path through the fields, downhill towards the river. After crossing the Don bridge, the way led up again to join the Penistone road at Springvale.

'Sit forrard.'

In 1904, when Grace was eleven, the Penistone Feast day coincided with the impending birth of yet another addition to the Spenceley family. Elizabeth was already confined to bed, so it was James who gave the children their money for the fair. Six of them were to enjoy the outing that day, the five Spenceleys who were of suitable age and cousin Madge who had come down from Copster in order to go with them. James gave each of the children a small, silver threepenny bit, evidently deciding this was enough for their requirements. The little group started out in happy, excited mood and hurried eagerly up the Jockey road. When they were halfway down the fields, alas, it was discovered that one of the younger children had accidentally dropped his threepence. It seemed this had happened while they were negotiating a stile, but in spite of prolonged searching in the tall grass around the stile and along the sides of the path, that tiny silver threepence was not brought to light. The idea of going back home for more money was briefly considered, but almost immediately abandoned. They were already nearly halfway to the Feast, and too much time would be lost by turning back. Added to this was the uncertainty of whether a further threepence would be forthcoming. Their father would no doubt take the view that, by having to go without the money, the unfortunate one would be more careful in future. So, after only short deliberation, it was decided to carry on to the Feast; each of them would donate a halfpenny to the penniless one when they got there. As there were five of them still with their threepences, it worked out exactly that all six had twopence-halfpenny to spend at the Feast.

In those days, however, a good deal of enjoyment could be had for a halfpenny. They could have a long ride on the roundabout or spend quite some time in a swingboat. Another halfpenny was usually invested in the 'peep show'. For this money they could gaze at very fat ladies and very small midget people, with possibly a 'black man' included. These were all objects of wonder and curiosity to Grace and her companions, since they never encountered such people outside the Feast. There was often a 'menagerie' too where, for a halfpenny, they could look at a collection of wild animals. One of the precious halfpennies was spent on gingerbread or jellies to take home. Despite their financial limitations, they were anxious that their mother should sample a little of the Feast too. Even if they did succumb to temptation and eat some on the way back there was still plenty left, since a considerable quantity could be obtained for a halfpenny. That particular outing to Penistone Feast was a memorable one for the Spenceley children, not only because of the lost threepence. Even that mishap seemed to lose some of its importance when, on returning home, they were given news of another baby brother. While Grace admired the new addition, along with the rest of her family, she also viewed him in terms of extra work in an already crowded and busy home. Frank was the tenth child to be born to Elizabeth Spenceley, and the ninth surviving at that time.

Following old tradition, Penistone Feast was, and still is, held on the last Saturday in June. The farmers around Penistone always regarded the Feast as a guide for their haymaking activities. According to custom they started cutting the grass on Penistone Feast Saturday, before going to the fair in the evening. The following day was the 'Sing', when hymns were sung outdoors by a large gathering of the towns-folk, augmented by other people from different parts of the Penistone area. Though not all the farmers patronised the Sing, they looked on it as a holiday event nevertheless. It afforded a chance to invite relatives or friends from further afield to have tea and talk with them. The grass, meanwhile, would be 'getting ready' for being dealt with later on in the week.

A whole week was allowed off school for Feast Week at that time. Grace recorded a pleasurable outing arranged by the Sunday School which took place in the middle of that week. She wrote:

> *On Wednesday I had to get up early because it was the*
> *trip morning. We went to Southport. It was a lovely day.*
> *We went on the car to the Botanic Gardens and while*
> *we were there we went through the museum. There were*
> *all sorts of butterflies and animals, and we went on the*
> *lake. We went through the Market hall and bought some*
> *presents to take home. We went home by the eight o'clock*
> *train. My father drove us to the station and fetched us back.*

Though she didn't specify which vehicle he drove, it could well have been that he borrowed William Herbert's horse and trap, and that cousin Madge went on the trip too. Grace did not mention seeing the sea at all in her written account, but it is thought this trip would be her first visit to the seaside. She was twelve at the time. These outings organised by the Sunday School provided the only opportunity then for the great majority of working-class children to visit the seaside.

Another day's outing organised by the Sunday School was a visit to Wharncliffe Crags. This took place on a day during the August holiday. On her return to school she wrote:

> *A fortnight last Saturday I went to Wharncliffe Crags*
> *with the Sunday School children on drays. The drays*
> *were kindly lent by Mr Peaker, Mr Webb, and Mr*
> *Fretwell. It was very lovely going, and coming back.*
> *When I got there I went with some of my friends on the*
> *rocks till the tea was ready. After I had had my tea I*
> *went on the rocks again. We saw the 'Old Wives Cellar.'*

We could go in at one end and come out at the other.
Then I went on and looked for some bilberries. I found
a lot. We went all among the rocks and then came out on
a foot-path. We saw some chestnut trees with little
chestnuts on, and some nut trees with nuts on. The
heather was all in bloom. We set off back at half-past six.

On a few occasions Grace and her eldest sister went to see their grandmother, Ann, who lived at Harrogate. They were taken there by their father. Grace described the journey by rail as very interesting. They were on the Barnsley line and had to go through the Hardlington tunnel. At Leeds they got out and looked through the market before resuming the journey to Harrogate.

James Spenceley's mother had lived for many years in the fashionable spa town, to which wealthy members of society came to take the waters. Leaving her son to be brought up by his grandmother, uncles and aunts, she had turned her back on Cranemoor long before, and looked on Harrogate as her home town. At first she worked as a maid, but eventually married a respectable man called Mr Wall. They had a son, Harry, but though he was James's half-brother there was never much contact between them. Grace's grandmother and her husband kept a boarding house at Harrogate. It was quite a reputable establishment overlooking the Stray, and attracted good-class clients. They gave it the name of 'Spencewall House', this being a combination of both their own. Ann had established herself as an excellent cook over the years. She did most of the boarding house catering herself, but had maids to assist generally. Her husband was an efficient administrator, so between them they kept Spencewall House running smoothly and profitably.

On her first visit to Harrogate, Grace had been more than a little puzzled. She had been told by her father that they were going to visit his mother who was, of course, her grandmother. Yet, when they arrived, that lady took her aside and told her quietly not to call her 'Grandma' but 'Auntie'. She said that to be addressed as Grandma made her feel too old, whereas Auntie sounded much nicer and younger. Grace accepted this explanation at the time. It was not until she grew older that she understood the real reason for her wanting to be known as Auntie. The truth was that their grandmother did not wish it known in her boarding house that she had an illegitimate son. This would have been obvious if she had allowed the children to call her Grandma. For her to admit to being James's mother might destroy, or at least harm, the good reputation for honesty and respectability which she had earned for herself by many years' work in Harrogate. She was held in high regard by staff and guests alike and wanted to remain so. If the indiscretion of her earlier life was uncovered she would go down sadly in their estimation. Perhaps the business would be in jeopardy too, for the type of people who patronised Spencewall House would not wish to associate themselves with a woman of doubtful character.

Harry Wall endorsed his mother's wishes that his half-brother and his family should conceal their true identities. He asked James outright not to reveal that he was also his mother's son. He told him that she was very well thought of by all who knew her and he didn't want his mother's name dishonoured in Harrogate.

If these words hurt James at all by implying that his presence meant dishonour, he had enough sense to know that he was not the guilty one. He knew too that he was leading a respectable life in spite of his bastard origin.

Whatever his feelings, he acceded to his brother's request. He had no desire to disrupt his mother's settled existence with her Harrogate family and situation. It was better to keep on friendly terms with his mother, even though she had abandoned him when young. Now she was growing old she encouraged him to visit her, and welcomed her grand-daughters when they accompanied him. The secret of their identities was always safely kept. Sometimes Grace's grandmother paid them a visit to Travellers Inn, staying for two or three days when she did so.

Elizabeth Spenceley did not travel very far afield as her family increased. She was mostly too preoccupied by home affairs to venture away often from Four Lane Ends. Only when something essential was needed, such as clothes or other goods that could not be obtained nearer home, did she make the journey to Barnsley. Grace was pleased when she was allowed to accompany her mother on these trips. The outings were so infrequent that they were regarded as special treats.

Barnsley is only a matter of six or seven miles from Travellers Inn, but at the beginning of the century the distance seemed much further. The journeys which Grace made with her mother were by waggonette. They occupied most of a day, since the plodding pace of the horses was ponderously slow. The waggonette in which they travelled came from Thurgoland every Wednesday morning, passing through Four Lane Ends at about ten o'clock. It returned from Barnsley at about four o'clock in the afternoon, so in winter it was dark by the time they reached home. The owner of the vehicle was Mr Joel Mellor, a Thurgoland man. He did the driving himself, but was invariably accompanied by his wife, who sat beside him up front. She was a cheery, energetic woman whose habitual attire on these journeys included a black bonnet and cape.

Not only did the waggonette carry passengers to Barnsley, but also farm produce such as butter and eggs. There was always some to be picked up at the end of the lane leading to Hadley House Farm at the bottom of Coates Lane. This was the long hill down which they travelled after first leaving Four Lane Ends. Further on during the journey other stops would be made at the ends of farm lanes to take on produce. This is where Mrs Mellor came in useful. She would jump quickly down from her seat, see that the goods were stowed safely on board, then climb back up beside her husband. As she did so she would invariably exclaim brightly, 'Right Joel', which was the signal for him to move the horses on again.

Those journeys in Mellor's wagonette were, in a sense, social events providing opportunity for the women to catch up with local gossip. Passengers were seated along the sides, facing one another, and could therefore talk easily together. The Spenceleys were sometimes given news by the Thurgoland women of recent happenings at Cranemoor, their old home. Occasionally there might even be one or two women from that village on the waggonette, in which case the news was had at first hand.

On fine days the vehicle was open to the air, but in wet or cold weather the Mellors put up a cover.

CHAPTER 5

Growing Up at Travellers Inn

WITH SCHOOLDAYS behind her, Grace had little time to regret that her education was at an end. Each day brought its own tasks, keeping her busily occupied. If Tilly had had plenty of work, her successor had more. After George was born in 1901 there were three further additions to the family, coming in quick succession. Elizabeth Spenceley had her last four children in a space of four years and was quite exhausted. In all, she had borne eleven children in sixteen years. Not surprisingly this had, to some extent, taken toll of her health. By the time Grace left school her mother looked far older than her forty years. She was often too tired or ill to cope with the large family she had brought into the world. It was therefore onto her daughter's shoulders that the heavy burden of bringing up the young ones fell, besides helping with the catering, washing and cleaning for all the rest of them.

The three youngest were all boys—Harry, Frank and Stanley. Sadly, little Harry was a handicapped child, which worry no doubt contributed to his mother's careworn appearance. The cause of his disability was never exactly specified. It was said he had suffered convulsion fits when a baby, but whether this was a cause of the trouble or a part of it is not certain. When he started walking it was noticed that he trailed or dragged one of his legs lamely. On becoming a little older he moved about quite quickly, almost running, but still with the leg trailing. Besides this handicap of movement there was also that of speech. Harry could not talk like a normal child of his age, even when he became older, and his powers of communication with other people were severely limited. Then, to add to the trouble, an accident happened to the little boy.

One day, as he was sitting near the fire with other members of the family around, someone accidentally knocked into the handle of a pan that was on the fire-bars. It was a large saucepan, full of hot soup which had been left to simmer. Harry was nearest to the pan, and the accident happened so suddenly that he had no chance to get out of the way. The scalding soup spilt all down one side of the poor child, badly hurting his arm and leg. It is not known for certain whether this accident caused Harry's handicap to worsen or whether his condition would have deteriorated in any case, but it seems likely that the scalding did have much ill-effect. The use in his arm diminished, as did his ability to run about. He was never able to go to school, being physically and mentally unfit. Much of his time, when the weather was nice, was spent sitting by the milepost across the road from the inn, near to Wright's cottage. He liked to play in the sand with an old spoon. His mother could see the milepost from a window, so was able to keep a check on what he was doing. She thought little harm could come to him as he played in this favourite place, for there was very little traffic on the roads then. Even so, there was one occasion which caused alarm. A horse and trap came quickly round the corner and only just missed knocking into Harry, who was about to re-cross the road to return home.

In 1906 when Grace took on the duties of second mother to the family there were twelve people in the Spenceley household, including two babies under two years old and three people incapacitated by ill-health. Besides her looking after all their various needs, the business of the inn had to be taken care of too.

James Spenceley was unable to give much help in the house, as he worked long hours at the wire mill and came home tired from standing all day at his workbench. He did usually take one of the young ones onto his knee whilst he ate his dinner, but this was the only brief interlude he could have with his children. After he had finished eating there were the inn duties to be attended to.

Herbert, the eldest boy of the family, had left school before Grace and was already working at Winterbottom's with his father. Willie, Mary and George, then aged ten, seven and five, were at school. The members of the family remaining at home all day were the mother, three daughters and three small sons.

Grace had experience long before she left school in helping with babies. As learned from her writing book, part of her Sundays and holidays were spent in nursing the baby or taking it out for a walk. At thirteen she was an invaluable help to her mother, being able to feed, bath and dress the three young ones. Harry still needed all these things doing for him throughout his life and, needless to say, it was Grace who did them. Her older sister Blanche could do light housework but had been forbidden to undertake heavy lifting and work requiring extra exertion, such as washing and scrubbing, on account of her weak heart. Emma was not expected to do anything apart from occasional washing up and sedentary occupations such as shelling peas or a little mending. She was only able to do these when feeling rather better. More often than not Emma herself would need looking after. She had to spend long periods in bed when her heart condition troubled her and breathing was difficult. Though by resting she temporarily improved, the doctor had told her parents that there was no cure for Emma. The most they could do for her was to keep her as comfortable and happy as possible. The doctor urged Elizabeth not to fret about her daughter too much because there was a little consolation, if she could regard it as such. He said that, with a heart like Emma's, she could die at any time, but when she did she would 'go like the crack out of a gun'. The end would be so quick that she would know nothing about it. His words did eventually prove to be true.

Grace had not left school very long when her small brother Frank was involved in serious misadventure which almost ended in tragedy. One morning at breakfast time there was rather more bustle than usual going on in Travellers Inn. The children's grandmother from Harrogate had been staying with them for a few days and was preparing to return home. Grace, her mother and sisters were helping to get her belongings together and making sure she had a good breakfast so that she would be ready to board the waggonette when it came. Frank and Stanley, the two youngest children, had been left upstairs whilst their grandmother was being attended to. There was a difference of only thirteen months in their ages, and it was thought they would amuse one another in the bedroom for a while without clamouring to come downstairs. This they seemed to be doing until, suddenly, the calm was shattered by piercing shrieks from the bedroom.

Without hesitation Grace went bounding up the stairs. Dashing into the room she saw with horror the two-year-old Frank standing up in bed with his nightgown on fire. Screaming with terror, he was beating the air with his hands as if to ward off the flames from reaching

Frank, Harry and Stanley

his face. Already the nightgown was flaring upwards, the fire threatening to catch hold of his long, fair hair. Grace yelled for her mother to come but Elizabeth had needed no one else to summon her. Her child's screams were more than enough. Realising the urgency, she followed her daughter up the stairs as fast as her tired legs would allow. In a matter of seconds she was hastening into the room after her. Quickly taking in the critical situation, the older, experienced woman showed great presence of mind in acting promptly. While her daughter stood petrified at the sight of her little brother in flames, Elizabeth snatched up the hearthrug from the floor and wrapped it around her son. So enveloped in the rug, the flames were smothered just in time. Another few seconds and his hair would have caught. It was lucky the boy had held up his head until help reached him, so everyone said afterwards.

Though Frank had been saved in the nick of time from being burnt to death, that day was only the beginning of weeks of anxiety. When the doctor came he was not too optimistic about the little boy's chances of recovery. The burns on his legs and lower body were very severe, giving him great pain. Added to this was the shock, which alone could kill such a small child.

The doctor visited his young patient every day for a fortnight, changing the bandages on his legs and attending to the massive blisters underneath. Grace recalled seeing him run a small pair of scissors up these blisters to let out the fluid they contained. During the long, slow recovery process, Frank suffered much discomfort. The mere sight of the doctor entering the room brought on more tears and crying, since he associated the man with his being hurt. The doctor cared well for his little patient however and, helped by the careful nursing of his mother and sisters, Frank was at last pronounced to be out of danger. On what was meant to be his final visit, the doctor brought him a box of sweets for his having been a good boy. As it transpired, the doctor did have one more visit to make.

A few weeks later, when the household had apparently returned to its normal routine, the family were seated to Sunday tea. Suddenly one of the older children cried, 'Look at our Frank,' whereupon the conversation stopped and everyone's gaze riveted on the boy. He was deathly pale and his eyes were rolling around, then staring upwards; his head lolled from side to side. He appeared to be unconscious and in danger of falling out of his chair. James took him up onto his knee while his wife hastened to get the smelling salts from the cupboard. Some of the family thought that Frank was going to die after all, but in a little while he began to revive. The doctor was called in, nevertheless, to ascertain if the boy was going to be alright. He told them it was delayed shock that had seized the child, but it had passed and he would be as well as before.

After that early misfortune Frank led a normally healthy life. He did however carry the terrible scars of that morning's mischief to the end of his days. For mischief it was that had caused the near tragedy. Elizabeth realised, after the incident, that a box of matches had been left within reach of the two children. They had been playing with them in bed, and when one was struck it had fallen onto Frank's nightgown. No one ever knew for certain just which of the brothers had acquired the matches or started the fire, but Grace had the feeling that it was Stanley, because he had the box in his hand. Neither of them was to blame for what happened, of course, since they were too young to realise the danger. The grown-ups had to feel thankful that a greater price had not been paid for their carelessness.

About that time, Grace acquired another best friend. This did not mean that her cousin Madge was held in any less affection. The new friendship was struck up with Frances because she and Grace had one big thing in common. They were both of them second mothers to their families. Frances Illingsworth lived at the top of Coates Hill, only two or three hundred yards away from Travellers Inn in the Barnsley direction. She was the same age as Grace and Madge, and eldest in her family of seven. Her father was a collier, who came home each evening black with coal dust. Frances and Grace, both having child-minding duties, would often join forces when it came to pushing out the babies on their walks.

The Spenceleys had a large perambulator, or bassinet as it was commonly called in those days. It was made to accommodate two babies at a time. This was just as well since, over quite a long period, there were always two contenders for places in it. Grace had wheeled out her four youngest brothers so often in the bassinet that, by the time Frank and Stanley were the occupants, she felt it was almost a part of her. The friends would usually take their charges up the Copster road to see Grandma Herbert, Aunt Blanche and cousin Madge. Sometimes Madge would join them in walking on as far as Thurgoland and back.

Like her friend Grace, Frances had also to leave school at thirteen. Unfortunately her mother died in childbirth at the early age of thirty-two, so for the next few years the girl tried to fill her place. The baby had been born dead, but Frances had a two-year-old sister Hannah to care for and the others were hardly old enough to fend for themselves. Arthur Illingsworth was a good father to them all, helping with the shopping and even with the washing. Yet his long hours at the pit, together with the walking time there and back, limited the time he had to spare with his children. Frances coped during the long days as bravely as she could, but welcomed the times she shared with the friend of her own age.

Though Elizabeth Spenceley had plenty of troubles of her own, she felt compassion for the Illingsworth children, and for Frances in particular. So, on Friday afternoons, she allowed Grace to go up to their house at Coates and help the motherless girl with cleaning and anything else that needed doing. Frances and Grace remained good friends throughout their younger days, and never lost touch during later life.

While Grace was young and her mother hard-pressed because of illness in the family, they would sometimes send out a small part of their washing to Mrs Marsh; this included items such as the girls' best white dresses, petticoats and other white things that needed special attention. Besides easing the burden a little at Travellers Inn, this was also helping Mrs Marsh by providing her with custom she needed.

Fetching water for the washing

This lady lived up a little lane off Bower Hill on the Oxspring road. Her husband was ill and unfit for work, so Mrs Marsh, helped by her daughter, took in washing to make ends meet. They had no water on tap in their small cottage, so her boys had to take a trolley carrying two tubs and buckets down to the roadside. Leaving the trolley and tubs near some steps, they then climbed over these into a field known as the Nelly, taking their buckets to fill at a well lower down. After carrying the full buckets up the bank and lifting them back over the steps, they proceeded to fill the tubs on the trolley. This necessitated several trips down to the well and back with their buckets before the tubs were full. The water was then transported up the lane to their home, one boy pulling the trolley and his brother pushing from behind. Mrs Marsh had to heat the water, of course, before she could begin washing. Sometimes the boys were dispatched to the Nelly for a further supply if there was a lot of washing to be done. Yet, despite the tedium of fetching and heating water, and the laborious work of washing by hand, Grace maintained that 'Mrs Marsh's washing was as white as the driven snow.' The articles she washed for their family were returned spotlessly clean and beautifully ironed.

When Grace and her cousin were about thirteen, the cloud, which had for some time hung over the house at Copster, darkened. It became necessary for Madge's mother to be sent to Storthes Hall, an institution for the mentally ill at Kirkburton near Huddersfield. The epileptic fits from which Blanche had suffered for so long were increasing in frequency and severity. As a result, her mind was often confused so as to make her irresponsible for her actions. These could sometimes have had dangerous consequences if she had been left on her own. It soon became clear that the poor woman was incapable of looking after herself. Her mother had tried to give her the care and attention she needed, but there were limits to what Mary Herbert could physically do. She was past seventy and often suffered from asthma. She worried about the idea of her youngest daughter going away from her, but had finally to agree with her husband that Blanche needed to be under constant supervision by someone fit enough to look after her. Reluctantly therefore, Madge's mother was given into the charge of the staff at Storthes Hall.

Mary Herbert

Her relatives were able to visit her there. Madge and her grandmother were occasionally taken to Kirkburton by William Herbert in his trap, pulled by the faithful Doc. The ride to Storthes Hall was made in pleasant anticipation of seeing Blanche, but the return journey was always a sad one. Having to leave her behind while they went home was upsetting, especially if she hadn't appeared very well.

The Spenceley family at Travellers Inn felt pity for their cousin. To be deprived of her mother seemed bad enough, but Madge had neither brother nor sister with whom to share the trouble. This made her plight infinitely worse. Her grandmother was invariably kind and good to her, but a young girl sometimes needed the company of other young people. Realising this, her Aunt Lizzie encouraged her to join their large family as often as she could. Grace, of course, continued to be a good friend, and sometimes accompanied Madge on the trips to see her mother.

The gloomy atmosphere at Copster never brightened again completely. Though Mary Herbert always retained patience and kindness towards her grandchildren, the despondency she experienced when thinking of her ailing daughter was not easy to overcome. On top of the anxiety she felt for Blanche, her asthma continued to be a trouble. Sometimes when Grace paid a visit to Copster she would find her grandmother seated up to the table, her face bent over a steaming basin. She said that by breathing in the vapours arising from the basin her breathing was made easier. This 'Potter's Asthma Cure' was a well-known remedy then for the complaint. Obviously it did not constitute a real cure, but it did have the effect of alleviating the suffering to some extent during a bad asthmatic attack.

After her daughter became an inmate of Storthes Hall, Mary's health deteriorated generally. Whether the worry and the asthma were contributing factors is not known. In any case, she had reached a good age for those days. It was in the spring of 1907, when she was seventy-three, that Grace's grandmother died and was buried in Thurgoland churchyard. Her death brought deep sorrow to her husband. Despite his generally stern character, which caused trepidation amongst the young ones, William Herbert had always been devoted to his wife. According to Grace, 'He wept like a child after she died.'

The Spenceley children felt the loss of their grandmother keenly, since she had been near at hand when they wanted to see her. Grace in particular was saddened because, being Madge's friend of the same age, she had been in closer contact with her Copster relatives than had her brothers and sisters. At fourteen, this was her first remembered experience of losing a close relative. The realisation that she would not see her grandma again brought with it a feeling of awe as well as sadness. When, years later, Grace's children asked her to describe to them how her grandmother had looked, she told them, 'I can still picture her sitting in the chair. She always wore an apron over her long frock and a lace-trimmed cap on her head. It had a band of mauve-coloured ribbon or velvet that fitted close to her forehead.'

The other girl whose life was greatly affected by her grandmother's death was, of course, Marjorie Buckle. They had lived under the same roof for as long as she could remember. They had shared the anxiety

of her mother's illness, taking comfort from each other. Life for Madge
had been tolerable whilst she had her grandma but, with her gone,
the prospect seemed dreary. At least, that is how it appeared to her
cousin. Yet oddly enough, Grace was surprised when Madge herself
did not bemoan her fate of being housekeeper to a cantankerous old
grandad. With her natural cheerfulness she continued to make the
best of a bad situation.

William Herbert really did become cantankerous in his last years.
He was difficult to please and ready to find fault just for the sake of it.
If he had been strict with his own children when young, he was even
stricter with Madge. One evening, when she and her cousin were about
fifteen, there was a concert due to take place at Oxspring. The per-
formers had come from outside the village and had a good reputation
for putting on a clean, enjoyable show. James Spenceley had therefore
given Grace permission to attend the concert with her friend Frances
Illingsworth, and his wife had persuaded her father, William, to allow
Madge to accompany them. The girl hardly went anywhere, she pointed
out. It was bad enough to have lost her mother and grandmother, without being deprived of her friends' company too. The old man had at
last relented and said Madge could go along with the others on condition she was back at nine o'clock. 'If she isn't, she'll feel this stick
across her back,' he had threatened.

In the event, they all enjoyed the concert, but the disturbing thing
was it didn't finish until well after nine o'clock. Although the girls
ran most of the way up Bower Hill on the way back, it was nearly
half-past nine when they reached Four Lane Ends. Grace and Frances
accompanied Madge up to Copster, only to find the door locked. It
was apparent that her grandfather had shut her out because she was
late. Not daring to bang on the door and ask for it to be opened,
Madge went back with the other two to Four Lane Ends. After they
had gone part way home with Frances, Grace took Madge into the
inn with her, where they related to her mother how Madge was locked
out. Elizabeth Spenceley remembered how her father had restricted
her outings when she was young, and took pity on her niece. Even she
thought nine o'clock had been an unreasonably early time to demand
their return home. As for leaving the concert before it was over, she
agreed they had done the correct thing to stay to the end and get their
money's worth.

To Madge's relief, Aunt Lizzie told her she must spend the night
with them at Travellers Inn. She could find her a place in one of their
beds, even if it did mean sleeping three together. So to bed Grace and

Madge went, but hardly had they done so when the loud knocking of a stick was heard on the downstairs door. Then followed their grandfather's irate voice, demanding to know where Madge had gone. He had evidently had second thoughts about leaving her out all night. As the girls listened apprehensively they wondered whether Madge would have to get dressed again to accompany the angry man back to Copster and perhaps feel his stick into the bargain. Their fears were soon allayed however, as they realised Elizabeth was ready to defend her niece. Her voice took on some of her father's own sharpness as she confronted him. Showing him defiance for one of the few times in her whole life when she risked his displeasure, her words could be clearly heard by the cousins upstairs. In reply to his question of Madge's whereabouts, Elizabeth told her father in no uncertain terms, 'I've put her to bed with our lot and that's where she's stopping till morning.' She followed this up with a tirade of plain speaking, condemning his treatment of Madge. The sight of his daughter thus aroused evidently had a sobering effect on William Herbert. His rage subsided, but before he made his departure back to Copster he was heard to mutter something about it being a disgrace for young folk to be stopping out till half-past nine. When he was their age they had all to be in bed by nine o'clock.

It was to Madge's credit that she continued to look after her grandfather as well as she could, despite his harshness and seeming ingratitude. No doubt she made allowances for the hard times he had experienced as a boy, and his loneliness in old age. His sight had become impaired too, which he found hard to accept.

Madge was pleased to have her cousin Grace's company on their journeys to Storthes Hall, since her grandfather's driving could be erratic due to his failing vision. The trap was sometimes in danger of knocking into the wall, in which case the girls had to warn him before it happened. Their cautionary words of 'Be careful Grandad, you're getting a bit too near t'wall,' would nevertheless bring a sharp retort from the old man, insisting he knew well enough what he was doing. The visits to Kirkburton gave very little joy as time went on. Sometimes Madge's mother seemed scarcely to know who her visitors were, when despite the hazards of travelling they finally got there. As it happened, they had not many more trips to make to that establishment which spelled unhappiness for them.

The year of 1910 was three days old when Blanche Buckle, at forty, was freed from her earthly troubles, having lived less than three years after her mother. She was buried at Dodworth with her husband Arthur and two-year-old daughter Lilian Emma. Then, before the year had run its course, the Spenceleys suffered another bereavement. In November, William Herbert died and was laid to rest with his wife at Thurgoland. He was seventy-seven. The house he had owned at Copster passed to his daughter, Elizabeth Spenceley, but it was felt by everyone that Madge was too young to live alone in the house. Madge herself was in agreement with the rest of the family. As the dwelling was set a little apart from its nearest neighbours it could be lonely and frightening for a young girl. In the end it was decided that Madge would go to live for a time with some relatives at Whaley Bridge.

CHAPTER 6

Later Days at Travellers Inn

FOR TWENTY YEARS Elizabeth Spenceley had babies and young children around her all day long. It seemed strange when the bassinet that had been an essential part of her life during those years was no longer needed. In the same year as her father died, her youngest son started school.

Frank and Stanley, the last two children to be born into the large family, were 'as different as chalk and cheese', according to Grace's description of her brothers. Frank, older by thirteen months, was slightly built and of a quiet, gentle nature. His mother often said he would have been better as a girl. Indeed, when he was at the toddler stage, people usually mistook him for one on account of his long, fair hair curling onto his shoulders. In those days small boys were dressed in frocks and skirts until they were two or three, so it was hard to tell the difference if the child had girlish looks too. Stanley, on the other hand, was a big boy for his age. He had a rougher, more boisterous temperament. No one would ever have mistaken him for a girl. His hair was fair but, since it was straight, with no curls to display, it had been cut shorter than his brother's. Although a year younger, he soon overtook Frank in size. His mother thought that perhaps the shock of those terrible burns which Frank had experienced had hindered his growth. Yet he was healthy enough as he grew up, and was seldom ill. Whereas Frank enjoyed books and lessons, Stanley much preferred to be outside doing something active. If this included a little harmless fighting with other boys, it was so much the better. He took an early dislike to school.

On one remembered occasion he was actually hankering after playing truant. His mother noticed him loitering around the milepost long after he had been dispatched for school with brothers Frank and George. Becoming aware of her son's intention to remain behind, she took up the fish-slice and hurried out to him. From the window Grace watched her mother go into action with her improvised goad. She saw the

delinquent hustled into the road and spurred quickly along by sharp
slaps across his seat from the fish-slice. His mother followed close
behind him as far as Bower Hill top, administering slaps all the way.
By the time they reached the hill, the message that he must go to
school had evidently been received by Stanley, for Elizabeth was seen
to turn back home. The episode caused Grace some amusement, as it
was one she often laughingly recalled. Though it probably did not
amuse Stanley at the time, the treatment had the desired effect. He
did not consider playing truant again, but accepted school like the
others. In time, he too became quite a good scholar. In the year that
Stanley started school there were five of the Spenceleys attending.
Emma had left, but Willie and Mary were still there besides George
and Frank.

Grace's eldest sister Blanche was a young woman of twenty-one
when the youngest member of the family was being initiated into
school life. She was taller than Grace and of slender figure. Her oval
face was delicately formed, showing grey-blue eyes and a nose that
was slightly aquiline without being big. Her hair, warm chestnut brown
in colour and inclined to wave, was parted over the centre of her forehead and complemented the shape of her face. Despite her indifferent
health, occasioned by three attacks of rheumatic fever during childhood, Blanche had excelled as a scholar. She had a particular talent
too—that of playing the piano. Her father allowed her to have lessons
when she was young, and such was her progress that, after only five
'quarters' tuition, her teacher declared he was unable to instruct her
further. She was already as good a pianist as he. Considering she often
practised with the crippled Harry on her knee, this was no mean achievement. What she needed then was a bit of high-class tuition from a
specialist, 'just to polish her up'. Unfortunately the funds at Fours
were insufficient to enable Blanche to pursue her piano studies any
further afield. She had to content herself by playing for the Sunday
School services and for her family. At home they usually had hymn
singing on Sundays, with Blanche accompanying on the piano. Besides
making music for the family she also entertained customers of the
inn by her playing. Her sister Grace had had piano lessons too for a
short while, but did not possess the same natural talent for playing.
Grace, however, had a nice voice which was often in demand at concert time for the singing of solos and duets.

When James Spenceley first took over Travellers Inn there was a
straight flight of steps leading up to the customers' door of the public
house. This was all very well for men entering the building, but presented something of a hazard to them on leaving. After an evening's

drinking, many of the better customers were not in a sober enough state to negotiate the descent safely, especially when two or three were coming out of the place together. Their joviality, induced by James's ale, sometimes came to an abrupt end when one or more of the drinkers took a nasty tumble straight down the steps onto the road below. These mishaps became rather too frequent for James's liking. Though none had suffered any serious consequences, he did not rule out the possibility of a really bad, if not fatal, accident. Rather than wait for this to happen he took action to avoid it. He had the steps turned and an iron handrail put up so that, on coming out of the door, there was only one forward step to take. The rail which faced them acted as a barrier to prevent anyone falling into the road, and enabled balance to be regained on the broader corner stone before turning to descend the remaining steps. The handrail continued to the bottom. There were no more accidents after this alteration, and the steps have remained the same ever since.

Inside the Travellers the taproom was the focal point where most of the local men congregated. During those years when James Spenceley was licensee, the floor of this room was stone-flagged and bare of any covering. The seats were wooden benches and stools. The tables were of wood too, but had metal legs which were bolted to the floor. Around the taproom were the spitoons. These were basin-shaped containers made of heavy metal, and were used mainly by the men who habitually chewed strong tobacco. This habit encouraged production of surplus saliva which needed to be got rid of from time to time. The spitoons were therefore regarded as a necessary convenience by these men. Persons inclined to bronchitis, who had phlegm to dispose of, could also make use of the spitoons. Men who worked among coal dust or in stone quarries often had need of them too. Since spitting in public was commonplace then, most of the inn's customers contributed to the spitoons quite frequently.

Some of the men would try to demonstrate their skill in spitting into them from a distance, but their aim was not always accurate, especially when they were a little the worse for drink. At such times, what was meant to go inside the spitoon finished up by dripping down the polished outside or on the floor. The fact that many of the drinkers were careless in their use of the spitoons was illustrated by the tale of a certain landlord. After having used them in his inn for a number of years he eventually had the spitoons removed. A little while later one of his customers was remarking that he had missed them a lot since their removal, upon which the landlord replied, 'Aye, but I remember thee missin' 'em a lot when we had 'em.'

As Grace Spenceley took over more duties from her mother she soon became responsible for the nightly cleaning of the taproom. This involved emptying the spitoons, a task that allowed no room for squeamishness. The contents often clung stubbornly and had to be removed by papers, or pieces of rag wrapped round a stick, which were then burnt. The insides of the spitoons were then washed clean and, when dry, had a little sawdust put in the bottom of each in readiness to absorb the next night's contents. After cleaning the outsides, Grace would renew the shine by polishing them again with black lead. She had of course to wash the bar and table tops, and wipe over the seats. Lastly the floor was cleaned. This meant sweeping up the dirty sawdust and putting down some fresh. Once a week the stone-flagged floor was scrubbed all over before the new sawdust was strewn. Grace accomplished this chore on hands and knees, the bucket of hot water beside her. It was always late at night when this task was performed, since it had to be done after the drinkers had gone home.

Apart from the drinking and conviviality there was entertainment to be enjoyed too at Travellers Inn, although it was the customers themselves who provided it. On a typical Saturday evening there would be singing to Blanche's accompaniment on the piano. Then certain individuals whose confidence had become sufficiently bolstered by the beer they had consumed would volunteer to give renderings of their favourite songs. These could be sung with or without accompaniment. An eager singer would not be deterred by having to rely solely on his own voice if there was no piano music available.

To add variety to the evening there was a unique performance put on by one of the regulars. He was a likeable if somewhat reckless character, who enjoyed showing off a clever act which always won him applause. A pint pot was placed, upturned, on a small table. The fellow then put his head on it and stood upside down, his legs straight up in the air and his hands flat on the table on either side of the pint pot. He would then begin turning round by moving his hands around the pot on the table, keeping his body straight with feet upwards. As he revolved, with head still downwards on the pot, he would sing his song which began, 'Upside down, upside down, the world is not the only thing that's going round and round . . .' He kept up the rotating movement for quite some time, all the while he was singing. James Spenceley was sufficiently impressed that he always called his children to come to the bar door when the 'Upside Down' performance was about to take place. Their wonder and amusement, added to the men's applause, pleased the singer greatly when he finished his performance by bringing his feet to the floor again and standing the right way up.

One night, however, that particular act could have come to an unpleasant end had not the landlord intervened. While 'Upside Down' was in progress, one of the drinkers who had become over-boisterous began to hit the pint pot with his stick as if trying to knock it from beneath the singer's head. This had the effect of increasing the amusement of the spectators, who appeared too befuddled to realise the danger if the pot should break. As the stick knocked on the pot, so they laughed aloud in heightened joviality. Without waiting for serious consequences to follow this horseplay, James Spenceley called his house to order and severely reprimanded the offender.

'*Upside Down*'

Another well-known character who frequented Travellers Inn was 'Bald-headed Jack'. He was a rough, strong, 'hard-as-nails' sort of fellow. Unlike Samson, his strength did not lie in his hair, as can be inferred from the nickname. Jack's speciality in the field of entertainment was a demonstration of strength and skill. The only requisites for his act were a chair and the Spenceley family's clothes line. He allowed himself to be tied to the chair with the line, then proceeded to prove his ability to work free. Various people would take turns at binding him as tightly as they could to secure him to the chair. Yet, though he resembled a trussed fowl, in the end Bald-headed Jack always managed to work the rope loose somehow. The whole length of the clothes line was never sufficient to constrict him for long. Jack's feat was well received by his fellows of the taproom. It was also one which Grace and others of the family were invited to witness.

One of the regular attenders at the Fours was a local man named Bill Brammer. His surname was really Bramall, but not one of his contemporaries ever referred to him by that name. To them he was either 'Brammer' or 'Owd Bill'. When Grace Spenceley first became aware of him as a customer he was a dark, stockily-built man of about forty-five. Her early impressions were that he was a rough, obstreperous fellow whom it was best to avoid. When drinking he soon became argumentative, even to the point of seeking a fight. His rising temper and threatening attitude were such as to strike fear into the children.

The older folk, however, who knew him better, had come to realise that his blusterings and rantings were only superficial. At heart Bill was far from being a dangerous man, and he never caused any real physical harm to anyone. The fights he got involved in were rather of the friendly variety and did not result in serious injury. At worst Bill Brammer was merely a noisy nuisance. At best his total lack of inhibition and blunt way of speaking his mind evoked a sneaking admiration from some. His unpretentiousness and bluff forthright manner even gained him a certain affection from those who knew him well.

Speculating as to how Bill Brammer had acquired his wild streak, some reckoned he had been over-indulged as a child, being the youngest member of his family. This may or may not have been true. His father, Joseph Bramall, had been a local farmer who had got on well through hard work and help from his wife. Bill's mother had been Harriet Dyson before her marriage. Her family had been highly respected in the Thurgoland area some years earlier, her brother John in particular being a person of social standing during his lifetime. He had owned a wire mill employing around a hundred workers, built a fine new house, and driven in his own carriage and pair. He was, moreover, a Justice of the Peace. One of John's sons, William Dyson, had become an eminent physician in Sheffield by the first decade of the twentieth century, after being educated at Wesley College, Sheffield and the University of London. He reached the top of the medical profession; one of his many offices in Sheffield was that of senior honorary physician of the Royal Infirmary. He was also president of Sheffield Literary and Philosophical Society and a staunch Wesleyan Methodist. William Dyson's character and lifestyle were in total contrast to those of his cousin, William Bramall. By the time the latter reached middle age, his contact with the Dyson relatives was almost negligible. They had their own circle of friends and professional colleagues who did not belong to the farming fraternity. Bill, on the other hand, had taken over his father's tenancy of the Oxspring farm, which he was working after a fashion.

His fondness for ale and careless self-indulgence often led Bill Brammer to neglect his farm. At times, when he got the urge, he would go 'on the spree' for whole days together, leaving home in the morning in his horse-drawn trap and returning late in the evening. His restlessness took him to taverns further afield during these trips 'abroad', often to Barnsley. Yet invariably he called in at Travellers Inn on his way home, infinitely worse for drink on those occasions. James Spenceley had sometimes to refuse to serve him then, despite Bill's entreaties and cajolings. It was not unusual for him to be in such a helpless state as rendered him incapable of driving himself home. Fortunately his horse was so accustomed to their wanderings that it had become familiar with the way and would convey him safely home of its own accord.

Bill was lucky too in having a patient, understanding wife. She and their young son always helped with the farm work and kept things on an even keel during his jaunts away from home. Mary, or Polly as she was usually called, was a member of the Watts family, who were farmers too, so she was used to the life. In appearance she typified the old concept of a farmer's wife as shown in children's nursery rhyme and story books. She was a short, plump woman with round, rosy-cheeked face, blue eyes and a pleasant smile. Her working dress was black and reached to her feet. Over it she wore a long apron of lighter colour and had a mobcap to cover her head.

For the most part Polly tolerated her husband's vagaries and prolonged sessions at the Fours. She enjoyed feeding their animals which, in winter, involved giving them their hay, corn and turnips. Admittedly, wheeling a large barrowful of turnips from their store place to the cow house was rather heavy work for a small woman, yet as a rule Polly didn't mind exerting her strength, and pushed the barrow cheerfully.

There was one occasion, however, when extra duties had cropped up and Polly decided she had done enough for a while. Bill was down at the Fours, had been there most of the day in fact, and she thought it was high time he was returning home. So, donning bonnet and shawl, she hurried down to the inn. As she bustled her dumpy little figure into the taproom, her usually placid face took on new animation. Ignoring the surprised stares of Bill's companions, who were not in the habit of seeing a woman in their midst when drinking, she spiritedly confronted her idling husband with words that came sharply. 'Cum thi ways hooam wi' thee, tha idle good for nowt. 'Ere am I wheelin' turmits into t'fodderem an' theear ar' thaar, sittin' wastin' thi time when we can do wi' thee up yonder. Tha silly, soft, fat-heeaded fooil tha ar' one.' When he had recovered from his initial amazement at the sight of his normally docile wife in such ruffled, agitated state, Bill Brammer appeared to be quite amused. Far from being annoyed at her intrusion into their sanctum of the taproom and her obvious desire to cut short his pleasures, he welcomed her into their midst, exclaiming cheerfully, 'Cum an' sit daarn 'ere at t'side o' me.' Polly shook him off as he put his arm around her waist and tried to draw her onto the bench beside him. Turning to the other men he continued pleasantly with a touch of genuine pride in his voice. 'You all know my missis 'ere, she's a real good 'un she is. Best day's waark ah ivver did i' mi' life were when ah wed ahr missis. An' ah'd go to t'same market ageean if ah'd mi time to cum o'er.' The words did not constitute an attempt to soften her anger. They were sincere, and Polly knew it. Her pink cheeks became suffused with deeper rose as she stood listening to Bill extolling her virtues to his companions. She became aware that they too were regarding her with happy appraisal, evidently pleased to be in agreement with Bill. None of them seemed to resent her presence in the least. Sensing the friendly atmosphere, Polly's expression softened. Her husband's words of praise had not been aimed at calming her anger, yet they did have that effect. In place of the heated annoyance she had first shown, her face took on a look of confused embarrassment. Needless to say, she did not accept Bill's invitation to sit down with them. Had she done so her good reputation in Oxspring would have been ruined for all time. In any case, it was enough for one member of the family to be neglecting work, she reflected. Seeing that her husband did not intend to leave until he was ready, and not wishing to chastise him further, Polly soon returned home. As she walked back up the Jockey to their farm at Tunnel Top she felt some gratification when she remembered how he had praised her in front of the others. At least it made her feel appreciated.

There was no denying that, in his prime and for many years afterwards, Bill Brammer was a physically strong man. Yet, to him the knowledge of his strength was not sufficient unless he took the opportunity from time to time to demonstrate it in public. It is on record that he and Ben Watts, Polly's brother, once accepted a wager to transport half a ton of coal from Bridge End at Penistone up to the workhouse. The distance was about a quarter of a mile and it was uphill all the way, the last part being very steep. The load of coal was in a horse-cart but there was no horse to pull it. Brammer took its place in the shafts, pulling all the way while Ben Watts pushed from behind. Through sheer strength and determination they managed to accomplish the arduous feat, thus proving their toughness to everyone watching. Unluckily though, they lost the bet because there had been a time limit set for the task and they were just outside it in finishing.

It was due to Bill Brammer's rough behaviour at Travellers Inn that the taproom tables were bolted to the floor. When the Spenceleys first took over the inn they had been movable. On becoming acquainted with Bill and his antics, James realised they would have to be fixed, the reason being that Bill in provocative mood thought nothing about tipping up a table or two, thus spilling the other men's beer.

The wager

Part of the farm buildings at Tunnel Top were used as butchering premises by Bill's brother, Joseph Dyson Bramall, who lived in a cottage nearby. There was a place for slaughtering the animals, and a 'shop' which was where the meat was cut up and made ready for sale. Dyson hawked most of it around Penistone with his horse and cart, but there were some local people who fetched it direct from the shop. His brother Bill found the arrangement convenient, on returning hungry from his late-night sprees, to appropriate meat from the shop. Polly had usually gone to bed on those occasions but she would learn next day how he had fried a pound or so of steak in some of her best butter, that being the nearest kind of fat to hand.

Bill Brammer must have come very close to being arrested many times during his life, yet there is only one known occasion when this did happen. He was quite a young man when, one day, his drunk and disorderly conduct warranted an appearance before the magistrates. Luckily for Bill, his uncle John Dyson was on the bench in his official capacity as Justice of the Peace. Consequently it was hardly surprising that the offender was exonerated. His uncle regarded him sternly, however, telling him firmly that he never wanted to see him in that place again. While Bill did not become an abstainer after that episode, his uncle's wish was gratified. John Dyson was never again put in the embarrassing position of having to pass judgement on his nephew.

'Owd Bill' was certainly a law unto himself. There was no one else quite like him at the time, and though a rascal in some of his ways, he was a likeable one. He was long remembered by the Fours fraternity and by many over a wide area. Grace Spenceley did not know it then, during those years at Travellers Inn, that one day she would become a member of the Bramall family.

Grace was seventeen when she was first escorted home by Ernest, a handsome, black-haired young man who was two years older. He was the elder son of Joseph Dyson Bramall the butcher, and therefore 'Owd Bill's' nephew. The young pair had walked up Bower Hill together, one particular night, after attending evening classes at Oxspring school. Ernest had given Grace an inkstand which he had won by playing

Grace at seventeen

dominoes. This friendly state of affairs was not allowed to continue, however. When James Spenceley became informed of the impending romance by one of the younger children, he declared firmly that it had to be stopped. 'Seventeen is too young to be going out wi' t'lads,' he maintained. Grace had to abide by this decision, since her father's word was the law in their household. Yet, though James temporarily checked the affair he did not entirely kill it. The sparks of romance still smouldered, but ten years more were to pass before they would be fanned into flame.

At seventeen Grace was full of energy and vitality. She was fortunate in having good physical health, being stronger than her figure would suggest. Her waist was trim but she had 'good legs', according to general opinion. Her face was round and full, too full for her own liking in fact. She maintained it was too fat and, contrary to what other folk said, thought her legs were too. It can be truthfully said that Grace had a 'bonny' face which, framed by plenty of luxuriant dark brown hair, was pleasingly attractive. When younger she had let it grow straight down her back, crimping it only for special occasions, but in keeping with the fashion had begun to 'put it up' when about fifteen or so. She never had her hair cut during the whole of her life.

Grace was very conscious of her appearance by the time she gained the attentions of Ernest Bramall. When 'dressed up' for church on Sundays and for the occasional outings, her attire would not have seemed complete without a large, elaborately decorated hat and gloves to match her dress or coat. Her boots of soft leather were polished till they shone their brightest. She was basically a cheerful girl, despite the worry and hardships of their family life, or maybe it was because of the day-to-day tedium of work at home that she was quick to enjoy the happier things in life when opportunities arose. One such opportunity was the celebration of George the Fifth's coronation in 1911 when she was eighteen. That occasion presented a good chance to show off one's finery.

In 1912 Blanche, the eldest of the family, married Frank Purseglove, a man the Spenceleys knew well as he had attended the inn frequently for some time. James had not voiced any objection to the match. Frank was popular with them all and, in any case, Blanche was twenty-three, the age at which he and his wife were when they married. The couple set up house in one of the three cottages near to Travellers Inn, all of which have in recent years been demolished.

Not long afterwards Herbert, the second in the family, got married too. His wife was Gertrude Illingsworth, a cousin of Grace's friend Frances. For a time they lived at the Copster cottage which the Herbert grandparents had previously occupied. Later on they moved into one of the cottages close to Winterbottom's wire mill at Oxspring.

Then, little more than a year afterwards, James Spenceley decided he had had enough of life as a publican. There were two main reasons for the decision. To begin with, he was no longer a young man. He felt that his work at Winterbottom's mill was sufficient without the extra evening duties as innkeeper. The other reason, equally if not more important, was that he was concerned about his wife. He had suspected correctly that she was taking rather more gin than was good for her health and their profits. Elizabeth probably felt overburdened at times by her large family, and in particular by the worry and anxiety over young Harry and Emma. The gin, so conveniently at hand, no doubt provided her with a little solace in an otherwise tedious existence. Her husband thought it would have an adverse effect if given the chance to become a habit so, after their stay of sixteen years, the Spenceleys left Travellers Inn. They had not far to travel to their next home, it being only a mile or so away.

For Grace, leaving the inn meant an end to the cleaning of spitoons, yet she knew with some regret she would miss the lively atmosphere of the Saturday-night jollifications. The Christmases there had been enjoyable too, when she and her mother had handed round the home-made spice cake to all their customers, and her father had made the ale hot by putting in the poker which he had heated in the fire.

CHAPTER 7

Tunnel Top

THE NEW MOVE took Grace and her family up the Jockey road to High Oxspring, or Tunnel Top as it was commonly called. It had acquired the name because the railway line between Barnsley and Penistone passed through a tunnel in that vicinity. The number of dwellings between Four Lane Ends and Tunnel Top can still be counted on one hand, as they could in 1914, for they are the same houses of seventy years ago.

Halfway up the Jockey, along a lane to the right, is Wraithe House Farm; further up and along the next little lane are two smallholdings: Clays Farm and Clays Green. At the top of the road is the red-brick Jockey House. Before the 1930s, when all this stretch of road was widened and new sections made as part of the Penistone Bypass, the route between Jockey House and Tunnel Top wound narrowly round to the left to pass in front of Willow Lane Farm. A quarter of a mile on, up a short lane to the right, are the three houses of Tunnel Top.

James Spenceley and his family settled in the first cottage at the top of the lane. This was the one in which Dyson Bramall the butcher had previously lived, and where his son Ernest had been born. Dyson had since taken over the tenancy of Willow Lane Farm, just back along the road, and was carrying on his butchering business there. His brother William, the notorious 'Owd Bill Brammer', still kept the Tunnel Top Farm, which was across a space of open ground from the cottage. He and Polly had plenty of help as their son Walter and daughter Bertha, both in their teens, were growing up to be useful and could tackle most of the work to be done. The third house stood on its own, being separated from the Spenceleys by garden and yard. It was occupied in those days and for a long time afterwards by a family named Bell, but is now derelict.

Unlike the earlier journey from Cranemoor to Oxspring, the move to Tunnel Top was less of an adventure. They had all travelled the road many times before, when walking to Penistone, so it was already familiar. Even the house to which they were going was well known to them.

Whilst understanding her father's reasons for wanting to move to Tunnel Top, Grace herself did not relish the idea. She would be further away from her friend Frances Illingsworth, so future outings with her seemed unlikely. When there had been concerts and magic lantern shows in Oxspring school, Grace and Frances had usually accompanied each other. Under new circumstances it looked as if even these simple pleasures would have to be curtailed. The road from Four Lane Ends to Tunnel Top was rather too lonely for a girl to be walking on her own at night. Her sister Emma, who was near to Grace in age, was seldom fit to go anywhere, while Mary was six years younger and hardly old enough to be a suitable companion. Though she resigned herself to moving with her family the prospect did look bleak.

At twenty-one Grace felt she would like to widen her horizons rather than be confined in a backwater like Tunnel Top. Two of her acquaintances had done just that, and hearing of their exploits had given Grace the incentive to do the same. These girls were not exactly her friends in the way that Frances was. They did not live nearby, but she often met them at the Oxspring functions and liked them well enough to be interested in their doings.

Fanny Vaughton was one of the girls. She had spoken quite enthusiastically about her situation, or 'place' as she called it, in a gentleman's service at a large house in Huddersfield. Many of the employers in that town were mill owners who could afford to treat their servants well. It was true that Fanny had to work long hours, but she had adequate food, a neat uniform to wear, and a half day off each week. Besides receiving free board and lodging she was also paid a wage. This was not large, but enough to evoke a feeling of satisfaction that she had independence from her parents and a little money of her own. Witnessing Fanny's enthusiasm over her situation, Grace thought she might like to go to 'place' too and earn money like the other girl. When she announced this intention to her mother, Elizabeth promptly dampened her enthusiasm. She hinted broadly that towns such as Huddersfield were full of undesirable characters. The men in particular were ready to take advantage of unsuspecting country girls. Moreover, if Fanny Vaughton had been fortunate in getting a good place, that did not necessarily mean everyone else would be. She had heard of girls in service who were worked harder and fed more frugally than her daughter would be at Tunnel Top.

Grace's other acquaintance who had left home had actually gone to Leeds in order to train for the nursing profession. According to reports received, she was enjoying her new life immensely. Grace had always had a strong desire to become a nurse, even before she was given this extra incentive. In view of her capabilities in tending the sick she would probably have made a good one. Yet, when she expressed to her parents this wish to take up nursing in a hospital, and informed them she had actually written off to Leeds for particulars, the only reply James Spenceley made was, 'I think there's enough nursing for you to do here at home, without going to Leeds to do it.' This was true and, though Grace had reached the age when she was not bound to conform to her father's wishes, her thoughts turned to her young brother Harry, who depended on her for daily care and attention. The bright lights of Leeds, which promised a bit of social life in addition to work, already began to recede. Of course she could not leave home when her mother sorely needed her help in looking after the young ones and her handicapped brother in particular. Pushing away her momentary disappointment, Grace's course at once seemed straight. Her duty clearly lay at Tunnel Top rather than in a city hospital. She realised that, by remaining with her family, the chance to see people and places further afield would have to be sacrificed. This she was willing to do in considering the wishes and needs of other people rather than her own. By showing some of the selflessness that characterised her whole life she quickly abandoned the idea of becoming a nurse.

The house at Tunnel Top was classed as a cottage, but it was large enough and quite adequate for the family of ten. Downstairs was a fair-sized main living room, a sitting room, a fairly big kitchen and a pantry. Cooking was done on the black range in the living room, there being no such facilities in the kitchen. The kitchen contained a large old stone sink, washing copper and items of household equipment. In the pantry a large stone table was a fixture on which food was stored. The downstairs rooms had stone floors. Upstairs were four bedrooms.

To one side of the cottage was a small garden surrounded by a wall. Grace's father was to derive much pleasure and satisfaction from gardening during his years at Tunnel Top. He had never had time nor opportunity when at Travellers, but at the cottage it became his hobby. Rose growing was something at which he excelled; in subsequent years he won many prizes for exhibiting these flowers at Penistone Show.

With Blanche and Herbert married, there were three daughters and five sons at home with their parents at the beginning of 1914. Willie and Mary had left school while the family was still at Travellers Inn. Willie had first begun work at a box mill in Springvale, between

Oxspring and Penistone, walking there early to arrive for six o'clock. After twelve hours at the mill his working day finished at six o'clock in the evening; then he had to walk home. For his work he was paid six shillings a week. When he had been at the mill for a while, Willie began to think that his long hours of labour were worth rather more than six shillings a week. His father was also in agreement, thinking likewise. So, plucking up his courage one day, Willie asked for a rise in wages. His employer told him bluntly that he couldn't have one and, according to a report of the incident, 'If he mentioned the matter again he would rise him under t'arse.' Willie Spenceley did not stay long at the box mill after that. Following in his father's footsteps, in both literal and metaphorical sense, he began to accompany James to the Winterbottom mill. There he started to serve an apprenticeship as a wiredrawer.

George was twelve when his family moved to Tunnel Top, so had one year more at school. He and his two youngest brothers, Frank and Stanley, continued to go to Oxspring. The distance was a little further than from their previous home, but the walk was pleasant. From Tunnel Top their way was by Willow Lane Farm and down the narrow lane just below. This lane was bordered on either side by hedges which included many holly bushes, so it was usually called by the name of Holly Lane rather than Willow Lane by local people. Whichever name is correct, it once formed part of an ancient packhorse trail. From the bottom of the lane the Spenceley children crossed over the mediaeval packhorse bridge spanning the Don to walk up the lane on the other side of the valley. This joined the main road not far from school. This route to Oxspring school was the same as Dyson Bramall's children had taken in earlier years when they lived at Tunnel Top cottage.

Despite her many bouts of ill-health, Grace's sister Emma had reached the age of eighteen when they moved house. James and Elizabeth would have liked to believe that the doctor had exaggerated the seriousness of their daughter's condition, but when they saw the attacks of breathlessness that seized her from time to time they did not doubt in their minds that what he said was true. As far as was possible they treated Emma as a normal girl along with the others, for her own sake and that of the other children, and did not openly dwell on her complaint. Subconsciously they were always prepared for the worst to happen. On her better days Emma did give the outward impression of being a smartly attractive girl who took a pride in her appearance. When she was well enough she liked to attend the Sunday School's afternoon service or the Church service in the evening. Grace and Mary were pleased when their sister was feeling fit to accompany them. They were careful to allow more time to get there on those occasions, since Emma was only permitted to walk steadily.

On the first Sunday in May of that year 1914 Emma was feeling comparatively well. In the afternoon she walked down to Oxspring with the others to join in the Sunday School worship. At tea-time, the weather being beautifully fine and spring-like, Grace and Mary announced their intention of going to Hoylandswaine church for the evening service. When the family lived at Four Lane Ends the girls had often gone to Thurgoland church on Sunday evenings if there was no service at Oxspring, but from Tunnel Top it was nearer to go to Hoylandswaine. On that particular May evening Emma expressed her desire to accompany her sisters to the Hoylandswaine church. She assured her mother that she did not feel at all tired, despite having walked to Oxspring and back in the afternoon. Grace thought that her sister really did look well that evening, as well as she had ever looked, in fact. So, allowing themselves plenty of time for the walk, they got ready early for church. Emma had picked some violets on her way home in the afternoon and, after making them into a little bunch, she pinned them onto her coat. They gave a pleasing finishing touch to her Sunday outfit, looking most appropriate for a spring evening.

Grace and her sisters made their way leisurely to Hoylandswaine. From Tunnel Top they walked up the road for half a mile in the Huddersfield direction until they reached the crossroads where the Huddersfield road is intersected by that from Barnsley to Manchester. Turning right at the crossroads they came to the village of Hoylandswaine another half mile or so further on. The church is situated down Haigh Lane, a minor road forking off to the left from the main road through the village.

The Spenceley girls reached the church on time without having to hurry. They enjoyed the service, which had for its concluding hymn the well-known 'Abide with Me'.

According to old, long-standing tradition, the first Sunday in May has always been known in the Penistone area as 'Spa Sunday'. At Gunthwaite, one of the outlying districts, is a spring whose waters have a peculiar 'rotten egg' kind of taste. This water is supposed to have medicinal, curative properties which could be beneficial for some types of ailments. Admittedly, no one claimed the spa water to be a cure-all, but it was generally regarded as an aid to good health. On Spa Sunday many people would walk from various places in and around Penistone

Emma

to Gunthwaite Spa in order to partake of the water. Most people drank a little on the spot and took some away in bottles too. Apart from going to taste the spa water, folk walked to Gunthwaite simply because it was a pleasurable walk on a nice spring evening and something of a social occasion too. One could meet friends and acquaintances who were seldom seen unless there was some such mutual attraction to draw them together. The young people in particular thought that the annual trek to the Spa on the first Sunday in May was an event not to be missed.

When the Spenceley sisters came out of Hoylandswaine church that evening, Emma declared she would like to walk to the spa. Grace was rather surprised at this. She thought her sister would be tiring after attending services at both Oxspring and Hoylandswaine. Strangely enough, Emma did not appear to be tired. In spite of this, however, Grace wisely insisted that she had done enough walking for that day, or at least she would have by the time they reached home. To go to the spa would mean another two miles walking, which would be too much for her. After only a little reluctance, Emma had to agree that what Grace had said made good sense. Putting thoughts of the spa out of their minds, they turned their steps homewards. They had enjoyed the day's outings and, on arriving home, it was good to see that the walking had apparently done none of them any harm.

Next morning Grace slept later than usual in the bed which she shared with her two sisters. On most mornings Emma was the first to wake, and she would tell the others when it was time to get up. That morning Grace was unaware of the time until she heard her father's stick knocking on the ceiling of the living room below to alert her into getting up. She thought it strange that Emma was not yet awake but was lying quietly still beside her. When her sister failed to respond to gentle efforts to awaken her, Grace called down to her father to tell him. The truth was already dawning tragically upon her, and when James went into the bedroom to look at his daughter he confirmed that Emma had died in her sleep. When her parents became aware of what had happened they were profoundly shocked. They had been told by the doctor long before to be prepared for her death happening suddenly, but when it finally happened they found it hard to believe. Emma had seemed so well on the previous day. Elizabeth realised the doctor's words 'She will go like the crack out of a gun' had proved to be only too true.

Later in the day, when Grace opened the wardrobe door, she saw Emma's coat which she had worn the previous night. The bunch of violets she had pinned on it was still fresh. Thinking sadly of their last visit to church together, Grace felt some relief in the knowledge that she had dissuaded Emma from walking to Gunthwaite. Had they gone to the spa she would have blamed the extra exertion for her death and felt herself guilty for having allowed it. She thought of the church service and that last hymn in particular. Its words held such strong significance that she could not doubt her sister was free of 'Earth's vain shadows' and had indeed been 'pointed to the skies'.

When James had to think of a last resting place for his daughter he decided to buy a double grave space in Thurgoland churchyard just across the path from where their little girl Flora was buried. Elizabeth's parents, William and Mary Herbert, were also not far away.

To Grace the shock of losing her sister was great, but the daily work of attending to the others had still to go on. Her father had certainly spoken the truth when he had declared there was plenty of nursing for her to do at home. As her brother Harry grew older, his handicap became worse instead of better. By the age of eleven he showed little ability or inclination to move about on his own. Much of his time would be spent sitting on the rug, propped against his mother's knees as she rested in her rocking chair near the fire. There was hardly any use in one of Harry's arms, his legs were incapable of walking, and he could not speak more than a few odd words at any time. One of the words he did know how to use was 'Grace'. This was understandable considering it was she who looked after all his physical needs of feeding, washing, toilet, dressing and undressing. Not only did she perform these essential duties for her helpless brother. She tried also to add a little brightness to his life by giving him some enjoyment outside the house.

On warm days Harry liked to go over the field and sit with her on the soft, grassy bank near the hedge. He could see the flowers, watch the farm animals grazing, and listen to the sound of the birds. Grace knew an area where, in June, the bluebells presented a delightful scene that pleased both sight and smell. Harry was happy when going to see the bluebells, so he was taken there when they were in flower. Because he also liked to watch the trains go by, Grace sometimes struggled to take him across to the railway line so that he could have a close view. These outings were only accomplished by a good deal of physical effort on Grace's part, since she had to carry her charge all the way as best she could. Though Harry was smaller and lighter than most boys of his age, he was nevertheless very heavy for her to carry, being almost dead weight. There was never any pushchair or wheelchair bought for the boy, and Grace continued to lift and carry him about to the end of his life. She considered the effort worthwhile if it brought a little pleasure into her unfortunate brother's life.

As all her other brothers grew older and bigger, so their appetites increased. At Tunnel Top Grace baked bread twice a week in addition to making a large quantity of pies, tarts and cakes.

She did the family washing each Monday. After filling the 'set-pot' with water and lighting a fire underneath, her next duty, while waiting for the water to heat, was to brush the Sunday clothes. These were the suits worn by her father and brothers the previous day. Although worn only for a few hours, they had to be meticulously inspected for bits of dust, fluff, or anything else that might mar their wearers' appearance when next put on. This would not be until the Sunday following, unless there happened to be some special occasion such as a marriage or funeral which warranted dressing up in one's best clothes. It never occurred to the menfolk to brush their suits themselves and put them away in the wardrobe. Grace accepted the brushing of clothes as part of her household duties. She considered her father and brothers were fully occupied with work and school while she, being at home all day, could find the time to do it. When she had given the five or six suits a thorough brushing she would hang them carefully again in their respective wardrobes until they were next needed. The water in the set-pot would be getting hot for the washing meanwhile. This took up the whole day on Monday because of the amount of clothes to be hand-washed and the fact that other work had to be done too. There were meals to prepare and clear away and Harry to attend to several times during the course of the day.

The set-pot was in use again on bath nights of course. Grace continued to light the fire, heat the water and fill the bath for each member of the family, emptying it again when each of them had finished as she had done when they were younger. Even when they grew quite big and were well able to lift the buckets themselves she continued willingly with the Friday night ritual of seeing they all had a comfortable bath.

Cleaning one's house in those days involved much rubbing, scrubbing, and use of 'elbow grease'. Grace Spenceley was always a fastidious person. Ever since their early days at Travellers, when she had been stood to the sink on a box to do the washing up, she had taken pride and pleasure in seeing things clean and tidy. While her mother also believed that 'cleanliness is next to godliness', the older woman, nearing fifty and having produced eleven children, had little strength or energy left to put the theory into practice. Fortunately, Grace did not mind doing the cleaning. She was young and healthy so took the floor scrubbing in her stride, though it meant much time spent on hands and knees. Years later she was heard to remark jokingly that the reason for her never growing tall was that she had spent so many hours kneeling on the floor when young and this had restricted her growth.

For a family as large as the Spenceleys there was a good deal of shopping to be done. Most of their provisions had to be fetched in, because Tunnel Top was somewhat off the track of the roundsmen at that time. One exception, luckily, was meat. Dyson Bramall, the butcher who lived just along the road at Willow Lane Farm, hawked meat to Hoylandswaine in a horse-drawn cart. He called at the Spenceleys and the other Tunnel Top houses on the way. If any extra meat was needed, apart from on the hawking days, it wasn't too far to go along the road for some. Milk, butter and eggs were three other important commodities near at hand. They could be obtained each day or when required from Bill's farm across the yard and round the corner, where a smiling Polly was always ready to oblige.

The nearest shop to their Tunnel Top house was the one at Four Lane Ends. This stocked most of the groceries that were needed by the family and other items besides. For goods which could not be obtained at that shop Grace walked to Penistone, going down the fields, across the river and up into Springvale, or 'Nibble Bottom' as it was commonly called then. The latter name had evolved from the local title given to Messrs Cammel Laird and Company's steelworks situated nearby. Most people around Penistone referred to the works as 't'Nibble', though why this was so is not certain. Whilst the walk to Penistone was enjoyable, the return journey, which involved carrying the shopping uphill, could be tiring. On the few occasions when something special had to be bought, trips to Barnsley were made. From Tunnel Top the most convenient way was to walk to the railway station at Silkstone Common and go by train. There were no buses in the area until several years later, and the Spenceleys had no wheeled transport of their own.

Every two or three weeks Graced walked to the cobbler's shop at Hoylandswaine, taking a short cut through a small plantation of trees just before reaching the crossroads. These visits to Joe Heeley the cobbler were to take or fetch back the boots needing repair. In those days, when most people's footwear was of leather, the uppers would last a long time. The soles wore out first due to the many miles of walking done then, and it was of course more economical to have new leather soles fitted rather than buy a new pair of boots if the upper parts were still good. Working folk would have their footwear re-soled and re-heeled several times and would never consider discarding a pair of boots until the uppers were wearing out too. When Grace was young the girls and women, as well as their menfolk, wore leather boots. Theirs not only covered the feet but also enclosed the bottom part of the leg. Sometimes they were fastened by being laced up the front, but it was fashionable too to have them buttoned up. The buttons were numerous, being fairly small and close together, and because the boots were tight-fitting a buttonhook was used as an aid in fastening them. Shoes did not come into fashion for general wear among the working-class folk until a short time later. Since the Spenceley family was large, and most of its members did a fair amount of walking, Grace's visits to Joe Heeley's were made quite frequently.

There was always plenty of sewing and mending to be done for the family. Elizabeth was able to undertake some of this as she was sitting in her chair, but had to admit that it was her daughter who could do the neatest darns and put on the best patches. Grace's early promise of skill with a needle, as shown in her schooldays, developed into real ability when she grew up. The task of mending clothes was performed mostly in the evenings, and often late at night, because the daytime hours were filled with all the many other duties.

Her father's working trousers and waistcoat often needed repair. The vitriol used in his wiredrawing work sometimes splashed onto them, burning holes in the garments. Patching these holes called for time and patience because the trousers were made of thick corduroy which, through constant rubbing against the workbench, became hard and shiny. It was difficult to push a sewing-needle through the material in some places, so the work of mending could only be done slowly with one stitch at a time. Sometimes the needle would break in the process. As James had only one pair of working trousers in use at one time, this necessitated his daughter's mending them at night after he had gone to bed. She would fetch them from outside his bedroom door, take them downstairs to mend, then put them outside his door again ready for his use early next day. Despite the difficulties encountered in the mending, the results were good enough to win genuine praise from her father. James was once heard to remark to a friend, 'Our Grace has put me some lovely patches on mi trousers.' When she was later told of the compliment, Grace felt genuine pleasure. The knowledge that her efforts were appreciated was reward enough for one who never asked for wages from her parents. Besides being fed and clothed she had only a half-crown spending money each week for herself. This proved to be adequate all the same, since she rarely went anywhere to spend it.

CHAPTER 8

Time of the Great War

THE SPENCELEYS WERE still feeling the loss of their daughter Emma when, three months after her death, the Great War broke out. At first this made little impact on the people at Tunnel Top, who were kept busy with their own day-to-day affairs. Towards the end of the year George, being thirteen, left school. He went to work as a 'farm lad' at the first farm up the road from his home. This was Whitefield Farm, occupied by a Mr Richardson who was a bachelor. George worked twelve hours a day for seven or eight shillings a week. He had his tea at the farm but was not provided with dinner. He went home for this meal in the middle of the day. George liked farm work and showed a natural aptitude in dealing with animals. Like the proverbial 'farmer's boy' he also learned to plough, sow, reap and mow, all these operations being performed with the help of horse power. He stayed at Whitefield for three years, and so became initiated into the farming way of life. Unhappily his employer died at the age of thirty-nine from cancer. This had started in his wrist and when George, seeing it bandaged, asked if he had cut himself, he merely shrugged the matter away by telling the boy to carry on with his work. Later on it caused him to go into hospital, where he lost his arm. Even then the trouble was not stopped, for the rest of his body was affected so that he died. After his three years' working for Mr Richardson, George decided to get a job at Cammel Laird's. As he himself put it, he 'went to work at t'Nibble.' He was better off financially at the ironworks, but some instinct told him that his farming days were far from being at an end.

His brother Willie was eighteen in November of that eventful year of 1914. Already the war against Germany had loomed larger into the view of Oxspring people. Seeming to draw nearer all the while and gaining momentum as it did so, it was soon touching even the quiet country places such as Tunnel Top. The Spenceleys became aware that this war, unlike the one in remote South Africa of a few years previously, was closer to them and could even affect their own lives. From the newspapers they learned of the country's need to train more young men as soldiers to augment the regular army. More volunteers were needed to ensure a quick victory.

If Willie Spenceley and his contemporaries entertained any doubt as to the truth of what they read and heard, these doubts were quickly dispelled when they saw the stern, moustached face of Lord Kitchener looking out at them from the posters on the wall. That great army field marshal was telling them seriously, 'Your country needs YOU', and they were quite convinced this was so because his finger was pointing directly at them. Willie and his friends were patriotic young men, eager to help their country. On being thus assured it really did want them, they showed no hesitation in offering their services. In January 1915, only a few weeks after his eighteenth birthday, Willie Spenceley broke off his wiredrawing apprenticeship at Winterbottom's to join the British Army. He enlisted as a private in the King's Own Yorkshire Light Infantry, along with two other young men he knew quite well. Albert Vaughton and Billy Tyas were both local boys who worked with him in the Oxspring wire mill and, for quite some time, the three had been good friends. They did their preliminary training at Strensall Barracks near York, where Willie became very proficient in the use of a rifle, so much so that he was awarded a stripe later on.

On completion of their training, the time came for them to go over to France, to put the training into practice by killing other young men like themselves but who happened to be Germans. Just before their departure for overseas, Willie's friends arrived at Tunnel Top to call on him so that they could all leave together. Elizabeth Spenceley expressed her anxiety for their safety, voicing her feelings of trepidation by saying she wished they hadn't to go. Albert Vaughton, trying to allay her fears, replied cheerily, 'Don't worry Missis, it won't be long before it's over and we're coming back again.'

The boys were all in good spirits, as if relishing the prospect of going to a foreign country. The travel in itself would be an adventure since none of them had even been to London, let alone sailed across the English Channel. There was another local man who, when he was about to go overseas, remarked that he was looking forward to going to France as it would be 'a nice little holiday'.

In spite of their misgivings as to what lay in store for the young men at the other side of the water, the Spenceley family could not help but admire the smart, well-groomed appearance they presented. Youthful exuberance at the prospect of unknown adventure awaiting just ahead was reflected in their bright, eager faces, while the army training just received was apparent in the straight, soldierly figures that carried the khaki uniforms so proudly. The shine on jacket buttons and on boots contributed to the boys' immaculate appearance. The uniform jackets fastened up to the neck in front by five brass buttons. They had four more such buttons, one on each of the two

Grace and Willie

top pockets and one on each bottom pocket. Round the bottom part of their legs the soldiers wore puttees. These were long strips of webbing material which were wound neatly round and round over the trouser bottoms from ankle to knee. Their boots were strongly made of black leather. Their hats, flat on top and peaked in front, bore the regimental badge. A short cane in the hand completed the dress uniform. The boys had had photographs taken in their new uniforms. Willie had one taken with his sister Grace too. Needless to say, this was one of the photographs she kept and treasured throughout her life.

Willie Spenceley and his friends were by no means the only men in their area to join the army. Throughout the district more and more of them exchanged their working clothes for khaki uniforms. In due course, Albert Vaughton's younger brother Clifford became a soldier too, joining the York and Lancaster regiment. As time went on, some women whose sons and brothers had become soldiers tended to cast hostile glances and make hurtful remarks towards the men remaining behind. There were excuses naturally for those engaged in vital work that only men could do. Wiredrawing was one skilled job that required long apprenticeship so, unlike some types of work, it could not be taken over at short notice by women. Herbert Spenceley considered that his work at Winterbottom's was sufficient reason for him to remain at home, apart from the fact of his having a wife and child to support.

After Grace's younger sister Mary left school, she spent part of her time helping at home, but went regularly down to Four Lane Ends to assist her married sister Blanche with the babies. During the war years, however, Mary obtained well-paid work in the railway company's offices at Penistone goods station. The men who had been employed in clerical work in all the railway offices had gone to the war and were being replaced by suitable girls. The railway at Penistone was busy. It carried a lot of traffic, both in goods and passengers, at the time of the Great War. Penistone was an important junction for the trains, and the railway company had to be discriminating in their choice of girls who were to take over the men's work. The girls had first to pass a test to prove their ability and fitness for their duties. Mary had travelled to Manchester to be interviewed, and was pleased to be told she had qualified for work with the company. She thought herself particularly lucky to be given a job at Penistone, because she could then continue to live at home and walk to her work each day. In winter. when her walk home had to be made in the dark, her brother George went down the fields to meet her and give company on the lonely part of the journey. Mary's wage from the railway company made a useful contribution to the family's finances.

As chief household help, Grace often found that adjustments had to be made, in those war years, to the running of the house. Certain provisions were hard to obtain. Sugar was in short supply. Flour appeared to have changed its quality for the worse, since when made into bread this was somewhat darker than before and did not taste as nice. However, the people at Tunnel Top were far from starving in spite of the many inconveniences. In common with other families, they felt that the discomforts they had to endure at home were not to be compared with those their menfolk in France were experiencing.

People were beginning to realise that the war was not going to be short with a quick victory after a few months. They learned that living in the trenches, under fire for day after day, was a far cry from the holiday that someone had at first anticipated.

Clifford Vaughton in 1915

Willie came home on leave tired and quiet, with a different look on his face. He seemed reluctant to speak of his experiences in France, but when pressed told them a little about life in the trenches and the mud that was so much a part of it all. He mentioned briefly the deadly effects of machine gun fire, and how at night the sky was so lit up by gunfire that it seemed as light as day.

Grace's first reaction when her brother came home was to light the set-pot fire and heat enough water for him to have a much-needed bath. Then, after he had put on a change of clean clothes, she took his dirty ones and put them in the copper to get rid of the lice. In all her washing experience she had never before dealt with clothes quite like them. It was not surprising that, at the end of his leave, Willie did not appear as keen to go back to France as he had done in the beginning.

Then in July of 1916 came news which Elizabeth had all along dreaded to hear. Willie had been wounded on the first day of the month in a fierce battle that raged along the River Somme. Whilst fearing the worst to begin with, she was later much relieved to learn that her son's wound was not too serious and that it would eventually heal. A bullet had passed straight through his left shoulder, entering at the front and coming out behind. He was brought home to England and kept in hospital for several weeks at Warrington, where his father was able to visit him. There were many young men of the King's Own Yorkshire Light Infantry who were killed and injured near the Somme on that first day of July.

While he was in hospital his regiment was involved in still more terrible fighting and slaughter. Willie's family came to regard his wound as a 'lucky' one, since it kept him out of action for three months and away from some of the worst destruction. In one 'big push' many of his comrades were killed, including his close friend and former workmate Albert Vaughton. On that same day in September when Albert was killed, his brother Clifford was gravely injured. He was brought back to an English hospital in Gloucester suffering from severe abdominal wounds. Though he lived for four more months, his condition deteriorated painfully so that even his family were in no doubt as to the tragic outcome. Clifford was brought back then to his home town of Penistone to be buried with full military honours in the cemetery there. The funeral service in Penistone church was attended by most of the townspeople, who found it hard to control their emotion. Some did not bother to try. According to Grace, 'There was not a dry eye in Penistone church that day.' Sympathies went out to the parents who had lost two fine sons. Though they knew there were countless others in like situation, this was small comfort to them. Albert and Clifford had been their boys.

The Spenceley family found it difficult to believe the loss of the two brothers they had known so well. Grace's thoughts turned back to the day, less than two years before, when Albert had called on Willie at Tunnel Top. He had been so full of life and optimistic about the future. Her mother showed feelings of anger as well as sorrow. She pointed out what a terrible waste it was when women spent time bringing sons into the world and rearing them, only to have them shot at when they grew up. Despite her views on the matter, Willie had been sent back to France to risk his life again when he was sufficiently recovered from his shoulder wound.

Besides taking over men's jobs during the war years, many of the girls contributed to the national effort by knitting for the soldiers. At Oxspring a group of knitters was organised by that benevolent lady Mrs Arthur Winterbottom. She invited girls who had been in her Sunday School class to her house each week where, together, they knitted socks and balaclava helmets for the troops abroad. Mrs Arthur of course provided the wool. Mary Spenceley was a member of that working party. Grace, being older and fully occupied at home, did not join them, though she had continued to go to Sunday School until the family left Travellers Inn, being a teacher during the last few years there. Mary walked down to the knitting sessions with three other girls of similar age. One of these was Bertha Bramall, daughter of Bill and Polly who lived across at the farm. Bertha was fair, smooth-haired, and had the kind of clear, fresh complexion usually associated with farmers' daughters. Her features resembled her mother's. It was easy to imagine that Polly when young had looked very much like her daughter. Bertha, however, was of bigger build. Having much of her father's physical strength she could work alongside her brother Walter, tackling almost any of the men's jobs on the farm. She enjoyed working outdoors and preferred it to being inside doing housework. Nevertheless, on the evenings at Mrs Arthur's she presented as feminine an appearance as any of the others in her neat white blouse, dark skirt, black stockings and shoes.

Most of the younger women and girls were beginning to wear shoes rather than boots by this time and their skirts, though still well below the knee in length, were a few inches shorter than before the war. Apart from economy of material this change in fashion was necessary when so many girls were becoming more mobile. Some were riding bicycles to get to their place of work more quickly and easily, and shorter skirts were more convenient for this activity.

Bertha, incidentally, had been wrongly named when a baby. Her mother had intended she should be called Laura after one of the six daughters of her brother, Ben Watts. Bill had been told this name when he was dispatched to register the birth, but after first calling in at the Fours for a few drinks he had forgotten the name by the time he reached the registry office. He remembered it was to be after one of Polly's nieces, but could not decide which one. Whereupon he made a guess and named the child after the eldest of Ben's daughters, who happened to be Bertha. No doubt 'Owd Bill' received some chastisement for his error, but this would not have bothered him greatly.

The other two girls who accompanied Mary and Bertha to the meetings at Mrs Arthur's were Gladys and Hilda Bramall of Willow Lane Farm. They were sisters of Ernest and Bertha's cousins since their father, Dyson the butcher, was brother to Bill. They had an older sister, Ethel, who was the same age as Grace. During their schooldays Grace and Ethel had been in the same class. Ethel had also taken part in that memorable 'Holiday Concert' put on by Mr Cooper their teacher. While Grace's role had been that of the flower girl, Ethel Bramall had been a 'fruit girl'. The Bramall sisters were always well groomed and spotlessly clean. When going to Mrs Winterbottom's house nothing less than perfection in appearance would have satisfied their mother.

Gladys and Hilda were both good-looking girls, though not alike. Hilda had beautiful, shining dark hair that was almost black, expressive brown eyes and a nose that was slightly aquiline. Her face was oval. She could have been described as a handsome girl rather than a pretty one. Gladys had hair of a lighter brown, blue eyes and a rounder face. Neither of the two girls went to any work outside her home, even during those war years. Living on a farm meant there was adequate employment on the spot, especially when a high standard of efficiency was insisted upon regarding the housework. So Hilda and Gladys stayed at home after leaving school to help their mother, while Ethel who had been at home left to go into service elsewhere. Gladys had been an exceptionally good scholar when at Oxspring school, winning a place from there to the Grammar School at Penistone in 1908. As she was the only person from the whole High Oxspring area to attend that school, she had to undertake the lonely walk on her own. In winter it was already dark by the time she reached Hoylandswaine crossroads on the return journey. She felt some apprehension on nearing the gloomy plantation a little further on, but the only thing to be done was to hasten her steps to pass those darkly looming trees as quickly as she could. Gladys did well at the Grammar School, being higher in her class than some girls who later became teachers, but the decision was taken that she should leave at fifteen. Her parents probably considered it more important for her to learn the household skills that she would be likely to need later on rather than subjects such as French and science which would never be of use to her.

The four girls from High Oxspring enjoyed their evenings at Mrs Arthur's. To them it was a pleasant change from work and family. Knitting stockings was not regarded as work but as a leisure occupation.

Mrs Arthur's knitting group

It afforded them a chance to talk with other girls from the Oxspring area, among whom were Alice Wray, Doris Vaughton, Reenie Brettoner, Martha Fretwell and Phyllis Senior. They all revered Mrs Arthur and regarded it a great privilege to be in her house. Grace often described that lady as 'a lovely woman' in every sense of the word, who put into practice those Christian ideals she tried to instil into her Sunday School classes.

One evening Mrs Arthur arranged for her knitting group to be photographed outside her house, much to everyone's delight. The picture shows the girls, some seated and others standing behind, with their teacher in the middle of the back row. All the girls look youthfully fresh and neat in long-sleeved white blouses above dark skirts. The only exception to this general attire is Reenie Brettoner who is wearing a white dress. She is positioned in the middle of the front row, presumably to balance the picture.

One of the prettiest faces on that photograph is Mary Spenceley's. Large grey eyes look out steadily from a gently contoured face, giving a look of dreamy innocence that is almost childlike. The brown hair framing her face is inclined to wave and arranged becomingly. The calm, gentle expression shown in the picture reflected Mary's whole personality. Throughout her life she was a patient, tolerant, good-natured person who never hurt anyone. At the time of the knitting evenings she was a sociable enough girl in her quiet way, being on friendly terms with most of her contemporaries. Because of this, together with her evenness of temper, she was generally well liked. Mary never possessed the vigour and boundless energy as did her sister Grace. She took things rather more steadily but was conscientious all the same in what she did, sometimes to the point of worrying overmuch.

Grace acquired another friend while living at Tunnel Top, a good friend who would remain so for the rest of her life. She was Betty Peaker who, when she married, became Betty Fieldsend. Frances Illingsworth was still a friend, but she and Grace were living rather too far apart then to be in regular contact. Betty Peaker had come to live at Jockey House, which was considerably nearer to Tunnel Top. She was the same age as Grace. Because her parents were dead, she lived at the Jockey with her uncle. It seemed he was a tolerant man for, when his business took him away from home, he allowed Betty to have her friends in the house. The fact that the company was not restricted to girls did not cause him undue concern. Grace was pleased to accept the invitations to the carefree gatherings. Betty's lively good humour was infectious, so the atmosphere on those occasions soon became quite jovial. After a while the rugs on the floor were rolled up and put out of the way, and furniture moved aside so that dancing could be practised.

Unfortunately for Grace, she had always to keep an eye on the clock. She was never able to stay to the end of those parties but had to return home when the jollifications were in full swing. Although she was over twenty-one, she would not risk her parents' displeasure by staying out too late. Yet despite the restrictions, her happy association with Betty Peaker did much to lighten the burdens of care and anxiety which surrounded her in the family home.

Elizabeth Spenceley never ceased to worry about her son Willie as the war continued its course. Her younger boy Harry was also a constant care. From time to time he had convulsion fits when he seemed insensible to everything around him. Grace felt great compassion for her brother when these occurred, but there seemed to be no way of preventing them. The doctors could offer no remedy at all. The best thing Grace could do was to make the boy as comfortable as possible afterwards, putting into practice the natural ability she had for nursing.

Apart from the anxiety over Willie and Harry, before the war was over another family trouble emerged disturbingly. The Spenceleys' eldest son, Herbert, married with two small boys, began to have fits too. He had reached the age of twenty-seven and had been until then a normally healthy young man. Elizabeth was naturally very upset at the prospect of yet another of her family suffering a handicap. Herbert's fits were the epileptic kind that had afflicted others of her own family, the Herberts. Remembering how sorely her sister Blanche had been afflicted by the fits, ending her life in an asylum, she feared for Herbert, wondering what the outcome was going to be in his case. Herbert received no warning when a fit was about to occur. He just fell down where he happened to be, often sustaining quite nasty injuries. He continued to work at Winterbottom's mill in spite of everything and tried to carry on as normally as possible. Having a wife and two young children he felt that the good wages he earned as a wiredrawer were needed to support them. The management at Winterbottom's were very understanding. They allowed him to continue for a while in the same job. After all, Herbert's fits did not happen too often to begin with. Later on, however, they increased in frequency and he sometimes took hard knocks resulting in bad bruises to his face.

Then one day at work he had a fit which caused injuries of even more serious nature. He fell forward with his hands going down flat onto the bottom of one of the ovens. The oven was quite hot so that Herbert's hands were badly burned. Of course he had to stay away from the mill until the terrible blisters healed. It was realised by his employers, and by his father too, that for Herbert to continue working as a wiredrawer would be courting disaster. There were too many possible dangers inside the mill. Yet no one wanted to stop him working there entirely. Herbert had been a conscientious worker, while his father James had been a valued employee of the firm for twenty years. After some deliberation it was agreed that Herbert Spenceley could remain at Winterbottom's, though not in his former capacity as a wiredrawer. He would be employed outside the mill, mainly in keeping the place tidy and helping with the gardening. There would be minimal risk of his being badly hurt during a fit. The fact that his father was working at the mill helped Herbert's case, since they all knew James would be readily available if his son needed him. Herbert was naturally perturbed to hear he hadn't to draw wire again. At the same time he was pleased that he still had work, and grateful that he hadn't to leave the mill.

Grace's eldest sister Blanche, who had married Frank Purseglove, became the mother of four daughters between the years 1913 and 1917. Because she had a weak heart and was in indifferent health for much of the time, Grace often walked down the Jockey road to her sister's house at Four Lane Ends to help her with the children after Mary went to work on the railway. Blanche followed the old custom, when choosing names for her daughters, of calling them after relatives. The eldest girl was named Flora Winifred, Flora being in memory of her little sister who had died from diphtheria at the age of four. Her second child was Mary Emma, named after two more sisters. The third daughter was Blanche Barbara Elizabeth who took the name Barbara for general use but had her mother's and grandmother's names included too. Blanche's youngest child was generally called Myrtle, but her full Christian name was Grace Myrtle.

When their children were all very small Blanche and Frank decided to move from their house near Travellers Inn to one at Coates, next door to the Illingsworths. This was only a short distance of two or three hundred yards higher up from the Four Lane Ends crossroads, being at the top of the hill before the road descended again in the direction of Silkstone Common, Dodworth and Barnsley. The small community at Near Coates comprised three roadside cottages and a small farm at the same side but just off the road on a short lane to the right. When the cottages were first built there had been five, but they had since been converted into three so as to give the families a little more living space. The Illingsworths lived in the middle house, Blanche moved into the end one nearest the farm and Four Lane Ends, while the cottage at the other end was occupied by Ned Thompson and his wife Annie. A larger farm and two more cottages were situated across a field at the other side of the road. A longer lane led to these houses which, presumably because they were further from the road, were called Far Coates. All the houses at both Near and Far Coates are still occupied and in good condition nearly seventy years after Blanche made her home there. The main change to the appearance of Near Coates generally is that two modern bungalows now stand on the piece of land that was formerly garden space for the three cottages.

While Blanche was getting her new home in order, Grace assisted her in moving furniture, cleaning, minding children and helping generally. Frank Purseglove worked at the 'Nibble' and did not get home until quite late because he had to walk from Penistone. He was good with the children when he was at home, taking them out for walks on Sundays, but like most husbands of that day had neither time nor inclination to undertake any cleaning or wallpapering jobs. It was Grace therefore who, when her sister wanted one of the bedrooms papered, volunteered to assist with the work and almost came to grief in doing so.

Blanche liked papering. It was something she could do well without its overtaxing her strength. She had, however, to avoid making too many journeys up and down stairs. When it was necessary for someone to go down to cut more paper it was Grace who did this. The cutting of the paper had to be done downstairs as there was shortage of space in the bedroom. The pasting equipment was there of course and, as the children were milling around at the same time, the room appeared rather full. There was the possibility too that either paper or children might be harmed by the scissors if Grace tried to do the cutting upstairs.

On that particular day she was just on the point of descending the stairs with the roll of wallpaper and scissors in hand when she realised that Myrtle, little more than a baby, was close behind her. Thinking the child would either fall downstairs or perhaps be accidentally pushed by one of the older ones, she decided to take Myrtle down with her. After all, she could manage to cut the paper and watch one child if the others stayed upstairs out of the way. They seemed to be engrossed in watching their mother doing the pasting. So, using the same arm and hand to carry paper and scissors, Grace picked up Myrtle in her other arm and took a step downwards.

Alarmingly she felt herself missing the step. The thought flashed through her mind in that one second that, whatever else happened, she must keep her small niece safe. The flight of steps was steep and made of stone. Somehow her instinct told her to jump clear of them and this she did, still clutching the child to her. Recounting the incident afterwards she would say, 'I jumped straight from top to bottom with Myrtle in my arm.' She landed at the bottom, more or less on her feet and with no broken bones, but her face banged into the side of the door as she did so, causing massive bruising all around one eye. In a matter of minutes the swelling became 'as big as a piesball.' Her only other injury was a cut to her elbow from the scissors, but this was bad enough to leave a small permanent scar. Miraculously, no harm whatsoever was done to Myrtle. She did not sustain even one small bruise because she had been so well cushioned against her aunt's body as they had hurtled downwards.

Despite the nasty, jarring experience which had happened so suddenly and unexpectedly, Grace felt thankful that things were no worse. Myrtle was unhurt, which was her main concern. Though she herself was temporarily shaken, with one eye so hugely puffed around that it seemed almost closed, at least she was still able to help her sister to finish the wallpapering.

Next day, back home at Tunnel Top, the Spenceleys' neighbour who lived in the other house across the garden went to ask for Grace's help. His wife was feeling ill that morning, too ill to knead her bread, in fact. He wondered if Grace could spare the time to do it for her. While he was making his request, he was looking quizzically at her black eye, so she told him briefly of the previous day's mishap. She said she would be only too pleased to knead the bread for his wife but felt rather self-conscious about going away from home lest anyone should see her face in its black-eyed, swollen state. The neighbour said he didn't know as they were expecting visitors that day, so Grace went across to help. In the middle of the bread kneading a knock on the door announced the arrival of an insurance man who began to make pleasant conversation. Grace, not wishing to appear deaf or unsociable, made suitable replies and comments as she vigorously continued to knead the dough. She kept her back turned all the while, fearful of the horror he might express if he saw the swollen, discoloured condition of her eye. Fortunately her neighbour was soon able to divert the man's attention from her, but she worried for a while after he had gone about what he would be thinking of her bad manners in not looking at him while they were talking.

CHAPTER 9

Later Years at Tunnel Top

IN COMMON WITH everyone else they knew, the Spenceley family were full of relief when the war came to an end. Willie came home to stay and never again showed any desire to leave his own country. Another young serviceman who came back from the war, fortunately unscathed, was Mrs Vaughton's third and last son, brother to Albert and Clifford who had died. Although she had lost two of her boys, the youngest was afterwards conscripted too by that unsparing, insatiable war-machine which neither heeded nor considered a mother's feelings.

For a short period Willie went back to Winterbottom's with the idea of continuing the wiredrawing apprenticeship that had been so suddenly interrupted when he became a soldier. His wartime experiences had, however, unsettled him to some extent. It wasn't long before he was changing his mind about becoming a wiredrawer and decided, to his father's annoyance, to leave Winterbottom's. Perhaps he thought that, at twenty-two, he was too old to be still an apprentice. There might also have been some truth in Grace's assumption that he didn't want his hands to be rough and sore again, which undoubtedly they would be if he was working with the wire. All wiredrawers in those days had to go through a stage of discomfort from soreness before their hands became sufficiently hardened to withstand the friction of the wire without its bothering them. Willie had been through that stage before, but his years in the army, despite the many horrors, had allowed his hands to soften again. Their appearance seemed to matter to him considerably, Grace observed, all the more so when he began courting Annie Whitfield, a pretty girl from Springvale. He had first met Annie before going away to the war, and was anxious to continue the relationship on a permanent basis when he returned. Annie was one of the girls who, like his sister Mary, had done a wartime job in the railway offices. At other times, being the eldest in her family of nine children, she, like Grace, stayed at home to help her mother and found plenty to do.

On leaving Winterbottom's Willie tried to get a job on the railway but did not succeed. He eventually found employment as a roadworker for the West Riding County Council. When his brother Frank left school at fourteen he did obtain a position on the Penistone railway. He was assigned to the signal box with a Mr Thompson who was to train him in the work. The youngest Spenceley brother, Stanley, went to work at Cammell Laird's as an apprentice boilermaker.

Grace was twenty-five when the Great War ended. After more than four years at Tunnel Top her way of life was showing little change. She continued to look after the daily needs of her family, which were somewhat greater than they had been before. With all her brothers growing up and going out to daily work there was more cooking and baking to be done, more shopping, and more washing and mending. She went to church on Sundays as usual and to the annual 'Feasts' as they came round.

Sometimes in the course of getting provisions, Grace had to go on to the Willow Lane Farm to buy meat from Dyson 'Brammer's' butcher's shop. Though most of their requirements were delivered by his son Ernest as he made his rounds, it was often necessary to fetch some extra in between times. 'Old Dyson' had taken a liking to Grace over the years and, on occasions, slyly asked if she would like to have 'a word with our Ernest', implying his willingness to give encouragement to any impending match. When an acquaintance remarked it was strange that a smart fellow such as Ernest should be approaching thirty and still be unattached, Dyson replied knowingly, 'Oh, he's only waiting for Grace to make her mind up.'

It wasn't until two years after the war ended that she and Ernest revived the romance that had first flickered into life ten years earlier. In the meantime a kind of silent understanding had existed between them. Though he sometimes went to a dance because he enjoyed the music and gaiety, he never had any other girlfriends whom he considered seriously. Grace had somehow never found time to learn to dance, though she too liked music well enough. The fact that ten years had to pass before Dyson Bramall's prediction was realised was basically because each of the pair was too fully preoccupied by home duties to spend time going courting. Ernest had been taking over the brunt of the butchering work from his father from the age of sixteen because Dyson's health was not good. There was farm work to be done too, including hand milking. His brother Willis took on the responsibility for this when he was old enough but, since he was ten years younger, there had been a period when Ernest was both butcher and farmer.

Unlike so many of his contemporaries, Ernest had not joined the army. The nature of his work was such that it could not have been undertaken by women. His father, Joseph Dyson, was having heart trouble by that time and was almost an invalid. Then he suffered a stroke, after which he had difficulty in walking. During one winter he was so ill that he was confined to bed for six months. In the February of 1920 he died. Ernest continued to run the business for his mother.

By the time he was twenty-nine he evidently thought he was entitled to think a little about his own life. Possibly Grace had begun to have similar views about hers too because, in that year of 1920, she allowed him to escort her home from Penistone Feast. That was the beginning of their three-year courtship.

One of their first outings together was a visit to the theatre in Sheffield. The variety performance was much enjoyed by them both, but in Grace's case the pleasure was somewhat adulterated by her mother's attitude afterwards. Elizabeth Spenceley was not in favour of her daughter's association with Ernest Bramall. She hardly spoke to her at all during the week following the theatre visit. When she did eventually break the silence it was to criticise not only Ernest but all his family too. Her remarks about them were far from complimentary.

Grace was intelligent enough to read into her mother's apparent displeasure. She knew it was not merely the Bramalls she was against. Elizabeth would have shown antagonism to any other man who wanted to form a serious attachment with her. Grace realised that her mother did not welcome the idea of her courting anyone because it posed a threat. One day she might actually leave home to get married. If this happened, who would take on all the many duties that Grace had fulfilled for so long? Perhaps the thought that was uppermost in her mind was the question of who could look after Harry. Mary would be there to render some assistance, but she had neither the energy nor the aptitude for doing all the things that her sister had been accustomed to doing. She had very little experience in dealing with her handicapped brother Harry. In fact the boy himself seemed to want no one else but Grace to attend to him.

Whilst admitting to herself that it would pose something of a problem to the family if she left them, Grace did feel she was entitled to some life of her own. After all, she had reached the age of twenty-seven. She thought her mother was acting selfishly but, understanding the predicament, did not reproach her. She said nothing untoward but waited hopefully for her to get over the shock and accept the situation with good grace. In a short time Elizabeth did.

Though there were more visits to the theatre they were only managed at irregular intervals. Going to Sheffield took up a lot of time. They had to walk to Penistone and go from there by train. It was late by the time they reached home again after walking back up the fields to Tunnel Top.

Outings to the pictures took place more often. In theory Grace and Ernest went each week, Tuesday being 'picture night'. The films were the silent variety in 1920 but they seemed then to be quite wonderful and an improvement on the magic lantern shows of earlier years.

The fact that Tuesday night was picture night did not mean that the plan was strictly and invariably adhered to. Quite often a little note would be handed in at Tunnel Top during Tuesday afternoon. It conveyed Ernest's regrets that he would be unable to finish work in time to go to the pictures that evening. All kinds of situations could arise on a farm, where looking after animals and crops took distinct priority over personal pleasures. In spring the lambing needed constant vigilance on Tuesdays as well as on all the other days. Haymaking and harvest time called for work to be carried out when the weather was right for it. Whatever the day or time of day, the state of crops and outdoor conditions dictated whether or not a few brief hours could be spared for something as unnecessary as going to the pictures.

Far from feeling disappointment when the notes arrived, Grace was usually relieved that she hadn't to rush her work in order to make the time to go out. It was always difficult for her to fit in the picture night at best of times. Apart from tending Harry and putting him to bed, her evenings were generally taken up with mending clothes or sewing some new article. Sometimes when they did go to the pictures she fell asleep halfway through the film simply because she was too tired to keep awake.

There was one evening in the week, however, when she seldom missed going out. That was Sunday evening. She went to church then as she had always done during the years since she was a young girl. In winter Grace and the other young women from High Oxspring, including the Bramalls, attended the services held in Oxspring school, but these were discontinued for the summer months. They would then walk to Thurgoland church or sometimes, for a change, to Hoylandswaine.

Thurgoland church had a good complement of single young men in the congregation in those days, as well as young women. It was the men's habit to sit together in the pews at the far side of the church so that they could unobtrusively eye the girls who, looking very modest in their Sunday finery, were seated in the nearer rows in full view of the parson. One might suspect that the young men's interest, though seeming to be focused in the parson's direction, was not entirely absorbed in his sermon. Another detection could also have been made by a close observer of the girls. Those angelic-looking creatures who appeared for the most part to be intent on listening to the parson were not devoid of human aspirations. Judging from the discreet sidelong glances that were cast across to the far row of pews when the parson turned his back, the observer could see the girls' interest was somewhat divided too.

Whatever attraction the religious service itself had for the young people, church was certainly a popular Sunday meeting place for many of them. When the service ended, they talked with one another outside, then usually formed small groups or pairs for taking a walk before returning home. Ernest Bramall was not amongst the men inside the church on those Sunday evenings, but he was waiting for Grace at the gates when she came out. Like everyone else, they would go for a walk before he took her back to Tunnel Top.

There were very few occasions when the pair ever went to a dance. Though she enjoyed the bright conviviality of seeing and talking to other people, Grace felt rather inadequate when it came to the actual dancing. Because she had never learned to dance when young, she thought that when one was nearing thirty it might seem too frivolous to start. Yet she did admit later that when Fred Hill showed her how to do the Waltz Cotillions she liked it very well. Fred was courting Ernest's sister Gladys and was reckoned to be a good dancer. Another dance that Grace enjoyed watching was the Lancers, because the movements were lively and the music tuneful.

At the beginning of 1923 plans were at last being made for her wedding to Ernest. They agreed that the end of May would be a suitable time. The sowing would have all been finished and haytime another month away. Ernest's youngest sister Hilda was to marry Joe Elsworth at Easter, so would be leaving Willow Lane. There would be ample accommodation there for Grace and Ernest. Since his work as a butcher was based there, it would be more convenient to continue living on the premises. Grace would have preferred a home of her own rather than share his mother's house, but she understood that it was the most practicable thing to do. His mother, being widowed, wished for their company, thinking rightly that the big house would seem empty and lonely if there were only her younger son Willis and herself left in it. Her older daughters, Ethel and Gladys, had married and left home some time before. Ethel's husband was Haydn Woodhead, a butcher from Penistone. Fred Hill, who married Gladys, was a farmer.

Ernest had also a stepsister, Emma, daughter of his father's first wife. Emma had married Charlie Hill, one of Fred's relatives, and was then living at Whitefield Farm.

With all his sisters married, it would have been the first time in his mother's life that she had been without female company near her. Bearing in mind she was sixty-two, a little help with the housework was also looked for. So it was that Grace Spenceley consented to live with her future mother-in-law.

Whilst looking forward pleasantly to getting married, there was one big worrying thought gnawing at the back of her mind. She was continually asking herself what was to become of young Harry when she wasn't around to feed, dress and wash him. Who would there be to carry him outside to see the bluebells and watch the trains go by? There were others who were asking themselves the same question. Her parents, brothers and sisters were feeling anxious because none of them had dealt with Harry before in the same way Grace had. Though handicapped physically and mentally, the boy must nevertheless have sensed it was his sister who understood him best. Her name was one of the few words he could say, and it was for her he called when he needed attention. Even when his mother and other members of the family were near him in the same room and Grace was further away in the next room, it was the latter name that was shouted. Showing the utmost patience and compassion when thus summoned, she would interrupt what she was doing to go to his side and, putting an arm around his shoulders ask, 'What is it love?' Although he could not tell her in so many words, such was the communication between them that she would usually understand his needs and do her best to meet them.

People outside the family who were strangers to Harry could not communicate with him at all, and he was not happy with them. Grace knew that her brother would lose what little pleasure he had in life if he were put into the care of some unknown stranger, assuming of course that someone could be found who was willing and able to undertake the caring for him. Many people would have been unable to lift Harry, let alone carry him for any distance. Those who saw Grace do this marvelled at the way she supported him on her hip and shoulders. Even her father remarked, 'I don't know how our Grace does it. It must be t'knack she has.' By the time he was nearing twenty, Harry was as tall as his sister, but the fits from which he suffered caused his condition to worsen so that he was as helpless as a baby. For much of the time he had to wear a large bib below his chin and across his chest to protect his clothes.

The wedding date was set for the 29th of May, despite the shadow of anxiety looming large in everyone's mind, Grace's most of all. Then, as if by some divine act of providence, the problem of who was to care for Harry was taken out of earthly hands. On the 22nd of March, after having several fits close together, Harry appeared to be recovering when, with Grace's arm around him, he turned his eyes towards her in recognition and, speaking her name slowly but distinctly, died peacefully with the word on his lips.

She felt the loss of her brother keenly, since his twenty years of restricted existence had been so much a part of her own daily life. People who knew their family situation said it was a blessing that the boy had been taken before Grace got married. They maintained it was fate who had decreed he would suffer no further miseries through being without his sister. While grieving for her brother, Grace thanked God for his mercy in taking Harry into his own care rather than leaving him to that of strangers.

Grace's wedding took place at Penistone church on the appointed day. It was not the joyful occasion which, under different circumstances, it might have been. The few short weeks since Harry's death had not been sufficient to banish entirely the air of sadness still hanging over the Spenceley family. The bride did not wear white. She thought that would have been completely wrong, considering she was mourning her brother. Instead, she chose a dress of heavy slate-grey silk. This was of fairly simple style, the skirt reaching almost to her ankles, being two-tiered yet not very full. What marked out the dress as being one for a special important event was the richness of the material, the embroidered roses and leaves design on the bodice front and the small beaded trimming round the neckline. These attributes set it apart from ordinary, everyday dresses. The sleeves, of below elbow length, had each a row of small buttons from elbow to hem. Her hat was grey to match the dress. It had a large brim which turned down slightly, yet not enough to conceal the silk ruching on its underside. Grace wore grey suede shoes and gloves to complete the outfit. On her dress she fastened the brooch that Ernest had given her, and on her left wrist she wore the gold watch that was also a present from him.

She looked very nice in her new attire but it could be noticed that the burdens she had carried over the preceding years and, in particular, during the previous weeks, had taken their toll. Her face had lost the round fullness it had shown when she first went to live at Tunnel Top, and appeared almost too thin and pale for a bride on her wedding day.

Ernest, at nearly thirty-two, was in his prime. Of medium build, he was physically a strong man. From an early age he had been used to exerting his strength and thereby increasing it during the course of his work as butcher and farmer. He had become a little heavier since first escorting Grace home from night school thirteen years earlier, but not too much so. His face, slightly fuller than it had been then, was strikingly handsome with blue-grey eyes, straight nose, firm mouth with good white teeth, and a strong chin. His black hair was cut short at back and sides after the fashion of the day. Above his forehead it was brushed over to the right and was quite thick with a natural wave. Ernest wore a grey suit at his wedding and looked impeccably smart. The chain of his gold pocket watch was fashionably visible across the waistcoat front, being secured at its end into one of the buttonholes.

Grace's two bridesmaids were her cousin Marjorie Buckle and Elsie Webb, the young lady who was later to become her brother George's wife. Elsie was a farmer's daughter. She was small, fair, blue-eyed and pretty with a quiet, pleasant manner. In her capacity as bridesmaid she too wore a grey dress which became her very well. An item of decoration she added to her outfit was a favourite necklace.

Grace was pleased that Madge, her cousin and childhood friend, was able to be in attendance at her wedding. The two still kept in close touch by frequent letters and occasional visits, though Madge had lived away from the Oxspring area ever since her grandad Herbert died. For her cousin's wedding she had come over by train from Wakefield, where she was helping her aunt Martha Herbert to keep house for her three sons. Madge's attire was very fashionable that day. On her head was a wide-brimmed hat trimmed with ribbon and floral decoration round the base of the crown. On the lapel of her blue two-piece suit was pinned a floral spray. Not only was Madge's outfit stylish, it also bordered on the affluent, for around her shoulders was draped a dark fur stole.

For his best man Ernest had chosen Haydn Woodhead, his sister Ethel's husband. His short, stocky frame gave first impressions that he, like Ernest, was a strong man, but Haydn was not as strong as he looked. He had been a soldier during the war and suffered the effects of gassing. Because of this he did not live many more years.

The journey to Penistone church was made in one of the early types of taxi, a large, high-sided, box-shaped vehicle. It was owned by Penneys of Springvale, who had bought it for the purpose of transporting local people on their special occasions. The ride was quite a novelty for the wedding group, as they had not been in a motor vehicle previously. It seemed to them the height of luxury to travel thus. During all her years at Tunnel Top Grace had seldom seen a motor car. The only person of her acquaintance to possess one had been the local doctor. Since

the end of the war, however, they learned that a few of the more affluent people in the area were also acquiring cars.

Before the marriage ceremony took place there was a disappointment which cast a shadow on the proceedings. The floral bouquets
that had been ordered for the bride and bridesmaids failed to arrive;
three wreaths were sent instead. Grace, whose feelings of happiness
for her wedding had already been mixed with those of despondency
over her brother, regarded this as an ill omen and wondered what the
future would hold for them. It renewed too a twinge of the guilt she
had first felt when Harry died. In her saddened state then, she had
partly blamed his death onto her own selfishness for planning to get
married when he needed her. Perhaps he would have lived longer if
she had been prepared to stay with him. These self-recriminations
had been only momentary of course, for her good sense told her that
Harry would not have had a long life in any case. Moreover, Ernest
had waited patiently for so many years, refraining from making any
other association, so she had a duty to him too. The wreaths had to be
sent back of course, but it was too late to obtain bouquets from elsewhere, so the ceremony had to take place without flowers.

The wedding reception at Tunnel Top was quiet and subdued as
Grace and her family intended it should be. In spite of the extra guests
the house seemed strangely empty without Harry's presence. Grace's
sister Mary had helped their mother prepare a tea for everyone when
the taxi brought the newly-married pair and their attendants back to
the house. The only other member of Ernest's family who was at the
reception, apart from his brother-in-law, was his mother. In the absence
of transport, his married sisters lived rather too far away to attend in
any case. Grace's own relatives were also absent for similar reason.
Though they lived nearer, Blanche, Herbert and Willie all had young
children who would have found the walk to Tunnel Top and back too
tiring even if they had been invited. As it was, Elizabeth did not want
grandchildren around that day. She felt that a large party, inclined to
merrymaking, would be completely inappropriate under the circumstances. The reception was therefore arranged on simple lines. The
members of Grace's family who were present included her mother
and father, sister Mary, and three youngest brothers, George, Frank
and Stanley.

Madge's presence at the tea table did much to warm and cheer what
might otherwise have been too sober a gathering. Whilst showing sym-
pathetic understanding to the recently bereaved family, and to her aunt
Lizzie in particular, she took the positive attitude that always seemed
to help in her own troubles. Madge's optimistic outlook and friendly

chatter served, to a large extent, to drive off her cousin's sense of fore-boding that the mistake over the flowers had caused, though that incident was never entirely forgotten.

Ernest, too, did his best to put his new wife in happy mood. During a brief period when they were in the sitting room with only their bridesmaid and best man present, he seated himself in one of the chairs and pulled her onto his knees. She, having been brought up to believe that it was only loose-living folk who demonstrated their affections in public, struggled to get free. Though she didn't really mind Elsie and Haydn Woodhead witnessing Ernest's innocent fun, she was fearful lest her parents or, worse still, her new mother-in-law, should enter the room. That would have caused the height of embarrassment to all concerned. Elsie could not control her laughter at the sight of the new bride struggling to be free of her husband. Seeing her bridesmaid's evident amusement, Grace became aware of the funny side too, and to her husband's delight joined in their laughter.

Photographs to commemorate the wedding day were taken in the garden just outside the house. There is one of Ernest and Grace on their own and another of everyone present at the reception. This group photograph shows the bride and groom seated in the middle of the picture, with Ernest's mother on his right and Grace's mother on her left.

Elizabeth is dressed entirely in black, her long-sleeved gown covering even her ankles. She looks far older than her fifty-seven years. Her figure which was straight and well proportioned in her younger days, has become stout with the passage of time and eleven children. Her shoulders appear somewhat bowed as if in resignation to the cares and troubles of her life weighing heavily upon them. Her face too reflects the sorrows she has borne by illness and handicap amongst five of her children and the loss of three of them while still young. From the haunted look in her eyes and the lines around her mouth can be read a lifetime full of worldly experiences that included grief in more than small proportion. Elizabeth's hair has thinned with age and ill-health; what little remains is almost white.

Ernest's mother, seated beside her son, also looks older than her actual age of sixty-two. The picture shows her wearing a long black skirt and grey, long-sleeved satin blouse. Her hair is dressed tightly back at each side from a centre forehead parting and, though very neat and tidy, gives her an air of severity. Her face is rather thin, probably due to her loss of teeth.

All the other members of the wedding party are standing in a line behind the four seated people. James Spenceley, in the centre of the row, presents a commanding figure. Tall, upright, well built and handsome still, he appears to have weathered the family misfortunes better than has his wife. It would seem apparent too that the long hours of work performed at his wiredrawer's bench had done him no harm. The picture shows James keeping to the old fashion of wearing a moustache, whereas Ernest and his young contemporaries are clean-shaven.

On James's right is the bridesmaid Elsie Webb, looking demurely pretty. At his other side is the son who was courting her. George was a tall, straight, good-looking young man in his twenty-second year. He was the same height as his father though not as broad. Fortunately he had inherited James's good health and physical stamina as his sister Grace had done. George was to be the longest-living member of the Spenceleys.

The two youngest brothers, Frank and Stanley, at nearly nineteen and eighteen years respectively, show happy smiles to the camera, suggesting that the resilience of youth had already pushed aside that sad-

The wedding party

ness that was still troubling their elders. Stanley was a half-head taller than Frank, being about the same height as his father and brother George. Both the boys look smart and well groomed in dark jackets, white shirts and black ties. Haydn Woodhead, at the end of the row, is in a dark suit that displays two watch chains across the waistcoat. His square-jawed face poses a serious, thoughtful expression. At the other end of the back row Mary Spenceley is also unsmiling, her large eyes having a wistful look. Mary wore a simple black dress with plain, collarless neckline and short sleeves. Her dress was a good deal shorter than those of the older women, reaching not much further than below her knees and so revealing her black stockings as well as shoes. The photograph serves to show that, while younger women such as Mary were keen to follow the new fashion of shorter clothes, the older ones were reluctant to do so. They evidently preferred to keep to styles to which they were accustomed. Their long-established views of showing one's legs in public remained unchanged.

Standing next to Mary in the picture is the other cheerful-looking member of the party, Marjorie Buckle. Her pleasant, smiling face surmounted by the gaily trimmed hat implied there were no doubts in her mind that Grace's wedding should be anything but a joyful occasion. Though she wore her fur stole with the air of a duchess, this aristocratic elegance did nothing to detract from the homely personality beneath. Her cousins were quick to recognise that, under all her finery, Madge was still the same kind-hearted, fun-loving girl who, when younger, had been so much amongst them as part of the large family. Grace was grateful for Madge's presence that day. Coming from outside their home, her cousin had not suffered the previous anxieties nor felt the bereavement as they had done. She was able, therefore, to add a little of her own natural brightness to the gathering.

On the photograph Ernest's expression is one of wellbeing and contentment at having achieved an important goal in life. Grace's face retained signs of the pressures under which she had so long been. Despite her natural toughness and strong stamina, the stresses and strains of the past years were not quickly nor easily overcome.

The couple did not go away on honeymoon. Few working-class people had money or time to spend on such luxuries then. Grace and Ernest considered themselves lucky that they were able to have a day at the seaside. They went by train to Cleethorpes. Grace said afterwards that the journey there seemed to take a very long time as the train made numerous stops along the way to take on more people. Apparently the day was half gone when they finally arrived at Cleethorpes, but they enjoyed the outing nevertheless. It was the first time they had been so far away from home together. Indeed, it was the first time in his life that Ernest Bramall saw the sea, and he was nearly thirty-two years old.

Chapter 10

Years at Willow Lane

WILLOW LANE FARM was, and still is, a place of some character. It occupies a commanding position all of its own at a bend in the old road between Jockey House and Tunnel Top. The outward appearance of the house has changed little since Grace Spenceley went to live there in 1923. Built of stone and red brick, it is high and stands four square to the winds that often blow along that hill-top.

The usual approach to the farmhouse then was from the roadside gate that opened into the yard. Across the yard one entered the house by way of the lower kitchen. There is a main door in the adjacent, south-facing wall of the house but it was rarely used when the Bramalls were tenants. They found it more convenient to use the farmyard door. By the roadside near the house front was the duckpond, an essential part of the rural scene in those days. At the western side of the house the fields slope down to the River Don in an expanse of green, gold or brown, depending on the time of year and to what use the land is being put. Between the fields passes the narrow Willow Lane or, as Ernest Bramall used to call it, Holly Lane, leading down to the packhorse bridge at the bottom. The land belonging to Willow Lane Farm amounted to about eighty acres.

When viewed from the present-day Oxspring village, lower down at the other side of the Don, the house and buildings seem to present a dominating appearance. Standing in lofty isolation against the sky-line, their elevated position at the head of Willow Lane is one of eminence. The general view of the well-built structure can be much enhanced on a summer's day when the rays of the afternoon sun glow warmly on the red-brick walls.

The house is not old as farmhouses go. When Grace and Ernest were married it had been built hardly more than a hundred years. The Bramalls were not the owners of the place but tenant farmers. Ernest's father, Joseph Dyson, had taken it over in 1912 when he left the cottage at Tunnel Top, but he was not the first of his family to live there.

An older sister, Sarah Dyson, and her husband Joe Beever Couldwell, were there as tenants in 1881 when they were a young couple with small children, but since that time other families had been in residence.

Joseph Dyson had moved to Willow Lane because he needed a place where there would be farm work for his younger son, Willis Dyson, and bigger premises for Ernest to carry on the business of butchering. Until then he had worked in conjunction with his brother Bill but, with Bill's son Walter and daughter Bertha growing up, the Tunnel Top farm was hardly big enough for them all. After 1912 Bill Bramall's place was a farm only, no butchering being done there except the occasional pig killing.

At Willow Lane the arrangement had worked very well. Though Willis was still at school when his family first moved there, it wasn't long before he was tackling the farm work with the help of a hired man. Ernest was responsible for the butchering. From the age of sixteen he had shouldered the bulk of the work because of his father's ill-health. He had hawked the meat to their customers by horse and cart unassisted by anyone else and, due to his diligence, the trade had expanded. The fact that he was butcher and brother Willis a farmer did not mean that each stuck rigidly to his own job. The arrangement had to be flexible because there were the busiest times on the farm such as haytime and harvest when extra help was appreciated. Ernest would lend his assistance during these periods and at any other time of crisis where the farm was concerned. In return Willis gave him help with the killing operations of his business.

Their father, Joseph Dyson, was twice married. At twenty-two his first wife had been Hannah Lovatt, also twenty-two and the daughter of an engine 'tenter'. Unfortunately Hannah was consumptive. She died at twenty-nine after having had five children. Three of them died in infancy. Dyson lost his wife and two of the children in a short space of six weeks. Another son died at nineteen. The only member of his first wife's family to live longer was a daughter, Emma.

After four years of widowhood, during which time a housekeeper looked after John and Emma, Dyson Bramall married again. His second wife was the woman who became Ernest's mother.

Ernest's parents would probably never have met if Dyson had not been a butcher. Besides his work at home he often earned a little extra money by killing pigs for other people. Quite a lot of folk fattened their own pig in those days but had neither the tools nor the knowledge and skill needed for the slaughtering of it.

It wasn't any man who could kill and cut up a pig cleanly and efficiently. Without the necessary expertise a real mess might be made of the job, unnecessary suffering caused to the pig, and the resulting meat badly cut. Dyson Bramall had acquired such skill and proficiency in his line of work that his services were much sought after. His pig-killing equipment included a piece of tough rope, a sticking knife, scraper, shaving knife, cutting-up knife, meat-saw and steel. The person who owned the pig provided the 'plonk', a low wooden bench on which the animal was killed. Plenty of boiling water had to be on hand too for the scalding.

When about to kill a pig the butcher would first fasten his rope tightly round the animal's nose to keep it under control. Then, assisted by its owner and another helper, they would drag it onto the plonk, the terrified creature giving vent to much squealing as if seeming to sense its fate. The piercing squeals finished only when the sticking knife found its mark in the pig's jugular vein and its throat was cut to let out the blood.

When the pig was dead, very hot water was poured over the carcass to loosen the bristles. These were then removed with the scraper, a sharp, broad-edged tool which had a small hook at the other side for pulling out the 'clears' or, in modern terms, the hooves. The butcher himself did the actual scalding while the helpers scraped off the bristles. Care was needed in pouring on the right amount of water at a time and to ensure that it was hot enough but not too much so. It had to be just off the boil, for to have poured it on boiling would have caused the bristles to become more firmly fixed. When one side of the pig had been scraped it was turned over so that the other side could be similarly treated. While the scalding process was going on the set-pot fire had to be well stoked up to keep the water boiling. Unless the place of slaughter had its own set-pot the water had to be carried in buckets from the house kitchen. It then needed to be boiling when it left the kitchen so as to allow for the loss of heat in transit. After the scraping the butcher would go over the carcass with his shaving knife to obtain a closer, cleaner finish. He next took a cambril: a straight, strong piece of wood that was thin enough to pass through the sinews of the back legs, yet stout enough to support the carcass when it was hung. With the cambril in place the butcher and helper heaved the carcass up onto a hook that was high enough to enable the pig's head to be off the floor. Taking his cutting knife, the butcher drew it straight down the front, opening up the pig. Then, using his meat-saw to divide the breast bone, he took out the 'pluck'—liver, lungs and heart—in one piece and hung them on a hook. These would be fit to use the next day if required. The intestines were taken out and the fat trimmed off. This was later used for rendering into cooking fat and scraps, though this fat was not of the best. The carcass was then left hanging in a cool outhouse for the rest of the day and throughout the following one. The butcher would be regaled with a drink of beer or whisky before returning home. Meanwhile the boys of the family would be busy blowing up the pig's bladder for use as a football. They accomplished this by blowing into the stem of an old clay pipe which they had inserted into the neck of the bladder.

Two days after the killing, the butcher made a second visit to complete his work. While the carcass still hung on the cambril he cut off the head. This was a stage where skill was called for if a clean job was to be made. The cutting had to be done in a certain place where there was a particular joint, and this was not always easy to find. The butcher then sawed down the backbone to make the carcass into two sides. Some assistance was required here to take hold of one side as it came off the cambril while the butcher supported the other half. One side was laid on the plonk which had, of course, been thoroughly washed and scrubbed after the killing. The other side of meat was put on a bench or trestle until it could be dealt with. Attending to the side on the plonk, the butcher cut off all the rich leaf fat that surrounded the kidneys. This was the best fat and, when rendered down, would be white and excellent for pastry making. The ham, hock and trotters were taken off and the ribs cut out. These could be eaten straight away, the spare rib or 'sparrib' as it was locally pronounced being shared with neighbours and relatives who would do the same when their pigs were killed. The head was 'dressed' last. The lower jaws, called 'chap', were cut off and salted. The upper jaws and ears, called 'pig face', were salted temporarily and, together with the tail and trimmings from the sides and hams, were made into brawn and potted meat. This was well seasoned, as the taste might not have been too popular otherwise. The sides of meat were put in the cellar on a clean, stone slab on which salt had been laid down. More salt was then put over the meat. After three weeks the salt was washed off and the sides hung up, usually in the coolest part of the kitchen or some other suitable room. The hams received similar treatment but, in addition, saltpetre was rubbed in around the bone. The hams needed to be in salt rather longer than the sides. Sometimes muslin covers were put over the meat during storage to keep off the flies.

One day during his period of widowhood Dyson Bramall was summoned on one of his pig-killing errands to the parish of Silkstone. Walter Helliwell, who worked the small farm of Doe Wells there, had

decided his pig was fat enough for the butcher. He knew that Dyson
had earned for himself a good reputation where slaughtering was concerned, so considered him to be the best man to engage.

Walter Helliwell had a busy household. His family was large, though
one or two of the older sons were sometimes 'farmed out' to work on
neighbouring farms. Walter strongly believed in having everyone gain-
fully employed. His wife Martha was a kindly woman. Where running the house was concerned she was very particular that everything
should be properly done, especially the cleaning and washing. This
might not have been easy to put into practice while her children were
small, and increases coming at close intervals, had it not been for the
help she received from her niece, Selina.

Selina Wragg was her brother John's daughter whom she had taken
under her wing when she was eight years old on the death of her
mother. When Martha Wragg married Walter Helliwell and went to
live at Doe Wells, Selina continued to stay with them. She had a great
liking for her aunt and repaid her kindness as she grew older by helping her with the work of the house. In particular she helped to bring
up her aunt Martha's many children. They tended to look on her as
an older sister, referring to her as 'our Lena'. Selina had often to manage the house and children on her own when her aunt was confined
to bed. Besides the numerous indoor duties that came her way, she
was frequently called on by Walter to assist with outdoor work too.
Consequently there were often days when she was working all hours,
from getting up in the morning until going to bed at night. Some folk
reckoned Walter Helliwell was a grasping man who was somewhat
over-keen when working people, and not averse to exploiting them.
While Selina felt this to be true, she had such high regard for her
aunt Martha that she continued willingly to live and work with the
Helliwells through twenty years of her early life.

Selina Wragg was in her late twenties when Dyson Bramall arrived
at Doe Wells to slaughter her uncle Walter's pig. No doubt she was
busy keeping the water boiling in the set-pot ready for the scalding. It
could have been she who carried out the buckets of hot water to Dyson,
but that we do not know for certain. It is likely that on his second
visit, when he went to cut up the carcass, she would be around to help
sort out the meat and take the fat away for rendering into lard. Whatever Selina's precise activities were during that pig killing, one indis-
putable fact emerged. That was, she made the acquaintance of Dyson
Bramall. The relationship developed on intimate lines until, at the
end of 1890, they became man and wife. Walter Helliwell was not

enthusiastic about the wedding since it meant the loss to him of some very cheap labour.

Selina settled into the cottage at Tunnel Top and cared for the two motherless children of her husband's first marriage. Then, in the summer of 1891, when she was thirty, the first of her own children was born. He was Ernest, who would later become the husband of Grace Spenceley.

Selina Bramall spent the next twenty years or so at the Tunnel Top cottage. After Ernest she had Ethel, Elsie, Gladys, Hilda and Willis in quick succession. Elsie died suddenly at four years old. No one seemed sure of the cause. According to what Ernest was told at the time, 'she fell out o' t'window bottom'. It was not clear to him whether the fall caused her death or whether she had some kind of condition which made her suddenly ill and she fell as a result of this. Grandfather Joseph came across from the farm, walking slowly with the aid of his stick, to condone with the bereaved parents, and told them 'I shan't be long after her.' He died a few weeks later, aged eighty-three.

Selina treated her stepchildren well as if they were her own but, in spite of her care, John died in his youth. It is possible he had inherited some of his mother's weakness. As the daughters grew up Emma and Ethel went into domestic service for a while before they married. Gladys and Hilda stayed at home to help their mother because, by the time they left school, the move had been made to Willow Lane where there was enough work to keep them all busy.

When Dyson died in 1920 and Gladys married not long afterwards the household was reduced to four occupants. Then at Easter 1923 Hilda married too, and Selina was more than pleased to welcome her new daughter-in-law Grace into the house. There was ample accommodation, Ernest would be still living where his work was and, also an important consideration, his mother would not be without female company. Throughout her life there had always been other such relatives around her. She would have felt strangely lonely had there not been another woman to talk to and work with during the long days, for she seldom left the farm.

Grace got on well with her husband's mother, mainly because she was prepared to fall in with her wishes and adapt her own ideas so as not to conflict with those of the older woman. She conceded that, although she and Ernest had been asked to make their home at Willow Lane, Selina had been there long before she had and was in fact still the mistress of the house. The methods she had employed in running it over the years were not to be changed. She told Grace firmly, 'I allus follow mi' Aunt Martha's ways and I've nivver seen none to beat 'em.' While Grace herself had been brought up in the belief that 'cleanliness is next to godliness', even she thought that 'Aunt Martha's ways' carried this to extremes. On washdays every seam of every garment had to be laid out on the rubbing board and meticulously scrubbed with a soapy clothes brush. Any dust or dirt that found its way into the house was swiftly and speedily attacked. When a caller suggested to Selina that perhaps she was rather too particular about her cleaning she retorted, 'Oh, but you can't be too particular.' She once referred to someone else's sheets as 'darkie white' because they fell short of her own snowy standard of whiteness. Of course, housework, children and farm had been Selina's whole life. Her satisfaction and pleasures had come, not from trips far afield, but from seeing a prospering farm, clean house, and in turning out to school well-fed, immaculately-groomed children.

Selina's own schooling had been negligible. Education was not compulsory when she was a girl. Her father, a farm labourer with many children, no doubt held the opinion that what she could learn from her aunt Martha would be of more use to her than reading and writing. She did learn to write her name in a good firm hand, but very little else. Her reading ability was also very limited, but this did not worry her. During her life she had had no time for reading and writing; in fact there had been no need for it. She had never had occasion to write a letter to anyone and, as for wanting to read a book or even a newspaper, she scoffed at the idea, maintaining that to sit down reading a book was a sheer waste of time. She had plenty of ability, nevertheless, in tackling the things that mattered to her and, where managing money was concerned, showed intelligence and common sense.

Ernest's father, on the other hand, had received some education. In the 1860s he and his brother Bill had attended the small 'dame school' near the top of Bower Hill. There, in return for a small fee of tuppence a week, they had been taught by an elderly lady called Rosamund Laycock, or 'Owd Ros' as she was named by the local folk. In after years Dyson Bramall used to tell his children that 'Owd Ros' didn't teach them much. The only thing he remembered her telling them was the ABCs. This she would impart as she sat by the fire with her knitting, the children seated around her in a circle. Ros taught them at the infant stage only. After that Dyson and Bill walked along the Copster road to attend the school at Thurgoland. Their father, Joseph, who had lived in Hunshelf when a boy and had probably been to the school there, believed that his children should also be able to read and write. It might one day serve them in good stead. Joseph Bramall was one of the Oxspring men who, as early as 1855, had signed a petition urging that village children should be allowed access to Penistone Grammar School. Yet, in spite of his belief in education, that had to take second place where the farm was concerned.

When there was urgent work to be done, such as leading in hay that was ready, they had to stay off school to help. Many of the farming operations could only be performed in fine, dry weather; so at the busy times, when the assistance of Dyson and Bill was required, it was their father's habit to look outside in the early morning to assess what kind of a day was promised. If it was raining he would promptly announce, 'There'll be nowt for you to do today; you might as well get off to school.' The thought of their getting wet while on the two-mile walk to Thurgoland did not enter into the matter, being quite beside the point. Like most farmers of long experience, Joseph was a good judge of what the weather was going to be by the look of the sky and the feel of the wind. When a day promised to be fair he would correctly predict, 'It's going to be fit to go in t'field later on, so you'd better not set off for school.' Despite these necessary interruptions, however, Dyson Bramall made the most of his schooling opportunities. He became a good scholar, well able to read a newspaper and anything else that interested him. The knowledge he gained at school did stand him in good stead. As time passed, and the twentieth century got under way, it became increasingly clear that such knowledge was essential for the efficient operation of his business.

After Dyson's death, Ernest continued to run the butchering for his mother until he was married. Then she decided to turn it over to him, but charge for the use of the slaughtering premises and for his and Grace's accommodation in the house. It was understood that Grace would give assistance with the housework.

As things transpired, Grace did not find it too difficult to fall in with 'Aunt Martha's ways', although she had thought them too fussy in the first place. She soon discovered that she and her mother-in-law had much in common. They were both tough, energetic women who held the view that to sit down during the day was little short of a crime, unless one's hands were occupied with sewing or mending. Even those tasks were not generally classed as daytime duties but as leisurely occupations that could be undertaken during the evenings while one was resting. Since Grace had always been accustomed to physical activity and had always followed the maxim 'If a job's worth doing it's worth doing right', the long hours spent in scrubbing, washing, cooking and sewing alongside her mother-in-law were nothing really new to her. There was, however, one other important duty that she was expected to take over after her marriage, one that she had never been previously called on to perform.

Selina had always been in the habit of making a quantity of potted meat each week for Ernest to sell on his meat round. The week after he was married she told Grace, 'You can make t'potted meat this week; it'll be your job from now on.' So after being shown how by her mother-in-law, Grace willingly undertook the new task. She supposed it was only fair that she should do the work since the business had become theirs. For many more weeks and years afterwards she made potted meat for the round. It was very popular amongst the customers, Ernest always having a ready sale for it, but the method of making it at that time was laborious and time-consuming. This seemed all the more so when it had to be fitted into an already busy routine.

Potted meat was made from odd pieces of meat which would otherwise have remained unsold. They were the rougher bits and the less palatable pieces which people did not readily buy unless they were transformed into potted meat. The whole operation of making it had to be done in the house using the black range for the preliminary cooking of the meat. Firstly the meat had to be put in a huge bucket kept solely for the purpose. It was covered with water, then lifted into the oven at the side of the coal fire. The meat was stewed for several hours until it was tender enough to come away easily from the bones. The bucket was then, with some effort, carefully lifted out onto the table which had been previously covered with old newspapers. The meat was transferred, a portion at a time, onto a large oval dish. Each dishful had to be carefully sorted, bones and skin taken out, and the remaining meat chopped finely with the use of knife and fork. Salt and pepper were added and mixed in well. The meat was then spooned into big, brown earthenware pots. Some of the liquid from the stewing process was stirred in too in order to make the correct setting consistency. When the potted meat was cold and solid, each potful was turned out onto clean trays ready for sale. It was easily cut into quarter pounds or whatever other quantity was asked for when the butcher was on his rounds.

Though Ernest's mother had delegated the potted meat making to her daughter-in-law, she still worked hard herself. She was not the sort of woman who would sit and watch other people working. She continued to make the butter most weeks, though Grace did learn how to do this too and often assisted in churning the cream. It was one of Grace's weekly errands to carry butter and eggs from the farm to sell in Penistone; these journeys had earlier been made by one or other of Ernest's sisters before they were married. The butter and eggs were packed into a large basket which on the return journey, would be filled with shopping done after the produce was sold. Grace quite enjoyed the outing when the weather was good. The walk in the fresh air was a pleasant change from being indoors. She walked along the road past her old home of Tunnel Top, then soon after turned by Whitefield Farm to go down the fields, over the river and so up to 'Nibble Bottom' where the customers lived. The basket was very heavy, of course, when filled with eggs and butter, while carrying the shopping uphill on the return journey could be quite exacting.

Having a person such as Grace for a daughter-in-law gave Selina Bramall a feeling of pleasant gratification. She watched how industriously Grace tackled her work, how particular she was where cleanliness was concerned, and how carefully she managed her money. Selina soon came to have a high regard for Grace's capabilities, realising there were many respects in which the two of them were alike. Each had spent hard years in early life looking after someone else's family for little monetary reward, and each had been thirty years old when married. One big difference, of course, was that Grace had schooling and the mother-in-law had not, but that seemed of little importance during their time at Willow Lane. The life that the two women led was essentially practical. On occasions, when their work was temporarily completed, Selina would tell her daughter-in-law, 'There, I think we've done for t'time being, so you might as well go on and help your mother a bit.' The idea that Grace would perhaps like to put her feet up and have a rest, or sit down to look at a paper, did not occur to either of them. Grace admitted long afterwards that being told what to do with her spare time did make her feel rather like a little girl instead of a married woman of thirty who could have chosen her own activities. Yet, realising that Selina meant well in thinking of the family at Tunnel Top, she carried out her orders and went on there to help her mother. As time went on, being in each other's daily company and, in a sense, sharing each other's lives, caused a close affinity to grow up between them.

Grace thought the house of Willow Lane rather grand when compared with the cottage at Tunnel Top. This was not simply because it was bigger, but because it supplied luxuries that had not existed at her former home. There was actually hot water on tap at Willow Lane, and an upstairs bathroom and lavatory! Very few rural homes boasted such modern conveniences in the 1920s, and those at Willow Lane were comparatively new. They had been added onto the original nine-teenth-century stone building around 1910 for Mr Ashton, who had been tenant of the farm just before Dyson Bramall. The newer part of the building also included a ground-floor larder, over which the bath-room and lavatory were built. It was this latest addition to the house that was built of red brick, whereas the original older part was of stone.

Though having hot water readily available did facilitate their wash-ing and cleaning operations, Willow Lane was not an easily-run house. Much time and energy had to be expended daily in going up and down the flight of stone steps between bottom and top kitchens. The bottom kitchen was the first place one entered when going into the house from the yard. In it was the big stone sink where most of the washing-up was done. There was a smaller, white wash-trough in the upper kitchen but this had only a cold water tap. As meals were eaten in the top kitchen, the crockery and cutlery were usually taken down the steps for washing and returned clean to the upper room for fur-ther use. Pans and other cooking equipment had also to be carried down the steps for washing in the low kitchen because the cooking was done on the range in the top one. Washing of clothes took place in the bottom kitchen too since the water was there and the set-pot or copper fixed in the corner nearby. The copper came into use for boil-ing the sheets, towels and other white cotton articles that required a snowy finish.

Ernest's mother brewed her home-made ale in this same copper. When she needed to brew she would do it on a washday evening after the washing was finished but while the fire underneath the set-pot was still burning. She then cleaned and rinsed out the copper before putting in fresh water for boiling up the hops and malt needed in the beer making. After the brewing was completed another thorough scrub-bing-out of the copper was necessary so that it would be clean for the next washday.

Standing conspicuously on the floor of the lower kitchen was the big end-over-end butter churn. This type of churn was barrel-shaped with a handle in the side and was fixed to a wooden frame that stood firmly on the floor. When the handle was operated, the ends of the churn turned over and over in clockwise motion. On one day each week the churn came into use for the butter making. All the cream which had been skimmed from the tops of the milk bowls was put into the barrel and the handle turned until the butter 'came'. Both energy and patience were called for by the operator, as turning a churn of that size could be quite an arm-aching occupation when it had to be kept up for a long time. Sometimes the cream was slow in changing into butter and the handle had to be kept turning for as long as half an hour.

The floor of the bottom kitchen was concrete. A second door at the far end gave access to the fields behind the house.

There were two cellars at Willow Lane with two doors leading down to them, one from the bottom kitchen and one from the top. The cellars were of great importance in farmhouses in that era before electricity and refrigerators came to be regarded as essentials in daily life. It was there, on stone slabs, that hams and bacon were put in salt after the pig killings. Bowls of milk were kept in the cellar until the cream formed on top, when it would be skimmed off for the weekly butter making. Food that needed to be kept cold would be stored in the cellar, particularly during the summer months. The womenfolk at Willow Lane had therefore to spend much of their time carrying things up and down the cellar steps in the course of their daily work, in addition to the many trips made up and down the steps between the two kitchens.

On ordinary working days the top kitchen was the focal point of the house. Indeed, it was often referred to as 't'house', it being the place where everyone assembled for meals during the day and where they sat to the fire to talk on an evening. The floor was stone-flagged but was partly covered by matting; across the front of the fireplace was spread a large home-pegged hearth rug made from cloth clippings obtained from old garments and fastened into a strong backing material called harding. The top kitchen was a cosy room as the coal fire, needed for cooking, was kept burning all day. The fireplace was set into the kind of black range typical of that period. Its oven had to rely solely on the fire for its heat, which meant that the fire had to be continually stoked up when baking was in progress. All roasting, stewing and baking was done in the side oven; frying was done on iron bars over the open fire. Pans of vegetables were also boiled over the fire, as was the kettle too.

Adjoining the top kitchen on one side was the larder. This served as a store place for most of the food, and for other things besides. Like the low kitchen, the larder had a concrete floor and was, on the whole, a cool room.

There were two more ground-floor rooms which came into occasional use. From the top kitchen a door opened into the sitting room, which in spite of its name was sometimes used as a dining or tea room when the advent of visitors warranted extra space. Beyond this was the 'far room', classed as the 'best' room in the house and only used on special occasions. Both these sitting rooms had wooden floors, were carpeted and nicely furnished.

Upstairs were four bedrooms. The bathroom and lavatory were separate places. Near the bathroom was another small, narrow room which was used as a store place.

Grace and her mother-in-law worked to a strict routine, performing certain duties on certain days. That way, nothing was missed. Yet, though each room was regularly cleaned throughout the year, the ritual of spring-cleaning was considered to be of vital importance. Ceilings would have to be whitened and some rooms have new wallpaper put on. Those rooms not requiring new wallpaper would have the existing paper well rubbed over with clean cloths. Floors would be scrubbed, paintwork washed and furniture polished; curtains and coverings would also be washed. The spring-cleaning occupied several weeks, as it had to be done in addition to the regular jobs. It was begun after Easter, and the aim was to finish by Whitsuntide. Then, any painting that needed doing was attended to. The deadline for completion of all spring-cleaning and painting was Penistone Feast. There were two main reasons for this.

One was that haymaking got into swing immediately afterwards. In fact, most farmers followed the traditional habit of starting the cutting on Feast Saturday. Once the haymaking started, the priority was to lend assistance to the menfolk in whatever ways were most needed. Keeping them well supplied with adequate refreshment to refuel their energy was all important. Haymaking was a tiring occupation involving hard manual labour when the only lifters and elevators were the men themselves using hay forks. On hot days, drinks would be taken into the field for them. Besides Ernest and his brother Willis there would probably be one or two casual helpers to cater for too during the haymaking. If there was a shortage of helpers the women would go into the field themselves to lend assistance.

The other reason why spring-cleaning had to be finished by Penistone Feast was that visitors were always invited to tea on 'Feast Sunday'. The house had therefore to be looking its best, since it would be subjected to extra scrutiny. This applied particularly when Aunt Martha happened to be one of the visitors. Ernest's mother took great pride in welcoming her aunt to a spotlessly clean house, knowing what pleasure it would give her aunt to see everything spick and span.

There was one occasion, however, when a visit by the Helliwells almost ended in disaster. The time of their stay had passed pleasantly enough. Everyone had partaken of the sumptuous fare which was always produced for important visitors. The menfolk had made their usual tour of the farm, and the women had enjoyed talking together of house and family matters. It was when Aunt Martha and the rest of the Helliwell relatives were seated in their cart ready for departure that trouble threatened. The horse, already harnessed to the cart, had somehow lost its blinkers. Known better by some people as bluffs, these were the strong leather pieces fitted to the bridle at each side of the horse's head near its eyes. The purpose of the blinkers was to restrict the animal's vision, allowing it to look only in front in the direction it was meant to go. With its blinkers gone suddenly awry, the Helliwells'

horse sensed a new measure of freedom. It tossed its head around excitedly, then glared wildly at the unfamiliar faces and strange surroundings. As if not liking what it saw, it began to shift about uneasily in the shafts, showing the whites of its eyes as it grew more agitated. Then, giving vent to a frightened whinney, it reared its fore-legs high in the air, causing the people in the cart to clutch tightly hold of the sides. Grace and Selina,

'Now for it!'

standing in the yard to watch the Helliwell family leave, were quite alarmed. Selina cried, 'Now for it!' as the horse, jerking the cart sharply after it, tried to bolt. She anticipated an overturned cart at least, with possible injuries or worse to the occupants. By lucky chance one of the men happened to be just near enough to grab the animal's head and get a firm hold over its nose. The others rushed to assist in getting it under control. They eventually calmed the horse down, re-adjusted its blinkers and, to everyone's relief, Aunt Martha and the rest of the Helliwell party, though still somewhat shaken, were able to make a safe journey home.

The corn harvesting was a busy time on the farm, when to get it in in good condition often meant a race against the weather. When weather conditions were adverse, nerves could be frayed and an atmosphere of tension could pervade the house. Corn was cut with a horse-drawn binder. This machine was an improvement on earlier reaping machines. which only cut the corn and left it to be bound into sheaves by hand. The binder not only cut it, but collected it up between canvas belts and tied it into sheaves with twine before discharging them onto the ground for stooking. This process had to be done by hand and was thirsty work on a hot day. Five pairs of sheaves were stood together on their ends to form a stook or 'kivver', this being the name more often used in the Penistone area. Corn was usually in stook for two or three weeks to dry, depending on the weather of course, but in exceptionally good weather, when there was enough sun and wind, it could be ready sooner. Quite often the stooks did get rained on before they were ready for carting in, and extra time had then to be spent in opening them out and setting them up again. When dry the sheaves were forked manually onto the waggons and taken to be forked off into the barn or onto a large corn stack.

At a later date the corn would be threshed to separate the grain from the straw and chaff. Threshing day began with the appearance of Mr Jackson's huge, box-shaped machine. Its approach had already been heralded when still some distance away by the loud snorting of the steam-engine drawing it steadily along. Charlie Jackson took his threshing machine to all the farms in the district where corn was grown, since no one else over a wide area owned one at the time. The machine was pulled by the engine alongside the stack of corn to be threshed. The engine man and one or two others who had come with him were given breakfast in the house, for they had been up some hours already. Sometimes the machine was brought to the farm on the evening prior to the threshing day, depending on the distance it had to come and the amount of corn to be dealt with. In that case the men would arrive early to stoke up the engine and have everything in readiness before eating breakfast. Soon afterwards the other helpers, numbering about ten, would arrive. They were all from neighbouring farms, so most of them were well known to the family. The system was for every farmer to help everybody else on the threshing days, exchanging labour instead of giving and receiving money payments. Willis Bramall would lend his assistance to all his helpers when it was their turn to thresh.

In those days, before the combine harvester was a part of the farm scene, many workers were required because much manual work was involved. Though the actual threshing operation had become mechanised, manpower was needed because grain and straw were still lifted and carried without the aid of machines.

When the team was assembled the men sorted themselves out to the various working positions. They had no need to be told where to go, for it was an accepted fact that the physically strongest men did the heaviest work. To have opted for less would have been degrading and an embarrassment. It was not that there were any easy jobs where threshing was concerned, but some were more arduous than others. Two or three of the younger men were employed in forking sheaves from the stack onto the threshing 'box'. This involved continuous arm lifting and body turning for two hours at a stretch without any rest. Towards the end of the day, when the stack level was lower than the box, the sheaves had all to be thrown upwards, which was quite exacting work. Standing on the box were two other men ready to receive the sheaves from the forkers. One was the band-cutter whose job, as might be imagined, was to cut the twine, or band, to loosen the corn. The other man then fed it down a space into the machine where the grain was separated from the straw. Men who were rather older could do these jobs, though they required skill nevertheless, and the continuity of working in a bending position for a long period was tiring. After being threshed inside the machine the grain flowed out in a steady stream at the front into sacks that were fastened onto hooks. As the sacks filled they were dealt with by the corn carriers. Two of the strongest men in the team took on the job of corn carrying. The heavy sacks of grain had to be hoisted onto their backs, carried from the stackyard, across the farmyard and up the steep steps to the corn-chamber, their ultimate destination. At Willow Lane the steps were open at the left side with no hand rail on which to grip, so the corn carriers had to be steady on their feet as well as strong. One redeeming feature was that they had chance to straighten their backs and have a little respite while walking back to the stackyard for the next sack. Straw emerged from the back of the machine tied in battens, or 'batts'. These were forked onto a waggon and moved to an inside store place, usually the loft above the cow house. Two or three workers were kept busy dealing with the straw. Yet another person, either a young boy or an older man, was responsible for moving chaff away from the machine and carrying it into one of the buildings.

Threshing was thirsty work due to the dusty atmosphere around the machine, so after about two hours a temporary halt was called while pint mugs of tea were dispensed to all the men. Work then continued for another two hours or so until word came from the house that dinner was ready. At the welcome news the machine was stopped, the men trooped into the house to sit down thankfully at the large table, and appetising food was put before them. As they had all expended considerable energy during the morning, they did full justice to the huge meal prepared for them. There was more tea handed round in the middle of the afternoon and another meal when the threshing was finished for the day. The women of the various farmhouses usually provided ample food for the hungry workers, especially at the dinner-time meal in the middle of the day, when there would be a huge joint of roast beef accompanied by Yorkshire Pudding. At Willow Lane Selina's threshing-day dinners were second to none. She would never have let it be said that the women at neighbouring farms were better cooks or more generous providers than she was.

If anyone did put on a dinner that was below standard, word about it was not slow in getting around, and it would be remembered long afterwards. Grace heard from her husband's family how, years before, when Dyson Bramall was alive and doing the butchering, one certain woman had made a meat and potato pie for the threshing dinner. At least, it was supposed to be meat and potato, but when everyone started to tuck in it was quite obvious that the cook had been far too sparing with the meat. Though the pie contained an ample filling of potato, the pieces of meat were few and far between. Most of the men were accustomed to good rations of meat when they were doing hard manual work, and felt rather cheated. One of them declared in exasperation, 'Well, ah've been up t'taty rows and dahn t'taty rows but ah 'aven't let o' Dyson yet.'

Though the threshing days involved hard work for the men, and for the women too in preparing extra food, there was generally an atmosphere of friendly conviviality on the farm then as each one was a member of the team. The meal-times and other breaks provided opportunity to talk to one's neighbours, and news was exchanged among them. At Willow Lane the food, of course, was always very well received. Grace and Selina no doubt felt satisfaction at the end of the day in knowing there had been a job of work well done.

Grace had become well accustomed to life with her mother-in-law and was very happy during that first year of marriage. Then came an event to give more joy. It needed exactly a week to their first wedding anniversary when, on the 22nd of May 1924, a child was born to Grace and Ernest Bramall. It was a daughter.

Ernest had been to Penistone early that day. It was Thursday and he had had business to do at the cattle market. On returning home to Willow Lane he was given the news by his mother, who told him, 'It's a lass, but it can't be helped.' Selina held the opinion that the birth of a daughter called for rather less joy than did that of a son. In those days there was strong belief in farming and butchering families that sons were needed to assist their fathers in work they had carried on from previous generations. Eventually the sons would take over from them and have sons of their own who, in turn, would do the same.

Such was the feeling of continuity then; even at the present time, sixty years later, it is still alive in many families. In other cases, due to education and wider opportunities, some farmers' sons have opted out of the rural life in preference to work involving less hours and more leisure or to work for which they have a greater interest and ability. Just what the descendants of Grace and Ernest chose to do with their lives will be told in due course.

Despite his mother's apparent lack of enthusiasm at the birth of a girl, Ernest himself seemed intensely proud on that spring day. If he had any feelings of disappointment he did not show them. Perhaps he thought there would be boys to follow; if he did, his thinking was later proved to be correct. The baby was a strong, healthy child whom they named Phyllis Mary.

Soon after she was born, Ernest's younger brother Willis got married to a Thurgoland girl called Jessie Grayson. Their first child was a boy, much to his grandmother's delight. He was given the name of Dyson, after his father, grandfather, and great-grandmother. As Willis also continued to live at Willow Lane with his family the household became somewhat busier with two babies near together in age. One advantage, however, was that the children often amused one another. At the baby stage they would be occupied merely by looking at one another as they sat in their prams. When they became more mobile they played together.

At the crawling and toddling stages restrictions had often to be imposed on the two infants for their own safety. To have given them the freedom of the house could have resulted in their falling down the steps into the bottom kitchen or in getting burned or scalded from the cooking. Their mothers were, of course, kept busy most of the time with other duties of the farmhouse, and time spent with the children had to be limited. It was therefore necessary to confine them for some periods during the day. There were no such things as play-pens then, at least not for families such as the Bramalls. Grace and Jessie had to think of other means of temporary confinement.

One method generally employed by hard-pressed mothers was to tie the child, on a short tether, to the table leg, but Grace and her sister-in-law adopted another idea which they considered rather better. Phyllis and Dyson were each stood up in an empty wooden 'peggy-tub' or wash tub. The tubs would be put close together with just a stool or chair inbetween. On this would be placed a few playthings. The fact that each child had a companion to look at while playing did much to keep them contented.

Though things went well on the whole during the children's first year, there was one temporary setback. When Phyllis was about eleven months old she was very ill with pneumonia. At one stage even the doctor feared she would not survive. The fact that she did was probably due to her being basically strong and being well nursed throughout the illness by her mother. Once recovered she retained no weakness other than a tendency to bronchial coughs during childhood; even this disappeared as she grew older.

Penistone Feast Sunday was once more a happy occasion that year. Phyllis was well again, the spring-cleaning finished in spite of the recent illness. Selina had been stoically carrying on with it, sometimes on her own if the pressures of nursing had greater demand on Grace's time. Because of her tenacity she had not failed in reaching her objective of finishing the cleaning on time. She had invited all her married daughters, their husbands and children, to tea on the Sunday.

The day before the family gathering was due to take place, Grace was speculating as to how she would dress her small daughter next day so that she would look her best in front of all the relatives. The trouble was she hadn't really got a nice 'best' frock for her. From habit formed by long necessity, Grace was always careful when it came to spending money. As a general rule she only bought new clothes for herself when the others were 'past mending', which meant they had become too old and worn to be mended any more. Regarding her daughter's frocks, it was not that they were old, but the ones which fitted her were ordinary 'everyday' frocks. She had outgrown her best baby dress, of course, by the time she was a year old. Grace did not want to appear extravagant by telling her husband that the child could really do with a new dress.

In the event it was Ernest himself who decided that a new one should be bought. 'They'll all be coming dressed up tomorrow,' he pointed out. 'We want her to look as fine as t'others so I'll take you to get one tonight when I've finished. We can't have her ta'en down by our Gladys's lass.' Learning that the dress problem was to be solved in such forthright manner gave Grace an immense feeling of pleasure as well as relief. She knew that Ernest, like herself, was far from being extravagant. His money was too hard-earned to be lightly or frivolously spent. Yet his ideas were clear as to priorities. The Feast Sunday occasion was undoubtedly one that warranted wearing of best clothes, so Ernest regarded the buying of a new dress as a necessity.

So strong was his view on this that, true to his word, when he had finished his meat hawking on the Saturday evening, he took his wife and child to Barnsley to buy one. Shops were kept open until eight or nine o'clock on Saturday nights in those days, so there was time enough. The frock, of good quality, pale pink crepe de Chine, and its wearer were much admired next day, to Grace's delight and Ernest's satisfaction. Their child, as it was obvious to see, compared favourably with all the other young ones at the tea party.

Grace and Ernest with their first child

The proud parents paid another visit to Barnsley soon afterwards, for the purpose of having photographs taken at Denton's, the most reputable studio in town. Soon afterwards a coloured enlargement of their small daughter wearing the best dress was to be seen in a conspicuous position on their bedroom wall, hanging in a big, oval, ornately-gilded frame. The picture shows her as having rounded cheeks, fine, straight, silky hair brushed smoothly into a fringe on the forehead, and large blue eyes whose expression was of solemn wonderment. Phyllis had defied all efforts to make her smile. The little face remained serious, with even a hint of a pout on the small mouth as if scorning their attempts and being bored by the whole procedure.

A second photograph which was also enlarged and framed shows Phyllis with her parents. This is a good picture of all three. Grace is seated, holding up the child in a standing position on her knee, while Ernest stands beside them. She presents an appearance of wellbeing and contentment, looking far happier and healthier than she did on her wedding photograph taken two years earlier. Her face is not as thin as it was then but appears a little fuller. The change was probably due in part to the absence of all her earlier anxieties and worries concerning her brother Harry; after two years the edge had been taken off that sorrow. The healthier look could also have been brought about by the good table at Willow Lane and by having a little more time to look after herself than she had had at Tunnel Top before her marriage. On her latest picture Grace had dressed her hair with side-combs to give a slightly puffed out look. This style contributed in giving her a more youthful appearance. For the photograph she wore her best long-sleeved blouse of cream silk. Her black skirt was of the shorter length that had become fashionable; her shoes and stockings were also black.

During the following year, 1926, the household at Willow Lane was further increased by the births of two more babies. In March Grace had the son to which her mother-in-law attached so much importance. She called him Frank, after her brother who had narrowly escaped being burned to death when an infant. The month after Frank was born, Jessie and Willis had their second child too, a girl to be named Freda. These new additions meant there were four children under two years old in the house, two sets of parents and grandma Selina who had reached the age of sixty-five.

As the months went by there were times when the atmosphere at Willow Lane was rather less than peaceable. It was only natural that four young infants should make a certain amount of noise, but Ernest sometimes found it irritating when he had been working hard at his job and was needing a little peace in which to study his business affairs. He thought too that his mother might also welcome more quiet as she grew older. Realising that both he and his brother would most likely have more children over the succeeding years, he feared that Willow Lane would soon be too overcrowded for comfort. Under the circumstances they had lived together amicably enough, but there was strong possibility that the good relationship might not continue if more children were born and they still lived together, not to mention a probable short-age of bedrooms.

Grace was of the same opinion as her husband. She had wanted a house of her own from the start. She had also a high enough regard for her mother-in-law to want her to have more comfort in her own home. So the pair began to think seriously about looking for some-where else to live. It would not have been practicable for Willis to have moved out, him being the farmer and needing to live on the place. In Ernest's case, his business as butcher could still be carried on providing suitable premises could be found. It so happened that good fortune was on his side.

His sister Gladys and her husband Fred Hill were soon able to tell him of a place which they considered ideal for his and Grace's require-ments. It was the small farm of Near Coates, only a few hundred yards distant from Grace's girlhood home of Travellers Inn, and hardly more than a mile from Willow Lane. Fred thought it was just the right sort of place in which to bring up a young family. Moreover, there was plenty of scope for the setting up of butchering premises. The reason why Fred was so well informed about Near Coates was that his aunt Emma and her husband George Senior were already the tenants there. They had lived at the place for a long time but, owing to advancing years, were wanting to leave and retire to Hoylandswaine.

Grace and Ernest went to look at Near Coates and discovered that, as Fred had shrewdly judged, it was exactly to their liking.

In the normal course of procedure the Seniors would have been required to give a year's notice to the landlord of their intention to leave, so that he would have plenty of time to appoint someone suit-able to take over the tenancy. The Bramalls could well have had to wait another year for a home of their own had it not been for Fred Hill's help. Being a nephew of the Seniors and brother-in-law to Ernest he was able to act as go-between, doing both parties a good turn by helping to speed up the changeover. As soon as the Bramalls decided they wanted to take Coates Farm, George Senior, accompanied by Fred, took Ernest to see the landlord directly. After explaining the case they asked if, under the circumstances, the usual year's notice could be waived. George Senior and his nephew were both able to vouch for Ernest's integrity and suitability as prospective tenant. Thus sponsored by the existing tenant and his relative, and no doubt creating a good impression himself, Ernest was told he could move into Coates as soon as the Seniors moved out. This they were free to do as soon as they wished. Feeling elated he hastened to tell his wife the good news that at last she was going to have her own home. Grace of course was delighted and excited at the prospect.

It was the spring of 1927 when George Senior and his wife left Coates Farm. Ernest and Grace Bramall moved in on the same day as their predecessors left. Although everyone at Willow Lane knew their going was all for the best, when it came to the actual leave-taking there were tears to be shed all the same. Some of these came from Selina as Phyllis, clinging to her, made it clear she didn't want to leave her grandma. Selina in her turn seemed equally reluctant to let the child go. Despite her initial disappointment at her grand-daughter's birth, Selina had become very fond of the little girl through the three years' daily contact with her.

Grace was somewhat perturbed at this sorrowful turn of events. Their faces brightened, however, when someone sensibly pointed out that they still wouldn't be far away. Visits could often be exchanged between Coates and Willow Lane, so Phyllis would still see her grandma quite frequently. This knowledge did help to cheer the situation, and it was on a happy note that Grace, with her husband and children, finally left Willow Lane after a four-year stay.

CHAPTER 11

A House of their Own

THE PROPER NAME for Grace's new home was Near Coates Farm, but it was seldom referred to by the full title. It was generally spoken of simply as Coates Farm. Its larger counterpart, being further away from the road, had the name of Far Coates and was usually known as such to distinguish it from its neighbour.

Both farms had cottages close by. These took the same name as the farms. All the local people living around Four Lane Ends at that time pronounced the word as 'Coits'. Even today it is still 'Coits' to the folk who wish to keep their dialect alive. Since this was actually the spelling on an old map of the 1770s, it would appear that theirs is the correct pronunciation. 'Coits', it seems, was the original name for the small group of dwellings on the hill-top above Travellers Inn. Later generations, because of educational influence, began calling their top garments by the standard English word 'coats' instead of using the dialect form 'coits', so it is most likely that the farm name became changed because of the similarity. Coates was therefore accepted as being correct speech for the word whether it referred to houses or top garments. The addition of the 'e' in the former case is the only distinguishing feature between the two.

On moving to her new home, Grace Bramall was still in the familiar surroundings she had known from the age of five when she had first come from Cranemoor to Four Lane Ends. Since then, her homes of Travellers Inn, Tunnel Top and Willow Lane were all within easy walking distance from one another and had Oxspring and Penistone as focal points for purposes of school, shopping, and the few entertainments to be occasionally enjoyed. This strong connection with the two places was to continue. Coates was actually just inside Thurgoland parish boundary but, being much nearer to Oxspring village, the Bramalls considered they would still have a closer association with the latter place.

By the year 1927 the crossroads at Four Lane Ends had hardly changed since the end of the previous century. Though the motor car had been invented, very few were seen on the roads around Oxspring. There was, however, one innovation of great importance to the local people. Bus services had begun to operate in the area. Travelling between Barnsley and Penistone the buses picked up and set down passengers at Four Lane Ends and Oxspring as they passed through. The first buses on that route were Harburn's 'Blue and Whites', but they were taken over by the Yorkshire Traction Company in 1925. Another proprietor, Arthur Walshaw, owned green and white buses which worked the same route. His service was taken over too by Yorkshire Traction in 1931, but the buses continued to be known as 'Walshaws' by the local folk until they were replaced. With the coming of the buses, Barnsley seemed a much nearer town than it did in Grace's early years when the journey by waggonette took nearly all day.

The little shop at Fours which, during Grace's childhood, had been kept by the Saunders, had since changed hands. A kindly woman named Phoebe Wray, her husband William and their family were installed as the new shopkeepers. They had previously lived in one of the cottages at Far Coates, next door to the Matthewmans.

Going to live at Coates Farm meant that Grace was near her eldest sister Blanche. She, with her husband Frank Purseglove and four daughters, lived in the first cottage nearest the farm. Myrtle, the youngest girl, was ten in that year and looked forward to playing with her small cousin Phyllis. In the middle cottage were the Illingsworth family. Frances, who had been one of Grace's best friends in her Travellers Inn days, had left Coates when she married, but her widowed father and his sons were helped in their housekeeping by the younger daughter Hannah. She had only been two years old when the family were left motherless. The cottage at the far end of the row was occupied by a childless couple, Annie and Ned Thompson, who were cousins. She was very deaf, and he stammered badly. They kept pretty much to themselves as a rule, but were helpful when needed and generally well liked by their neighbours.

Coates Farm is older than Willow Lane. The date of building is not certain, but evidence from the old map shows it was there as early as 1770. It could well have been built a good deal earlier, but of that we cannot be sure.

From the Barnsley road above Four Lane Ends, at the very top of the hill, the farm is approached along a short lane to the right. This leads into the yard at one end of the house. The yard extends along the whole frontage of house and farm buildings to the field gate at the other end.

When Grace first went to live at Coates there was a picturesque little pond just through the gate. At the far side, where the water was deepest, it was backed by a hedge. Immediately in front of the house, an area of flagstones was separated from the yard by a surrounding wall. Access to the house door was through a little gate in the wall and across the 'flags'. Another gate, at the lower end of the wall, was convenient for anyone entering the house from the bottom part of the yard. The wall served to protect the house windows from animals that might sometimes be running loose in the yard. It also made the 'flags' a safe play area for young children.

The front of the house faces east, in the direction of Coates Lane, which is that part of the Barnsley road leading downhill towards Silkstone Common. When viewed from the top of Coates Lane, the dwelling has a long appearance due to the farm buildings and house being one continuous structure. Behind it to the west, and also at the southern end of the farm, are grass fields comprising about twenty-four acres. The only grass directly in front of the house is the small croft across the yard. The land between croft and road was formerly garden belonging to the three cottages. These have since been sold and are now owner-occupied. Two modern bungalows have been built on the site of the original gardens.

The situation of Coates Farm was ideal as far as Grace and her family were concerned. Being just off the road and surrounded by its own land, it afforded privacy without isolation. The new bus transport was near enough to be convenient, yet not too near for its noise to cause disturbance. Though the farmhouse was set apart, Grace's cottage neighbours were near enough to prevent any feeling of loneliness she might otherwise have had.

Her first weeks at Coates were essentially happy ones. The spring evenings being light, she would take her children down the yard after tea to watch her husband milking the cows in the mistal. Seated on his three-legged stool, he drew out the milk by hand, causing it to swish rhythmically into the piggen between his knees. This was a straight-sided metal container which had a wide rim at the top and a handle at the side. From the piggen the milk was poured into a larger bucket set down on the floor. Besides watching the actual milking process, Grace enjoyed looking through the mistal window because its outlook was so pleasing to her. In the foreground was the pond with low bushes around part of its perimeter. Beyond were the fields with their hedges and walls. It was good to gaze on them for a while, after being busy inside the house all day. The peaceful scene outside, added to the cosy warmth within the mistal, gave her a pleasant feeling of contentment.

The house itself was basically to her liking. It had three main downstairs rooms, a pantry and a cellar. There were three bedrooms, two of them quite big and the other small. Unlike the house at Willow Lane, there was no bathroom at Coates Farm and no indoor lavatory. The Bramalls had therefore to revert to bathing in a tin bath, as they had done when living in the cottage at Tunnel Top. The lavatory was of the earth variety and not quickly reached, since one had to traverse both yard and croft in order to get to the small closet. The wooden seat inside provided accommodation for a child and adult at the same time, there being two holes of different sizes. Adjoining the farm closet was the one belonging to Purseglove's cottage. The yard, which was communally shared by all three cottages, was just over the wall of that side of the Bramalls' croft, so the conveniences were sited to suit all concerned. The Illingsworth and Thompson families had adjoining closets reached from their back yard as was the Pursegloves'. Cleaning-out of all four conveniences had to be done from the farm croft, as the doors for that purpose were all at the croft side.

Despite the primitive toilet facilities, Grace was delighted to be in her new home, pleased with the knowledge that she could organise the running of it herself. At the same time she thought that keeping to some of the methods employed at Willow Lane would be a good thing. She had admired Selina's thoroughness in all she did and, while thinking at times she was rather too particular in some respects, admitted to herself that, if fussiness was a fault, at least it was a good one.

In comparison with the house at Willow Lane there was plenty to be done at Coates to bring the rooms up to anything like acceptable standards. The Seniors, being elderly and knowing the end of their time at the farm was in sight, had not bothered much about changing their interior decor. What had sufficed for them over the years had continued to do so. The inside walls were colour-washed, some rooms in pink and some in blue. While they did look clean and colourful there was a big disadvantage where young children were concerned. The type of colour-wash used was the sort that rubbed off onto one's clothes if one was standing against the wall. Phyllis, at three years old, often forgot she wasn't meant to go near the walls and would unthinkingly lean against them, to the detriment of her dresses and pinafores. These garments quickly acquired large pinky patches that were not meant to be there and were difficult to remove. Grace decided the best solution to that problem would be to cover the walls with wallpaper. The paintwork which was looking worn and shabby would need to be renewed. If it was painted, grained and varnished by a professional man it would look good for years, only needing to be washed from time to time. The cost would be less in the long run because woodwork treated in that way remained sound and durable. Ernest was in agreement that to have the job done properly would be money well spent. Another improvement that they considered necessary was the erection of a partition in the first bedroom at the top of the stairs. This required the services of a joiner. The stairs opened directly into the bedroom and were not enclosed in any way. Because there was no landing at the top, the Seniors had, during their days at Coates Farm, walked through the first bedroom to get into the second one. This did not allow for privacy on the part of the first bedroom's occupants. Grace thought the open stairs presented a hazard to young children, so commissioned the joiner to fix a permanent wooden barricade round the stair-top. This was also painted and varnished in due course. He put up the partition on that side of the bedroom nearest the stairs so that, on ascending, one came onto a landing. The first bedroom was entered by a door in the partition, and the second bedroom from the original door which was now at the end of the landing.

While the improvements were being carried out Coates was a very busy place. The joiner and painters did their work to Grace's satisfaction. Yet little did she think then that the happiness she was experiencing through having a home of her own was so soon to be shattered.

CHAPTER 12

Dark Days

THAT YEAR OF 1927 proved to be an eventful one, during which Grace felt joy and sorrow to extreme degree. The painters had hardly finished their work when her little son Frank became ill. He was a fair, sweet-faced boy who until then had been healthy enough. At fifteen months he was walking well and quite advanced in talking, showing good understanding for a child of his age. He and his sister Phyllis were already becoming playmates for one another. Their cousin, Flora Purseglove, who was the eldest of Blanche's four daughters, sometimes went across to the farm and, holding Frank on her knee, would help to feed him. Being thus pleasantly acquainted, Flora too was sorry to hear her small cousin was ill.

When Frank first showed signs of being unwell, Grace thought it was perhaps due to his teething. She soon grew more concerned when he suffered a bout of diarrhoea that seemed to persist. She wondered whether the smell of the new painting had brought this about. The doctor was called in and the little boy confined to bed. It was obvious that he was far from well. Feverishness, headache and vomiting added to his discomfort. When he showed no signs of improvement Grace began to fear that the complaint might be serious. This fear was soon confirmed by the doctor, who pronounced Frank's illness to be meningitis. Grace's initial alarm on hearing the diagnosis was quickly suppressed by her determination to do her utmost to make him well again.

At times when he seemed a little better she would be optimistic about his recovery but, when he screamed for three hours at a time because of the searing pain in his head, she suffered too. The doctor told her that if she could see inside the little boy's head she would not wonder that he had periods of screaming. The inflammation of the brain would feel similar to a burning fire. While telling Grace this, the doctor seemed unable to do anything to ease her son's distress.

One day, after three or four weeks had passed, he told her of his surprise that Frank's illness was carrying on so long. Often children with meningitis died after a few days; it was unusual for them to live with it for more than two weeks. Grace took this as a good sign, thinking that, as Frank had survived longer than the expected time, he might recover. Still the illness continued as before. Frank had a long screaming bout at some part of every twenty-four hours; if not during the daytime it happened at night. At these distressing times Illingsworth's dog would bark from across the cottagers' yard, adding to the pain of it all.

Frank became wan and pale. His once plump little limbs grew thin and wasted until he seemed to be only skin and bone. The food his mother managed to get into him was often vomited back.

While she was spending much of her time by Frank's bedside, Grace did not neglect her husband's meals. Many were the trips up and down stairs she made during their preparation. At breakfast time she set the frying pan over the fire and put in the bacon for Ernest and the boy who helped him with the outside work. She then went upstairs to attend to Frank, coming down again when she judged the bacon was ready to be turned over and the eggs needing to go in. After a few more minutes snatched upstairs she came down again to serve out the breakfast and mash the tea to go with it. The same procedure would be followed at dinner and tea-time too if Frank was awake and needing her. Her own meals were often neglected, but that she didn't mind.

As she cared for her son who was so gravely ill, Grace had to endure another sorrow. One day in July her cousin Madge appeared in the yard at Coates Farm. Madge had come over from Wakefield and was staying for a while at Tunnel Top to keep house for her Aunt Lizzy and Uncle Jimmy. Elizabeth Spenceley had been a semi-invalid for several years, and since her daughter Mary had also married not long after Grace she had no woman's help in the house. There was less to do of course because Willie and George had both married and left home. Her son Frank, because of his work on the railway, also left Tunnel Top to live in lodgings in Sheffield. He found it more convenient since his work was transferred there, but came back to Tunnel Top at weekends. The only Spenceley son to remain at home with his parents was Grace's youngest brother Stanley. He and his father had of necessity to attend to their own needs when Elizabeth was unfit, but they welcomed a visit from Madge now and then. Besides attending to the housekeeping she brightened the place with her cheery presence and was an ideal companion for her Aunt Lizzy, who had always been fond of her. Since Grace was in no position to help her mother just then, Madge had undertaken to assist for a while at Tunnel Top until Elizabeth was in better form. The trouble was her heart was not good and she was inclined to dropsy.

On that particular July day she had told Madge to 'go over to t'Coits and see how our Grace's little lad's getting on.' Stanley and his father were at home so Madge, knowing her aunt was not alone, had hurried down the Jockey to Coates Farm. Just as she was crossing the yard on her arrival, Stanley came running along the lane after her in great agitation. Turning at his shout, she listened unbelievingly while he told her that his mother had just died. It appeared that Elizabeth had gone very suddenly. James had been reading the newspaper and discussing with her some items of interest it contained. 'Have you seen this, Lizzie?' he went on, reading further. Getting no reply he looked up, only to see she had slumped over and was dead. Grace, already greatly troubled, had nevertheless to be told the sad news.

She was naturally very upset at her mother's death and wished she could have done more to help her in the last weeks but, as everyone realised, her first duty lay with her sick child. She was grateful for Madge's company during that dark time. Elizabeth was buried at Thurgoland in the family grave that already held two of her children, Emma and Harry. Grace did not attend the funeral, because she could not leave her son. She did, however, take Phyllis down to the bottom yard gate from where they had a view over the fields to Copster top. She pointed across in that direction, telling the child that her Grandma Spenceley was going along that way to Thurgoland. As Copster was quite steep in those days, before the road was altered, the funeral cortege could be seen as it topped the hill. Viewing it thus from the bottom yard gate was the only way Grace was able to share in her mother's passing.

Phyllis remembered visiting her grandma Spenceley not long before Frank fell poorly. On that occasion she was seated in a big chair pulled up to the table. She spread butter on a cream cracker biscuit, then smiling kindly gave it to her. Phyllis thought her grandma looked a very old lady. She was rather fat, her hair was grey and scanty, and her smile showed gaps in her mouth. Elizabeth Spenceley was sixty-one when she died.

Grace had little time to grieve for her mother as Frank's condition deteriorated. She continued bravely up and down the stairs, though often feeling tired. This was partly due to the fact that her next child was expected at the end of September. The doctor had told her she needed rest, but she found that impossible. Even when Frank was asleep there was Phyllis to be looked after, as well as the baking, cooking, cleaning and washing. Ernest was fully occupied in earning their living, and she did not expect him to give any assistance in the house.

Bravely she carried on alone for a while, regarding it as entirely her duty. Then Selina Bramall and Jessie, her son Willis's wife showed compassion for Grace in her pitiful situation. They eased the burden by taking Phyllis back to Willow Lane with them, promising to care for her until such time as Grace was better able to cope. Phyllis was happy to play with her cousin Dyson again, and went willingly to her Grandma's.

The meningitis had such bad effect that it took the sight from one of Frank's eyes. The doctor tried to reassure Grace by telling her that it might come back, yet she hardly believed him. Although the doctor visited frequently he could offer no remedies for the disease as it pursued its ravaging course. Grace nursed her child often, doing her best to soothe his pain and bring him comfort, but soon she noticed that the sight in his other eye was being threatened.

Then came a day in August when she thought he was a little better. She fed him some milk pudding, which he seemed to enjoy. On telling the doctor this she was disappointed in his reaction. It was evident he did not share her optimism that her son might, after all, have taken a turn for the better. A day or two later she knew why, for Frank passed away as she held him in her arms. He had been ill for nine weeks. The doctor told her that what she had thought of as an improvement in her son's condition was only a 'lightening'. It was not unusual for this to happen just before a person died. Grace was overwhelmed with grief. The only slight consolation the doctor could offer was to say that, if Frank had recovered from the meningitis, he would probably have been blind and his brain badly affected. 'He would not have been the child you would wish him to be,' were the doctor's words. Grace had to think that, for the little boy's own sake, it was for the best that he was at peace.

Frank was buried in Penistone's Stottercliffe cemetery. Most of the Bramalls are at Penistone, the earlier generations in the churchyard quite close to the church and the later ones in the cemetery as the churchyard became full. Ernest, showing foresight, bought a family plot of ground at Stottercliffe. Grace was too heartbroken to go to the little boy's funeral. She had kept up bravely during the nine weeks of that terrible illness, but had not been outside the farm gate during the whole of that time. Now she was desolate. It seemed as if the happy little world which had been hers not so very long ago had suddenly fallen apart.

After a short while Phyllis returned from Willow Lane. On going upstairs with her mother to make the beds, she noticed that the small bed in which she had last seen her young brother was empty. 'Where's little Frank?' she asked. Her mother replied, 'Mr Tinker's taken him.' 'Well, if I'd been here I wouldn't have let him taked him,' said the three-year-old girl assertively. Then, in childish innocence, she wondered why her mother started weeping.

It was not until after Frank had left her and she knew she could do no more for him that Grace spared much thought for the new life she was soon to bring into the world. There were people around Four Lane Ends who, knowing of the physical and mental hardships she had just undergone, hinted to one another that the next baby's health might not be good because of them. When Grace finally turned her thoughts onto the matter she admitted to herself that it would be a wonder if the child was alright. She had so often been driven to the point of exhaustion, and had utterly disregarded the doctor's orders to get some rest.

At the end of September, just five weeks after Frank's death, she was blessed with another son. Despite all the general apprehension to the contrary, he was a fine, healthy boy. He was a contented baby, sleeping for most of the time and being little trouble. As she gradually regained her sense of humour Grace told people, 'He didn't get much rest before he was born, so he's catching up on it now.' Although she had got another boy, he never took the place of the one she had lost. That sorrowful time of their first summer at Coates Farm left a scar on Grace's mind that never did completely fade away.

Her second son was named Norman. This caused her some annoyance, because that was not the name she had chosen. She had wanted him called George after one of her brothers, and Ernest had seemed to be in agreement. He set off to register the baby but, on his way to Penistone to do this, he called in at Willow Lane. There he was persuaded that George might not be a good idea, as the boy would be in danger of being nicknamed 'Jud'. Someone suggested Norman for a name and, thinking the objection to George a feasible one, Ernest continued his journey to Penistone to record the new alternative. Grace was far from pleased when he returned home and informed her of the change, but allowed the name of Norman to remain. Ernest received stern admonition all the same for allowing himself to be swayed by the in-laws. Grace accused him of being as bad as his uncle, 'Owd Bill Brammer', in his failure to register the child correctly. In fact she considered him rather worse than his uncle. That individual had actually forgotten the name that his wife Polly had chosen, so he had some excuse for getting it wrong.

When Norman was born an Oxspring woman known as Bethann was engaged to take over the housekeeping duties until Grace was up and about again. Her full name was Elizabeth Ann Taylor but, as her family always used the shortened form of 'Bethann', everyone else tended to give her that name too. She was a talkative, gossipy soul but bustlingly efficient at the same time. Having such a person as Bethann in the house helped to cheer Grace up to some degree. Ernest had engaged her for the temporary work at Coates because, apart from her suitability for the job, the Taylors patronised him as meat customers. Phyllis was too young at the time to remember much about Bethann. The one memory she did retain was not of her face but of plump arms bathing her. The arms, unlike her mother's, were covered in freckles—which Phyllis didn't really like. She was glad when the bathing was finished.

Owing to her good constitution Grace was seldom ill, yet there was one time during their early period at Coates when she did have a day or two in bed. On the first morning of her enforced lie-in, she was pleasantly surprised to see Ernest bringing a cup of tea into the bedroom for her. It was not, alas, a cup that she enjoyed. In fact she had never had one quite like it before. Tea leaves were floating on top of the too-milky, lukewarm liquid, some of which had spilled into the saucer during its journey up the stairs. It was quite evident that her husband was unused to making tea. Indeed, that was the first time he had ever attempted to make any. He hadn't known that the water should be actually boiling when poured onto the tea leaves, hence the pathetic result. Grace, realising his intentions were good, had not the heart to criticise or chide him for domestic shortcomings. After all, making tea was not his job.

When later that day her mother-in-law came down from Willow Lane to see how she was getting on, Grace told her of the morning's tea episode. Selina, a little embarrassed at her son's helplessness in this respect, defensively made the excuse that mashing tea was something new to him. She had always done it for him before he was married and of course Grace had done it since. While both of them agreed that tea making was not really within a man's province, they grudgingly admitted that a knowledge of how to do it could prove useful in times of crisis. Before leaving, Selina told her daughter-in-law that she would see to it that a proper cup of tea would be forthcoming on the following morning.

Grace wondered whether that meant she was going to instruct her son in the art of tea mashing; if so, the idea was quite out of keeping with her traditional beliefs. Next morning, however, she and Ernest were awakened quite early by the sound of pebbles being thrown up against their bedroom window. Then Selina's voice was heard, urging

Ernest to hurry up and let her in. Selina had been up betimes and had walked the distance from Willow Lane to Coates especially to make the promised cup of tea. Rather than trust her son to do it, she was relying on her own efforts to ensure that Grace got the good cup of tea she deserved.

CHAPTER 13

Continuing at Coates

GRACE OFTEN SAID that having Norman was, in a way, like starting all over again with Frank. She had reared her first son through the baby stage to the point where he was walking, talking, and becoming more interesting, only to lose him. Having another son just afterwards meant going through it all again, which at first brought hurt as well as joy.

In the following year it was decided that Grace should have some permanent help in the house. Her sister Blanche's second daughter, Mary Emma, had reached the age of fourteen, so was wanting a job on leaving school. She was pleased to accept her aunt's offer of work as day-girl in her house. Living so near to the farm was convenient, since no travel was involved. Her sister Flora, who had a job in a Barnsley shirt factory, had to be up very early to get to her work on time. She had to walk to Silkstone Common to catch a train there at half-past seven because, though the bus company was in operation, there wasn't a bus so early in the morning that would enable her to reach work soon enough. In Mary Emma's case she could be at the farm in a minute, literally speaking, since she had only to walk along the few yards from her door before turning onto the farm lane. Mary Emma was a pleasant good-looking girl, with round smiling face, grey eyes and brown hair. She was willing to follow her aunt's instructions regarding the work and be patient with the children. Having Mary Emma to take on routine tasks such as washing-up, helping with meals, cleaning and ironing, gave Grace a little more time to take out her children.

The walk she usually took with them was down a pleasant country lane not far from their home. This lane forked off from the main road at Coates Lane top and was called, appropriately enough, Bird Lane. There were hedges as well as walls at the sides of Bird Lane. These and some taller trees growing alongside provided ideal habitats for those small feathered creatures which, in springtime, made the lane

come joyfully alive with birdsong and the busy activity of nest building. The left side of the lane was hedged all the way along. At the
other side there were low-walled gaps through which could be seen
the fields belonging to Houghlands' farm. There was life in the fields
too in the shape of cows, sheep and lambs. Several hen huts housed a
large number of egg-laying birds at nights, but during the daytime
the hens ranged over the grassy fields at will, only going back into the
huts to lay or if the weather became bad.

Apart from the birds and beasts there were flowers too to colour the
Bird Lane wayside in the spring and summer months. Bright sun-
faces of dandelions, shining boldly upwards, enriched the laneside
with yellow-gold display, as did the buttercups in their turn. Daisies,
daintily pretty with their white, pink-tipped petals peeped shyly from
the grass. Clumps of milk-white stitchwort showed pure, star-like flowers on the grassy bank beneath the hedge. In one certain place a plantation adjoined the laneside above the bank. Here, in late May and
early June, bluebells grew thickly under the trees' shade, exuding into
the soft warm air their sweet, heady scent. In summer the lower part
of Bird Lane was bordered by tall hemlocks, with foxgloves here and
there. Except for the sounds of nature the lane was a quiet place. The
only wheeled traffic to be encountered along it then were the slow-
moving, horse-drawn carts and implements belonging to Houghlands'
farm. Now, more than a half-century later, cars sometimes pass through
and something of the old charm has been lost. Yet, in spite of changes,
Bird Lane is still quite a delightful place for a pleasant summer walk.

During the spring and summer following Frank's death, Grace found
that going down Bird Lane with Norman in the pram and Phyllis walking beside did help to heal the devastation she had first felt. Quite
often on her way down the lane she would meet with Laura Hough-
land, one of the daughters from the farm further along. Laura, a bucket
in each hand, would be taking corn up to the hen huts to feed the
hens and collect the eggs. Laura invariably appeared smiling and unhurried. As she and Grace were about to meet, she set down her buckets
methodically, signifying she was ready to pass the time of day and
partake of a little conversation besides. The Houghlands rarely left
Bird Lane apart from going to market, for the purposes of shopping, and
special occasions such as Penistone Show and Penistone Feast. Laura
welcomed, therefore, a chance to see a new face and learn fresh news.

Grace did not always manage to go the whole length of the lane.
After a quarter-mile or so she came to the place where another short
lane led up to Houghlands' farm on the left. Immediately past that

point a gateway gave access to a cottage with its yard and garden, occupied by the Darwents or 'Darrins' as they were locally called. Mrs 'Darrin' was a middle-aged, motherly woman who, like the Hough-lands, seldom left the lane but enjoyed a gossip with anyone passing by. If she happened to be outside her house when Grace was coming along, she would bustle down to her gate and, leaning plump arms across its top, proceed to enquire after her welfare. She usually wore a mobcap to cover her head, while her long skirt was protected by a clean apron tied round her middle. Mrs Dar-rin's ample figure and full, kindly face beneath the mobcap evoked a feeling of comfort even before she began to speak. When she did her words were reassuringly optimistic. While sympa-thising with Grace over the loss of her first son, she tried also to cheer her by pointing out, 'God's sent you another healthy 'un in his place.' Sometimes she would urge her to 'Look after yerself, Grace lass. Get a drop o' gruel into yerself; it'll do yer good.' Mrs Darwent's friendly concern

Meeting with Laura in Bird Lane

did much to help Grace over those difficult days when she was com-ing to terms with life as it was. When time had been spent talking with her, Grace would turn the pram around and hasten back home, judging she had been out long enough. At times when Mrs Darwent was not about, she would continue further, down the next part of the lane as far as Hollin Dyke.

That part was of steeper gradient, the trees at the sides taller and thicker, excluding much of the light, so the way in that place was always in shade and appeared a little gloomy. The silence there could have created an almost eerie or 'spooky' atmosphere had it not been for the friendly babble of running water. This came from a little stream that gurgled its way down the right side of the lane as far as Hollin Dyke, where two adjoining water troughs stood. The trees finished just before the troughs were reached, so it was lighter there. Catching the sun's rays, the water in the troughs flashed and sparkled in crystal clearness as Grace paused for a moment to let her small daughter look. One trough supplied drinking water for the family at the small-holding across the lane and for three other families living in the 'poor row' a little further on, where the lane turned uphill again before ending at Pinfold crossroads. People from these families carried their buckets of water back uphill on a wooden yoke fixed across their shoulders; a hook at each end of the yoke meant the two buckets were evenly balanced. Use of a yoke made water carrying easier, as it took the weight from the carrier's arms. The trough adjoining the people's water supply was for horses to drink from. As there was a constant supply of fresh water trickling into the troughs to replace that taken out, the water drunk by the people was always clean. Surplus water from their trough passed into the horse trough. When this was full, the surplus trickled slowly over the side to join another stream. At that lowest part of Bird Lane the continuous gurgling and trickling sound of water, added to Nature's other pleasant voices, gave a soothing sense of timelessness.

While Grace enjoyed her outings with the children, she did not always accompany them herself. Thinking rightly that her niece also would appreciate the delights of Bird Lane, she allowed Mary Emma to take the children sometimes while she carried on with housework.

She was far from being lonely in those early days at Coates Farm. Mary Emma appeared before breakfast and stayed until after tea, taking all three meals with her employers. So did the boy Alf who helped Ernest with the butchering and farm work. Alf was one of the Matthewmans and, though his own home was only just across the field at Far Coates, it was Grace who provided all his meals too. He was a year older than Mary Emma and, like her, had come to work at the farm when he left school the year before.

There was always close contact with the Pursegloves of course. Grace was able to speak most days with her sister Blanche when she came to the farm for milk. When Myrtle was not at school she frequently played with Phyllis. Myrtle was a gentle, helpful girl, with a face as lovely as her nature. She often read stories to her small cousin, and taught her all the letters before she started school. By the time Phyllis was five she was able to read many short words, thanks to Myrtle.

The Illingsworths and Thompsons from the other two cottages came to buy milk too. Hannah would usually spare time for a chat, but Mrs Thompson, who was so very deaf, could only exchange smiles and, after the milk was put in her jug, she made her silent departure. Her husband Ned was a sociable man who, despite his speech impediment, was naturally talkative. When he fetched the milk he would usually embark on some topic of conversation, but it required time and patience all round before Ned had finished what he wanted to say.

Just before Phyllis started school, another daughter was born at Coates Farm. She was named Betty. Of all Grace's children, Betty was the most difficult to rear as a baby. Different brands of food were tried but none seemed to satisfy her. She cried a lot and was failing to gain the weight she ought to have reached. In desperation Grace took more new advice from the doctor. He told her to put the baby back onto cow's milk but add a lump of butter to it. Whether it was this change in food that did the trick or whether she would have improved in any case we do not know. The fact is, after the change to cow's milk with butter, Betty began to thrive and continued to do so.

An Oxspring woman by name of Mrs Jagger helped in the house when Betty was born and, while Mary Emma was still only young, she came on Mondays for quite some time afterwards to assist with washing. Mrs Jagger was industrious and thorough, particularly where washing was concerned. She was glad of the work at Coates, because her husband was not in good health and she needed the money.

Phyllis was pleased to be going to school. Her mother had told her well in advance that she would be able to go, and had said it was a nice place where she would learn to read books for herself. It was the same school she went to when she was a little girl, though she had been to another one to begin with because they lived at another place then. Grace told her daughter how she had wanted to go to school when she was only three and had in fact gone there, only to be told to return home.

This implication that school was a desirable place prompted her child's eagerness to attend. Another reason why Phyllis was willing to start school was that she would be walking there and back in the company of her cousin Myrtle.

Grace never took her children to school in the mornings because there were always other older ones to accompany them in the walk down Bower Hill. There was also very little traffic on the roads before 1930. Oxspring School accommodated all children up to fourteen years old until then, and there was quite a little contingent went from the houses at Four Lane Ends and Coates. The Naylor family who lived in one of the cottages near to Travellers Inn had nine children; some were attending school in 1930, though the eldest few had already left and the two youngest hadn't started. There were Jack and Irene Langley from the tiny house that was actually part of the Travellers Inn building then, but is now incorporated into the inn. The Hustlers who, for a time, kept Travellers Inn, later moved into a small wooden bungalow just off the Copster road not far from the crossroads, so their children attended Oxspring school too. At Far Coates Farm the tenant was Bert Milnes. His son Donald, who was the same age as Phyllis Bramall, and daughter Margaret, two years older, were amongst the band of scholars who made the daily journey down Bower Hill.

Halfway down Bower Hill, on the right-hand side, were other houses from which children went to Oxspring school. Among these, the Marshes were most prolific. There were three families of them living in Bower Hill at that time, the fathers—Ben, George and Joel—being brothers. Ben died comparatively young, leaving seven children for his widow to bring up. The eldest had only just left school to begin work at Winterbottom's wire mill, while the youngest was a small baby. Mrs Marsh ran a mail-order clothing club as one means of helping her finances, but had a hard struggle to make ends meet. It is to her credit that when the children grew up they became useful and highly-respected members of the Oxspring community.

Phyllis and Norman Bramall in 1929

Across a field at the other side of Bower Hill the two houses of High Pickliffes stood in elevated position above the 'Nelly' stream. The older house was inhabited by another family of Illingsworths who were relatives of those at Coates cottages. The newer house belonged to Randolph Fieldsend who had married Grace's friend, Betty Peaker, from Jockey House. Their daughter Joan was attending Oxspring school at the time when Phyllis started there, as was Stanley Illingsworth from the other house.

The walk to school which Phyllis took followed exactly the same way as her mother's had done thirty years earlier. At the bottom of Bower Hill the twisting road past the old corn mill and over the narrow humped-back bridge spanning the Don was still adequate for the amount of traffic it carried. More recently, a section of straight road and wider bridge have been built to comply with modern needs, but happily the old route has been allowed to remain too. Anyone, if so inclined, can still wander along the quiet, picturesque way into the time of fifty years past. The older Oxspring people perhaps feel some nostalgia as they remember childhood companions whose hurrying feet crossed over the old bridge on that daily walk to school so long ago. Phyllis's five-year-old legs traversed the route up and down Bower Hill on six days out of the seven, for she was soon initiated into attending Sunday School as well as the weekday one.

One of Grace's regrets was that she had never had a photograph taken of Frank. Not wishing to chance a similar happening where Norman was concerned, she and Ernest took both children to Woodhead's studio in Penistone, where they had a photograph taken together. It turned out to be quite a good one, and copies were duly distributed to the various relatives.

When Christmas came round they all went to the pantomime in Sheffield. The show was Cinderella. By all accounts Phyllis enjoyed her introduction to the theatre immensely, joining in whole-heartedly with the grown-ups' applause. Norman, being rather too young to appreciate the pantomime fully, occupied himself happily all the same by discovering how the empty seats moved up and down when he pushed them.

CHAPTER 14

Ernest's Work as a Butcher

WHEN HE WAS quite a young boy, Ernest Bramall helped his father in the small family meat business and, when not at school, accompanied him on his hawking rounds. On Saturday nights, when the Penistone round was finished, it was his duty to stand with the left-over pieces of meat in order to sell as many as he could before returning home. His father had the use, for that one night each week, of a small cabin situated on the flags near the Old Crown Inn in Market Street.

At the beginning of the twentieth century, and until 1910, the cattle market was held in the whole of that area near the Old Crown. On market days pens of animals would occupy the stretches of roadside, while the road itself would be filled with cows, sheep and pigs being taken to their place of sale, and by butchers and farmers engaged in the serious business of buying and selling.

The place in which Ernest took up his Saturday night stand was referred to as 'the shop', though its size hardly warranted that name. It was only big enough to accommodate two or three people together, but at least it provided a roof over one's head while waiting for customers and was adequate for their needs. Much of the left-over meat was sold in this way, for there were women of limited means who were glad to buy those rougher pieces as a cheap means of filling their large families' stomachs, even though it did mean going to the 'shop' late on a Saturday night. From the butcher's point of view it was better to sell the meat at a lower price than have too much to take back home, since there was no means of keeping it fresh until the following week. For the butcher's boy, standing in the shop waiting for customers could be a cold, lonely occupation on a winter's night, but this fact was never taken into consideration. Only when it was realised that no more customers were forthcoming, could the journey home be made. Any 'scrag ends' still remaining would be converted into potted meat.

From the age of sixteen Ernest did the rounds on his own because Dyson's health began to fail. In fact, he had to shoulder most of the physical work involved from that time. Though Dyson lived for another thirteen years and was able to advise, it was his son who did the slaughtering, cutting-up and selling too. Ernest had, of course, been well instructed by his father, just as Dyson had earlier been by his father, Joseph. Through the years of his youth at Tunnel Top, and young manhood at Willow Lane, he had become master of his trade.

When he and Grace moved to Coates Farm, Ernest had, for a time, to continue to operate his business from the Willow Lane premises, until the necessary conversions could be made at Coates. At the top end of the farmyard, just to the right of the gate-entry from the lane, were old farm buildings which had been in use many years earlier and had fallen into disrepair. Ernest had these converted into two sound, higher places adjoining each other and connected by an interior door. Each building had also its own exterior door into the yard. Commonly called the 'clammin' 'oil' and 'shop', the names given to the new places were rather misleading, since Ernest did not 'clam' his animals there just prior to slaughter. The bullocks and cows were 'clammed' in the mistal down at the bottom end of the farmyard. That is, they were shut up without food for the whole of the previous day so there would be less waste material for the butcher to dispose of after the killing. Also, to have slaughtered a cow with its stomach full of grass would have had an adverse effect on the meat, particularly in hot weather. Another consideration was that there was no point in wasting food on the last day of the animal's life, since it would not be put to good use anyway. Sheep and pigs due to be killed would be housed in old buildings at the far side of the 'clammin' 'oil'. The 'shop' was that part of the new premises nearer to the farm gate, and therefore conveniently situated for local people to fetch their own meat. In this sense it was a shop, but that was not the only use to which it was put. The 'shop' was also the place where the actual slaughtering and cutting-up were done. The adjoining part of the premises was used for storing equipment and as a place of transit on killing days.

It is not known why the new buildings were so inappropriately named. Perhaps the original intention had been to keep animals in the one place during the starving period so as to be near the point of slaughter. What seems a more likely reason is that the Bramalls' earlier butchering premises at Willow Lane and Tunnel Top had been so called because they were sited to fit the description and, from long habit, Ernest continued to refer to his new buildings by the old names. Whatever the reason, those names were in almost daily use at Coates Farm in the 1930s and during the thirty years afterwards too.

When Ernest established himself at Coates he had the walls of both 'clammin' 'oil' and 'shop' lime-washed and the floors concreted. His equipment was then transferred from Willow Lane. This included the 'plonks' or low wooden benches on which sheep and pigs were killed, and the higher cutting-up benches. An important item was the pulley and chain for hoisting up the heavy carcasses of cattle. There were also the cambrils and hooks, knives, saw, cleavers, choppers and poleaxe. The grindstone, turned by a handle, was a familiar fixture at the side of the yard in those days. As the butcher's knives had to be kept sharp, the grindstone was put to frequent use.

To be a successful family butcher required mental alertness as well as physical strength. Ernest carried out all the various activities connected with the work. He did the buying, killing, cutting-up and selling himself, with some assistance from his brother Willis and the boy Alf. Until Alf was older and better able to help, Willis came to Coates on killing days and on Tuesday evenings to take out orders.

Having the twenty-four acres of land at Coates Farm meant that Ernest could feed some of his own animals to supply part of the butchering requirements. He would therefore buy young, partly-grown stock to utilise his grass. With the addition of bought-in 'cake', cereals and supplements, they were eventually converted into good meat. Quite often he would buy animals from his farming neighbours; these transactions were of mutual benefit because marketing expenses were not incurred. Of course Ernest did need to buy many of his animals in the market in addition to those he obtained locally or reared at home.

The weekly routine began with the Monday morning's killing, when Willis came down from Willow Lane to help. The bullock, heifer, or cow to be slaughtered would have been confined since the previous day in the mistal in the bottom yard. The butcher and his assistant had to put a rope round its neck and bring it up into the top yard. The beast was usually unwilling to comply. It was only after hard pulling on the rope by the man in front and repeated beating from the stick of the man behind that the poor creature was dragged and pushed up the yard, past the house front and towards the clammin' 'oil door. Once inside that place, the long rope was taken through the connecting door into the shop. There its end was passed through an iron ring bolted in a low position to the outer wall. Near the ring was a small hole left deliberately by the builders for the purpose of passing the rope outside after it had been put through the ring. At this point Ernest's helpers stayed outside to draw the rope through the hole in the wall. He remained inside to push the animal into the shop as the

others drew it on from outside. By the time it reached the middle of
the slaughter place it had been pulled into a lower position due to the
ring being fixed low on the wall. Sometimes a beast would slither to
its knees in the process, but with the rope held taughtly by the people
outside it was rendered helpless. Its head was kept steady while the
butcher lifted his poleaxe and, with a swift hard blow aimed at the
middle of its forehead, knocked it down unconscious.

The poleaxe was the accepted implement of all butchers for slaughtering beasts when Ernest went to Coates, though it was not unknown
for hammers to be used by some who were less concerned with the
suffering they might cause to the animal. Ernest followed the methods of his forebears. The poleaxe had been in use for centuries and, if
skillfully employed, was not thought of as a cruel thing, at least not
by the people most closely concerned. It was quite a heavy implement. The strong wooden handle had at its end an axe-head with a
straight metal piece attached, about six inches long. This was rather
like a gun barrel, being hollow along its length. It was this end of the
poleaxe that struck the animal between its eyes. If the butcher's aim
was true the animal did not suffer further. On some occasions at Coates,
presumably when the beast to be killed was an exceptionally heavy
one, Grace and Mary Emma were summoned from the house to lend
their weight at the rope's end for the final pulling-in. If the small
daughter happened to be at home she would 'help' too.

When the beast was on the shop floor, Ernest inserted a thin cane
into the hole in its forehead and moved it around to quicken the death.
Then came the messy part of the work. Its throat was cut and, as the
blood gushed out, it was Alf's duty to shovel it into buckets and dispose of it at the bottom of the yard. For a while he was kept on the
run as several trips were made. Unlike most of the town butchers,
Ernest did not use the blood for making into black pudding. It was
not entirely wasted, though. Along with other killing remains it was
of benefit to the farm hens that pecked among it afterwards.

After being bled, the beast was partly skinned while still on the
floor, and part of the legs were taken off. Then, by dint of great physical effort on the butcher's part, it was hoisted up into mid-air by means
of pulley and chain. There the skinning process was completed and
the animal opened up to allow the stomachs, intestines and various
organs to be taken out. At that point the atmosphere in the shop grew
steamy and reeked with the most unpleasant smell. Ernest and his
brother never showed any revulsion at this stage nor at any other;
they had experienced the nasty side of the business from boyhood and

had become hardened to it. The beast's liver was hung on a hook in the shop to await sale, but the unusable inside parts were dealt with by Alf, who barrowed them to the bottom yard. After being pecked over by the hens, they were later shovelled into the manure heap to rot down with the muck, so were eventually recycled onto the land again.

When all waste had been removed from the shop floor, this was thoroughly cleaned down. The carcass, after being wiped clean too, was left to hang until next day. The butcher's blood-stained smock and apron would soon find their way into Grace's washtub. Ernest killed one beast each week during his years at Coates. This, together with sheep and sometimes a pig, was adequate for his customers' needs. It provided sufficient work too in that age before electric saws and other devices began to speed up and lighten what had previously been slow, laborious tasks.

Occasionally something extra was asked for. At Whitsuntide there was a demand from customers for veal, so one or two calves would be killed then. The method of killing was to tie the calf up by the back legs so the head hung down. Its throat was cut and the blood drained downwards into a bucket placed beneath. The general demand and expectation for veal to be white meat necessitated that method of killing in order to achieve the required result.

For special occasions such as family parties or wedding teas, Ernest was often asked to supply a tongue. He kept one or two of these in reserve to meet such emergencies, though most people would order them in advance. A cow's tongue would keep for some time if immersed in brine solution. Ernest had a large, earthenware brine pot for that purpose. After partially filling it with water he would carefully put an egg at the bottom. He proceeded to add salt until the egg came to the top, which signified the amount of salt was adequate to keep the tongue from going bad. When a tongue was needed for a customer it was taken out of the brine, washed, boiled and pressed. This was done by Grace in the house.

When the Monday's slaughtering work was done, Ernest would go to Penistone market in the afternoon, either to buy for future requirements or merely to keep abreast of current prices and talk with other butchers and farmers. In the 1930s the fatstock market was always held on Mondays and a dairy market on Thursdays. Two decades later the selling of dairy cows was stopped at Penistone because of new testing regulations. The Holmfirth market then accommodated dairy cows from the Penistone area while the Penistone one specialised in fatstock and was held, from that time, on Thursdays instead of Mondays.

Tuesday was cutting-up day. The benches that had been moved next door to make killing space on the previous day were brought back into the shop. Using cleaver, saw and knives Ernest had to quarter the huge carcass, then reduce it to smaller, more manageable pieces. Boning-out and cutting into saleable portions was skillful work which needed time and practice before it was perfected. When Alf grew older he was gradually initiated into the butcher's art so that he could help with the cutting and boning if need be.

On Wednesdays and Thursdays there were the midweek orders to be taken out. These were prepared in the shop, wrapped in grease-proof paper, and the customers' names written on. They were then put into the large meat delivery baskets which fitted in the two-wheeled spring cart. Taking out orders was a comparatively easy job, since the real work of cutting, weighing and pricing had already been done.

Friday and Saturday were the main hawking days. Grace took a real pride in ensuring that her husband was immaculately turned out to meet the customers. His blue and white striped smock was freshly clean and well ironed. Over it was a spotless, white starched apron, the tapes of which Grace tied for him behind his waist. His black boots and leather leggings which covered the bottom parts of his trousers had been blacked, brushed and polished to give the highest shine that Grace could achieve.

Ernest's rounds covered a wide area, including Oxspring, Penistone, Hoylandswaine, and many outlying farms besides. Travelling around with horse and cart took a long time on Fridays and Saturdays because it was then that the women bought their bigger weekend supply of meat. Most of them came out to the cart to choose what they wanted on the spot and Ernest cut it for them while they waited. All the meat, including Grace's dishes of potted meat, was arranged on cleanly-scrubbed boards and covered over between customers. At some houses the customers would be watching for the butcher's arrival and come to his cart immediately. At others he had to go to their doors to let them know he was at hand and ready to serve them.

On Fridays Ernest covered the greater distance, as his round included the scattered area of Hoylandswaine. He left home after breakfast and did not return until ten o'clock at night. Alf accompanied him until afternoon but then got a bus back from Penistone so he could do the milking and attend to the other farm jobs before going home. The butcher and his boy took packed sandwiches and flasks of tea with them on Fridays because they were too far from home by mid-day to warrant a return home for dinner. When Ernest finally reached home at the end of his long day out, Grace had to go outside with the storm lantern to hold the cart shafts while he released the horse. With her help the shafts were lowered steadily to the ground. Had they been allowed to drop heavily while the horse was being led out, they might have cracked. Grace had a cooked supper ready for her husband on Friday nights, since he had eaten only cold food during the day.

Penistone Market Day (prior to 1910)

The Saturday round was mostly around the Oxspring and Penistone districts. He came back home for dinner on that day and finished selling in the early evening. It was his custom then to have a drink at the White Hart and reach home about eight o'clock. In the Willow Lane days his way home had been up the long, steep hill from Penistone Bridge End to the crossroads above Tunnel Top. Ernest had always climbed down from his seat when at the bottom of the hill and walked beside his horse all the way to the top so as to spare it the extra fatigue of carrying his weight. No doubt he realised the horse felt as tired as he did after a long day in the shafts. On moving to Coates Farm it was more convenient to go home by way of Oxspring and Bower Hill, a route that was less exacting for the horse. He still walked part of the way in cold weather, however, in order to keep warm, because sitting up in front of the cart could be chilly on winter nights. Over the years he had grown accustomed to being out with the horse and cart in all weathers. Although the cart had a top cover that extended over the driver too, Ernest often reached home in a soaking wet state if the day had been one of heavy rain. There was no way of avoiding it when he had to go knocking on doors and stand behind the cart attending to customers for long periods at a time.

Though he suffered from chills and heavy colds because of his working conditions, he always managed to avoid having time off. He insisted that no one else was able to do his job, which was probably true. From being sixteen years old, Ernest Bramall went out on his meat-hawking rounds every Friday and every Saturday for thirty years without a single break.

CHAPTER 15

Grace's Duties in Early Years at Coates

GRACE'S HOUSEWORK IN the thirties was hard, to say the least, even when compared with some of her own contemporaries. The fact that she was wife of a butcher and farmer brought duties that were unknown to women who lived in cottages and whose husbands went elsewhere to work. While many people in towns had gas or electricity by that time, Grace had neither. She had to wait several more years before the magical flick of a switch would flood her room with instant light, not to mention all the other assets to be regarded as luxuries later on.

When so much had to be done with one's own two hands, even allowing for the other two that belonged to a willing Mary Emma, a rigid programme had to be worked out and strictly adhered to if the house was to be well run. The chief aims were to provide an adequate supply of good, nourishing food for the household in as economical a way as possible, to maintain a high standard of cleanliness for the house itself and the people in it, to help her husband, and to see that the children were properly brought up. The workload fell into three basic categories. There were the essential daily chores, the weekly or fortnightly ones, and the seasonal work which had to be done in addition at certain times of the year.

Grace's day always began before seven o'clock in the morning. Her first job was to make a coal fire in the living room, or 'house' as it was called. She would have ensured that enough coal and sticks were fetched in for this on the previous evening. The house was the place between the kitchen and the third downstairs room. In it was the traditional black range where all cooking and baking was done. Not only were the meals prepared in the house, but they were eaten there too. The place also served as a sitting room in the evenings because the 'room', or sitting room of later years, was not furnished to begin with. When Grace had got the fire burning brightly, she put water in the iron kettle and set it on the bar to boil for a cup of tea. Of course it was a while before that happened so, in the meantime, she cleaned out the previous day's ashes from beneath the fire and carried them across yard and croft, where she riddled them over a grating into the earth closet. She brought back the pieces of coke that were too big to fall through the riddle and added them to the new fire. Grace always wore a dust-cap when emptying the ashes. Her next daily job was to give the black range a good brushing over and rub up the steel fender top. By the time she had washed the hearth-plate, the kettle would be boiling so, after being up for about half an hour, she was able to enjoy her first cup of tea. Sitting for a few brief moments while she drank it, she would view with satisfaction the shine on her fireplace and alert her mind to the day's tasks that lay ahead.

Mary Emma arrived soon afterwards and washed up the previous night's supper pots. She set the table for breakfast, cleaned the children's school shoes and packed their lunch of potted meat sandwiches and cake. Grace got the children up and dressed the young ones in front of the house fire, since there was no heating in the bedrooms. Each bedroom did have a fireplace, but fires were only made upstairs when anyone was ill in bed. Before eating breakfast the children were ushered up the step into the kitchen to 'have t'bed washed off their faces', at the cold water tap over the big stone sink. Grace would make porridge for them if the weather was cold, but on most mornings they were satisfied with bread and dripping—or bread and jam. That was an excellent meal in those days when all three constituents—bread, butter and jam—were home-made from only nourishing ingredients. While the children were eating, Grace set a large frying pan on the fire-bar and put in rashers of bacon which she cut from the home-cured flitch. Alf brought up the milk about that time from the mistal at the bottom of the yard. It frothed warmly as it was poured from the aluminium bucket, through the 'sile' or sieve, into wide earthenware bowls. Some was put into a jug for use in the house, but the children liked to take their mugs up into the kitchen and have them filled while the milk was still frothing. That drink of milk, warm and fresh from the cow, seemed the perfect complement to the bread and jam breakfast.

By the time Phyllis was seven, her cousin Myrtle had left Oxspring school. Under re-organisation, it became an infant and junior school only. It wasn't long before Norman was accompanying her though, and there were the Four Lane Ends children with whom they could walk down the hill. Grace was always at the door to watch her children start out for school. As they crossed the yard she usually called, 'Have you got a clean handkerchief?' Having obtained a satisfactory answer to that question, her parting instruction then was, 'Mind t'motors.' There were a few more cars on the roads after 1930 and, although they did not travel very fast, it was well that the children were made aware of potential hazards.

Mary Emma in the 1930s

After the schoolchildren had left at half-past eight, Ernest and Alf came in from their work and sat down with Grace and Mary Emma to a breakfast of 'home-fed' bacon and eggs. The bacon was mostly fat, but that was how the menfolk preferred it.

Mary Emma then cleared away the breakfast things, taking the pots up into the kitchen. Washing-up was done in an enamelled bowl on the stone sink, but as there was only cold water in the kitchen tap she had to take a lading can down into the house, fill it with hot water from the fireside boiler, then carry this back up into the kitchen again. When hot water was required for household cleaning, such as washing of floors and scrubbing out cupboards, it was obtained from the house boiler. Then the person who took out the water had to be sure to put in more from the kitchen tap. This had to be carried down by bucket and lifted into the boiler with extreme care so as to let no spills run down the shining black front. Since there was a good fire burning for most of the time, the boiler water remained constantly hot, but much energy and time were expended during the course of a day in journeying between house boiler and kitchen sink and in going up and down the step from one room to the other. Neither Grace nor her niece ever complained about the inconvenience then, because they had not experienced anything easier. Grace probably looked on the situation at Coates as being easy in comparison with that at Willow Lane, where one had to carry things up and down a whole flight of steps instead of merely one.

One of Grace's daily morning jobs was the bed making. In the absence of any indoor toilet facilities, that duty was combined with the other essential one of slop emptying. To this end she made her morning ascent to the bedrooms equipped with the slop bucket and a lading can of hot water in which soda crystals were dissolving. After emptying the contents of the chamber pots into the bucket, Grace rinsed each pot thoroughly with the hot soda water and replaced it under the bed where it belonged. Then she donned her 'bed-making apron'. This was an apron kept upstairs entirely for that purpose and worn over her general pinafore so that no speck of dirt came in contact with the bedclothes. The actual bed making was quite a lengthy ritual if properly carried out. First the eiderdown was removed onto a chair, then the quilt, blankets and top sheet individually turned back over the foot of the bed. The pillows were removed to the chair, then the bottom sheet lifted off and shaken through the window to get rid of any bits of fluff. It was placed on the chair while the next, and perhaps the most important, part of the ritual was performed. That was the turning over and shaking of the bed. Grace and Ernest slept on a large, double feather bed which, though very comfortable, needed to be completely turned over each day, then shaken and smoothed over to distribute the feathers evenly again. Considerable energy was expended at that stage of the proceedings. The children slept on flock beds instead of feather ones, but they also underwent the daily treatment of turning and shaking to prevent the flocks lumping together. All the pillows were feather-filled and these were well plumped up as they were put back on the beds. When all the covers had been neatly replaced ready for the next night's sleep, Grace took off her apron and folded it carefully away. Picking up her lading can and slop bucket, she carried them steadily downstairs, continuing outside with the bucket to the bottom yard where she slung the contents onto the muck heap.

Once the children had come downstairs in the mornings, they were not allowed to go up again until they went to bed. Grace did not want her stair carpet to be prematurely worn out, neither did she want toys upstairs. Bedrooms were the places where they slept, not played. In any case there was the unfurnished 'room' downstairs which served admirably as a playroom on wet days. Ernest had that idea in mind when he refused to buy good furniture for it. There was an old, plain wooden table on which the children could write, draw and play games, and a desk that had belonged to Ernest as a boy. This held books and came into use when they were playing at 'school'. Two or three chairs and stools were the only other furniture in the room. A big, rectangular wooden box held all the toys. The floor was of white wooden planks and uncovered. The whiteness was maintained by frequent scrubbings with hot soda water.

Another daily task was fetching in the buckets of coal to keep the house fire continuously burning throughout the day until bedtime. This was heavy work when two buckets at a time were carried from the coal-place across the top yard. The coal buckets were large because a great amount of coal was used. On the house fire depended all the cooking and baking for the household, which was considerable as the family increased.

Except for Fridays, when Ernest and Alf took packed lunches on the meat round, a substantial dinner was cooked daily for around half-past twelve. There was always meat in plenty at this meal. On Sunday a large joint of beef was roasted and accompanied by the traditional Yorkshire puddings. The remains were eaten cold on the next day. Tuesday's dinner meat was fresh steak, chops, or liver from the previous day's killing. The other days' dinners consisted of appetising stews and meat and potato pies. The usual Saturday dinner was hash, made from leftovers but very nourishing all the same. It was eaten on thick slices of toasted bread, through which the tasty gravy soaked deliciously. Potatoes were invariably cooked at the dinnertime meal with one or more other vegetables besides. To complete the meal Grace provided apple pie and rice pudding on most days, but varied it occasionally by an apple sponge or a jam roly-poly. The latter was popular in cold weather because it was warmly filling. It had suet in the crust and, after being rolled and tied up in a floured cloth, was boiled in a big saucepan.

Tea at five o'clock was the other main meal of the day when everyone, including children, sat down to eat together. On cold days this was also a hot meal, bearing in mind that the children who had been to school had eaten only cold food in the middle of the day. For tea there might be chips, scalloped potatoes, fish, eggs, ham or sausages. Younger children who had been at home all day and eaten hot dinner with the adults would often enjoy a cut-up banana with cream for tea. There was cheese to be had too, and always a plentiful supply of Grace's home-made bread, butter and jam, with a variety of cakes, buns and tarts to complete the meal. In summer the family ate a lot of stewed fruit as it came into season, with jellies, blancmanges and trifles. Grace bought very little tinned food. In fact the only time she opened a tin in those days was at Sunday tea, when she treated the family to a large tin of salmon. If no fresh fruit was available, the salmon would often be followed by a big tin of fruit salad.

After the tea things were cleared away and the washing-up done, Mary Emma was free to go home unless there was extra work as in spring-cleaning, haytime, and when preparing for Christmas. Then she willingly stayed on longer to help her aunt. Even at less busy times she sometimes opted to stay after tea of her own accord, which pleased the children. They regarded their cousin as one of the family during those years and liked her because she was always cheerful and even-tempered.

Every evening the house was lit by the shiny brass hanging-up lamp which was suspended from a hook in the middle of the ceiling. In winter, when the days were short and the lamp had to be lighted earlier, it needed filling with paraffin every day. During the longer days, when it was used for fewer hours, one filling would serve for two days. The lamp's wick had to be kept trimmed so that the flame burned evenly, and the glass washed frequently for a good light to be obtained. Tiny paraffin lamps were put on the bedside tables at nights so that the children would not be in total darkness should they happen to wake. Apart from the paraffin lamps, candles were in general use for lesser lighting requirements. In winter, one candle in its blue enamelled candlestick was set on the stone slab in the pantry to enable Mary Emma to see where she was returning food after tea. She then took the same candle up into the kitchen and stood it on the set-pot top near the sink. The kitchen, with its almost bare, stone-flagged floor was bitterly cold on a winter's night. Washing-up in it by the feeble light of one candle was a cheerless occupation to say the least. and not one to be lingered over. The only thing that could be said in its favour

was that it made one doubly appreciative of the lamp-light and the
fire's cosy warmth when one had finished a stint in the kitchen and
could return to the comforts of the house. Candles were of course
used to light everyone to bed, but were not left burning all night.

At Coates Farm, and probably at every other farm in the area at that
time, was a storm lantern, also paraffin filled. It was used by the men
on dark nights to show them a light in the outbuildings and their way
about the yard. On winter nights Grace had sometimes to light the
lantern in order to accompany one of her children across yard and
croft on an essential journey to the closet, or 'nessy' as she often called
that small place. To leave the cosiness of the warm house and trudge
through wind, rain or snow by lantern-light was not an enviable occupation, yet again it did make one value the fireside all the more when
one reached it afterwards.

When the children's bedtime came round, Grace saw they all had a
good wash before going upstairs. Until they were about ten she washed
them all herself, necks, ears, feet and legs included. The water for
washing was heated in the kettle on the fire and poured into the enamelled bowl that she brought down from the kitchen and put upon the
house table. The children could therefore remain reasonably warm
while being undressed and washed. Only when they grew older were
they banished into the cold kitchen to wash. After a drink of milk or
cocoa and a piece of cake or biscuits to eat, they were ushered up to
bed by their mother with her lighted candle. They did not all go at
the same time but went in order of age. Grace made individual journeys with them up the stairs and before
getting them into bed spent much time
and patience teaching them prayers.
These were said as the children knelt
by the bedside. They enjoyed their
prayers and learnt quite a few. Apart
from the spoken ones that asked God's
blessing on members of the family,
friends and other people they knew,
there was a hymn that was sung too.
It was really a prayer in that it thanked

'Bless the little lamp tonight.'

God for things he had given and asked Him to look after them, but
the children liked it because of the tune to which it was sung and
because their mother sang it with them. The first line of the hymn
was, 'Jesu, tender Shepherd, hear me, bless thy little lamb tonight.'
Years later the family had a good laugh at Betty's expense when she

revealed that, for a long time during her childhood, she had been singing, 'bless the little lamp tonight', thinking the prayer referred to the small nightlight on the table by her bed.

With her children safely tucked in bed, Grace's daily work was not always finished. On most nights there was sewing and mending to be done. Clothes were never discarded until they had been patched or darned several times. The fact that the Bramall children sometimes appeared in school with mended clothes put no stigma on their parents. On the contrary, it testified to their mother's diligence at a time when some school contemporaries had holes showing in their clothes. Unless she was very tired, Grace looked on her sewing as a pleasurable occupation. It could be done while she sat to the fire in her rocking chair and talked with her husband at the same time. Ernest had a rocking chair too. Pulling it up to the fire, he sat relaxed with legs outstretched to rest his feet on top of the fireguard. He rarely missed reading the papers on an evening, and particularly enjoyed studying the business pages. Though much of Grace's sewing and most of her mending were done by hand, she did have a sewing machine in which she took great pride. It was a treadle-type machine and very useful for making the household furnishings such as curtains and cushion covers, as well as new clothes for the family. On one occasion she stayed up all night through to make a dress for her daughter to wear on a school outing next day. The dress fitted perfectly and looked very nice, which said much for Grace's sewing ability since it had not been tried on the wearer because she was fast asleep in bed. The treadle machine was always kept well maintained and highly polished. It is still in good working order after fifty years.

As a farmer's wife Grace had to deal with the daily milk yield from their cows. After putting enough aside for the neighbours who fetched it, she left the rest of it standing in the wide earthenware bowls on the cellar stone. The cellar was four steps down from the back of the kitchen. It was similar to the pantry in that it was cool, had a stone slab on which to put things, and a stone-flagged floor, but was twice as big. On the following day the cream which had formed thickly on top of the bowl was skimmed off with a saucer into another smaller bowl. Some of the old milk that had been skimmed was sold for a halfpenny a jugful to neighbours who were anxious to economise in their housekeeping. Grace would often use some too in her own baking, then the remainder was fed to the pigs. Resulting from the daily skimmings was sufficient cream to be made into butter when churning morning came round.

Whilst all the daily indoor activities at Coates Farm were vital and necessary, the weekly work was equally important and had to be fitted in between the other duties. Monday was invariably washday whatever the weather. Grace had to rise a little earlier than usual on Monday mornings because she had to light two fires instead of one. In addition to the house fire she had to make one under the set-pot in the kitchen after first filling it with water. While the water was heating she assembled the washing equipment which included two wooden tubs, rubbing board and 'peggy', the mangle with its huge wooden rollers, and various bowls for processes of rinsing, bluing and starching. Another indispensable item was the clothes brush used in conjunction with the rubbing board. The large clothes basket containing the dirty washing was put in the middle of the floor and the clothes sorted into neat piles according to colour and treatment needed. The white things, including Ernest's hawking aprons, had priority of the clean water. Until Phyllis was seven or eight she wore a clean white pinafore for school each day and they came into the same category too. The hawking smocks of course received meticulous attention, but the badly-soiled killing smocks and aprons were relegated to the last batch.

Two washtubs were in operation because every garment was washed twice. In one tub the first wash involved a good soaping, general rubbing, and prolonged agitation by means of the wooden peggy. This was moved up and down amongst the clothes to release the dirt that was fairly loose. In the second washtub each article was laid individually on the rubbing board of corrugated zinc and inspected carefully for any more stubborn marks of dirt that had resisted the first onslaught. Once detected these were vigorously attacked with clothes brush, soap, and that other commodity much used in those days—'elbow grease'. As the clothes of each batch were finished they were put through the mangle which pressed out the water. Unless there was another person available to turn the handle, mangling was not an easy job. A woman on her own would lift the clothes up from the tub and feed them through the large wooden rollers with her left hand while turning the handle with her right. After the first mangling everything had to go through two lots of rinsing water and then be mangled again.

The set-pot fire had to be continually stoked up during the day and extra coal fetched in for that purpose. As water was ladled out of the set-pot into buckets and poured into the tubs, more water had to be drawn from the cold tap into the bucket and poured back into the set-pot. Besides heating enough water to keep the tubs well supplied, the set-pot was used for boiling certain things. On a normal washday Grace would have three different boilings. The first one would include the smaller white cotton articles, the second the sheets which filled the set-pot on their own, and the third the towels. There was usually room in the first boiling for the two white tablecloths that had been in use at meal-times during the week. After being boiled, the white things were rinsed twice and then put through a final blue rinse to maintain their whiteness. This was made by squeezing a little blue colouring from a small dye-bag which was commonly known as 'dolly-blue', but care had to be taken as to how much was put into the water. If the rinse was too blue the clothes would come out a shade darker than the snowy whiteness aimed at. Items such as aprons, tablecloths, pillow-cases and the hawking attire would also be dipped in a starch solution before being hung outside. A popular brand of starch at that time was 'Robin Starch'. The small, white, chalky pieces were sold in little boxes with the bird's picture on the side. To make the solution, a few pieces were put in the bottom of a bowl and boiling water poured over. When cool it was a thin, jelly-like liquid. Woollen articles such as jumpers, socks and stockings were washed separately in the enam-elled bowl on the sink.

On fine Mondays the clothesline was put out in the croft. Grace and Mary Emma made many trips across the yard in the course of the day when hanging out and fetching in the washing. On wet days the tall clotheshorse or 'winter hedge' was set round the fire and filled with washing, which needed to be frequently turned before it was dry. The atmosphere on those days was steamy and unpleasant in the house because the fire was hidden by the washing. Yet such a situa-tion was unavoidable on rainy days and had to be accepted. The clothes had to be dried on Monday, or at least as many of them as possible had to be, because Tuesday brought its own duties.

Washday at Coates in the thirties meant just that. It lasted all day from just turned seven in the morning until tea-time. Of course there were the daily jobs to be fitted in too, causing interruptions to the washing. When the actual washing was finished, the set-pot was emp-tied with lading can and bucket, rinsed out and dried, the tubs emp-tied down the sink, wiped out and stood outside to dry, and all the other equipment carefully dried and put away. The stone-flagged floor of the kitchen was scrubbed thoroughly all over. Grace did this while Mary Emma got tea ready, or sometimes the jobs would be reversed for a change. After such an energetic day as theirs had been, it can be imagined how greatly they enjoyed the meal which would restore spent energy. As they ate their well-earned tea, the sight of neat piles of

clothes made spotless by their manual efforts evoked feelings of achievement in work well done, even though it did result in sore, red hands.

Mary Emma usually stayed for an hour or so after tea on Mondays
to get the ironing started. The rest of it was finished on Tuesday morning. Ironing was only a slow process during those years when irons
had to be heated from the fire. Grace used the same type of iron that
her mother and grandmother had used before her. The flat iron, as it
was called, had been in existence for longer than anyone living could
remember. Two irons were employed simultaneously, since one was
re-heating while the other was in use. When ironing, an iron-stand
was hooked onto the front of the fire-bars so that the irons, when set
on it, had their flat bases towards the fire's heat. It was necessary, of
course, to grip the handle with a padded iron-holder made from several layers of thick material as the handle was very hot too. As each
iron was removed from the fire it was tested for heat. An experienced
ironer would generally be able to judge the heat of an iron by the
state of the fire and the length of time the iron had been on the stand.
In cases of uncertainty she would hold the palm of her other hand
close to the iron's base in order to feel the heat. If it was suspected
that the iron had perhaps become too hot, a quick little spit onto the
flat base would ascertain whether it was safe to proceed, depending on
how quickly the spit sizzled away. Before the iron was put onto the
clothes it was rubbed over with beeswax and given a quick wipe. The
wax facilitated the iron's smooth gliding over the clothes and the wipe
ensured that no speck of soot reached them. A newly-heated iron would
be used first on cotton and linen things which required the greatest
heat. Large articles such as Ernest's hawking smocks often needed a
change of iron before they were finished.

Grace had no special board on which to iron. Everything was done
on her solid, square house table. Standing in the middle of the room,
it was an all-purpose table. Meals were eaten from it and, apart from
being used for the ironing, it served on baking days too, and for many
other activities. When the children were older they did their homework on it. The Monday night homework, however, was allowed only
a small strip of one side of the table because ironing was in full swing
on the rest of it. The white wooden table top was generally covered
with a patterned oilcloth but this was taken off for ironing and replaced
by a piece of thick blanket material over which was spread the white
ironing sheet. A metal stand was in use for resting the iron while a
finished article was put aside and the next one laid in place. Another
requisite on the ironing table was a basin containing water. This was

for damping articles that had become too dry. The starched things especially were better ironed while slightly damp if a smooth, glossy finish was to be achieved. This applied particularly to Ernest's white hawking aprons. Even the tapes of those aprons were meticulously pressed out and smoothed over until they shone.

Grace's other main Tuesday work was the butter making. Unlike the barrel-shaped end-over-end churn in use at Willow Lane, her churn was smaller and stood on the sink instead of the floor. There was less cream to be made into butter at Coates, as farming there was subsidiary to the main occupation of butchering. Fewer milk cows were kept on the smaller farm and some of the milk was sold new to the families who lived near. Yet there was always enough cream from the bowls' daily skimmings to warrant a weekly butter making in the little churn. The type Grace used was a rounded version of the box churn. It was made of white wood that was kept white by the scrubbings it always received after use. The flat lid at the top lifted off completely to allow the cream to be poured in. A handle at the side rotated the paddles that agitated the cream. This had to be kept turning at a steady pace until the butter 'came', which was a tiring occupation. One could tell when the butter had 'come' by the different sound it made inside the churn. That sound was gladly heard because it meant the laborious job of handle turning was at an end. The buttermilk, or liquid part of the cream that had become separated from the solid, was drained off through a small bunghole in the churn bottom. To stop the butter sticking to the inside of the churn it was washed in a solution of brine. At this stage Grace had ready a large, cleanly-scalded slate on the stone slab adjoining the sink. Transferring the butter from churn to slate, she squeezed and pressed it to extract surplus liquid and worked it about with her two wooden butter pats, one held in each hand. Those vital pieces of equipment were flat, rectangular-shaped boards of about six inches by four in dimension and perhaps a quarter of an inch thick, with a short handle of three inches or so that was continuous with the rest of the board. One side of the butter pat was smoothly flat and the other was ridged. Grace added a little salt to the butter as she worked it about with the pats. At no time did she touch the butter with her hands. It was then weighed and patted up into half-pound blocks. The top of each rectangular block was imprinted with the ribbed side of the butter pat. Sufficient butter was made at Coates for the weekly household consumption, with the surplus being sold to neighbours. It was pale cream in colour, as no artificial additives were included. Grace had no need to spoil the excellence of that natural product with any other substance. When Grace had transformed the lump from the churn into a slateful of neat, rectangular blocks, she carried the slate down onto the cellar stone. Then she thoroughly scrubbed her churn and butter pats, finally giving them a scalding from the kettle of boiling water before setting them on the wall outside to dry and 'sweeten' in the air.

Wednesday was 'upstairs day', which meant that the bedrooms, landing and stairs received their weekly cleaning. The day's activities were not confined solely to that work though. Before tackling the upstairs cleaning, all rugs from the house were taken outside and well shaken in the yard before being relaid. The furniture was dusted and the kitchen doorway scrubbed clean. The morning was half gone by the time Grace and Mary Emma were able to concentrate on the main job of the day. As there was soon a breaking-off for preparation and eating of dinner, the 'upstairs' was mostly done in the afternoon. Grace stood the clotheshorse round the fire on Wednesday afternoons to give the clothes a good airing before they were put away. It was better to have the fire monopolised for airing whilst no one was in the house, but it did involve someone going downstairs at intervals to turn the articles round and keep the fire stoked up.

The big bedroom accommodated two beds, the large double one used by Grace and Ernest, and a smaller one for the youngest children. The suite of furniture was of high quality. Made from dark, polished walnut, it comprised a tall, double wardrobe with long oval mirror in the front, a dressing table with a wide oval mirror at the back, and a washstand. The drawers and back surround of this were polished too, but the top which held the large flowered jug and washbowl was of smooth, grey and white patterned marble, while green splash-proof tiles completed the back. The china jug and washbasin only came into use in cases where someone was ill in bed. As may be imagined, Grace took extreme care of her best bedroom suite. It was always kept well polished with Min Cream during spring-cleaning sessions. On the weekly 'upstairs' days it was dusted and rubbed with the best duster in the house. The children were not allowed to touch that bedroom furniture at all until they were old enough to help with the maintaining of it. Now, sixty years after the furniture was bought, it is still in Grace's family, still highly polished and looking very well, with hardly a scratch anywhere on it. There was also a round-topped bedside table in the big bedroom, plus a couple of single chairs to match. The brown woollen hearth rug was a treasured possession. It had been hand-made by Selina, Grace's mother-in-law, and given to her as a present when she was at Willow Lane. Measuring about a yard by almost two, it was well made and hard-wearing. The fact that it is still in use after so long testifies to its quality.

The second bedroom, where the older children slept, contained only a bed, small chest of drawers, wardrobe and chair; yet these were adequate for their needs. The small third bedroom was not generally used except as a store-place. It was reached before one got to the top of the stairs by a door on the left, being above the pantry. One thing that Ernest stored in that small room was his greaseproof paper which he bought in bulk periodically. The sheets were large and came in thick, blue-wrapped packages that were heavy to lift and stack. Ernest moved one large package at a time when needed, from the spare bedroom into the shop.

Only the big bedroom had carpet over most of the floor. The uncovered surrounding parts were darkly varnished in a shade that matched the furniture. The other two bedroom floors were covered with linoleum. All the rooms had small bedside mats and a few woollen rugs. On the weekly cleaning day these were all rolled up, carried downstairs, and placed on the wall that surrounded the flags. Then Grace or Mary Emma would go all over the bedroom carpet on hands and knees with a hard hand-brush and shovel to sweep up dust and bits. The dusting that followed was methodically done. Ornaments and other objects were completely removed from surfaces to be dusted before the job was attempted. To have dusted around the things while they were still in place was unthinkable.

The varnished floorboards were dusted twice. The person performing that part of the work had a duster in each hand, the idea being that the first duster took up most of the dust while the second captured any specks that might have escaped. In the other bedrooms the linoleum was also cleaned over with two dusters. The floor dusting resembled an obstacle course in that it involved crawling under beds and around furniture to reach far corners where a little dust might be lurking. One of the beds was rather low, so it was fortunate that neither Grace nor Mary Emma was too fat to wriggle beneath it. The landing had a strip of carpet with varnished surround, and this received the same sweeping and dusting treatment as the bedrooms. So did the stairs, which had carpet down the middle and glossy varnished sides. When everything was considered dust-free, the mats that had been taken outside were spread on the wall to be brushed, then shaken in the yard before being carried back upstairs.

Keeping to the tradition of her Willow Lane years, Grace continued to make potted meat on Thursdays so that it would be ready and fresh enough for the Friday and Saturday rounds. It was always taken down into the cellar of course after being made, and only fetched up again when the butcher was actually ready to set out. Grace stewed all the leftover meat in her coal oven as Selina had done, but before she had been long at Coates Farm she acquired an innovation that speeded up the next stage of the operation considerably. Whereas at Willow Lane she had followed Selina's tedious, time-consuming method of chopping up the meat by hand, using knife and fork until it was of the required fineness, at Coates she invested in a small mincing machine. It was bought with Ernest's full approval and encouragement. The machine could be screwed to the house table in a matter of seconds, and taken off as quickly when the mincing was finished. Though it had to be manually operated by turning a handle, it was a vast improvement on the former method, being far less tedious and much quicker. Having the mincing machine enabled Grace to continue with the other duties sooner than before. These included the important weekly work of baking, as that was invariably on the Thursday programme.

Grace preferred to make the bread herself, not that she thought her niece unequal to the task but rather because she felt it to be her own duty. Mary Emma helped with all the other baking, and excelled at pastry and cake making. Before she had been working very long at the farm she could be safely entrusted to carry on with those items if her aunt was otherwise engaged.

Before the actual baking commenced Grace raked out all the previous week's accumulation of soot from the flues into a bucket and disposed of it in the bottom yard. It amounted to a good half-bucket or so, which was not surprising considering the quantity of coal burned throughout the week. After scraping out the bulk of the soot with the rake, she finished the cleaning by brushing out the flues with a long, wire-handled flue-brush. She had to be up rather earlier on Thursdays to allow for this extra weekly job, because flues could not be cleaned while a fire was burning. Consequently the fire could not be lit for boiling the kettle and cooking breakfast until the soot had been taken out in addition to the ashes. When the fire was finally lit it roared away fiercely and, as more fuel was added, the oven soon grew hot enough to receive the baking.

Every Thursday three huge apple pies were made in deep enamelled dishes. This necessitated the peeling and slicing of a great quantity of apples, and much rubbing of lard into flour. The pastry was rolled out on a sizeable wooden baking board placed on the house table. Other items frequently made with the pastry were Bakewell tarts. jam tarts, mince pies, date or currant pasties, and egg custards. All these confections were mouthwatering because the pastry was made with lard that had been 'home-rendered' from one of their own pigs. When the pastry items were completed, scones were sometimes made before the baking board was removed to make room for the cake-making requisites.

As the baking progressed to cakes and buns the house table could soon have been in chaotic state, owing to so much activity going on in restricted space. Grace did not allow such a state to occur because she followed a rule that, from experience, she knew would work, particularly when applied to her table on Thursdays. The rule was: 'Clear as you go; muddle makes more muddle.' During the baking, things were tidied away into the cupboard as they were finished with, so allowing enough space for articles brought out later.

With her niece's loyal assistance Grace Bramall made many delicious cakes and buns of various kinds during those years of the 1930s when her children were growing and the household increased to nine. Fortunately she enjoyed baking, and so did Mary Emma. Grace was sometimes heard to remark that she would have quite liked to have done confectionery for a living. However, her abilities in that respect were put to good use in her own household, being highly appreciated by the family. Sandwich cakes, both plain and chocolate, were made. The plain ones were filled with jam afterwards and sprinkled over with icing sugar. Parkin and ginger cake were baked in the large rectangular 'pudding tin' which, on Sundays, was used for the Yorkshire pudding. Cake made in that tin was later cut into squares and stored in a deeper tin with a lid. Some types of cake were baked in loaf tins, two popular kinds being fruit loaves and seed cake. There was another cake she often made especially to please her children. It was 'ribbon cake'. Made from three separate cakes of white, pink and brown, sandwiched together with jam, its appearance when cut pleased the children as much as its taste. For birthday occasions there was always a round, deep fruit cake which received on its top the full treatment of almond paste, icing, cachous and edible flower decorations.

Throughout the years nothing but home-made confectionery appeared on the table at Coates. To have bought cakes and pastries from a shop would have been uneconomical when they could be made more cheaply at home. This apart, Grace scorned 'bought stuff' as being inferior to her own, maintaining 'You never know what they put in it.'

After their weekly baking, Grace and her niece had certainly something worthwhile to show for their day when tea-time came round. As the children came home from school on Thursday they would be greeted by the delicious smell of newly-baked bread even before they reached the door. That smell was nostalgically remembered by some of them after half a century and more. It signified their mother's presence in the house and was indeed a part of their childhood that spelt happy security.

The weekly cleaning of places and things downstairs was undertaken on Fridays with the exception of the house. That room, being most in use, was cleaned to some degree on Wednesdays, its furniture dusted every day, and given its thorough clean on Saturdays. The fire-range however was black-leaded on Friday because that was the only day in the week when a dinner had not to be cooked on it. After breakfast was cooked on Friday, the fire was allowed to go out. Mary Emma would prepare sandwiches and fill flasks with tea for the butchers' lunch, while her aunt fetched up the dishes of potted meat from the cellar and helped her husband get ready for his round. After he and Alf had left, Grace set to work with brushes, cloths and Zebo, which was the 'black lead' liquid contained in a tin. She poured a little onto her cloth and rubbed it onto the range, applying more from time to time as she progressed until boiler, oven door, fire-bars and shelf above the fire were covered. The tidy, which stood on the floor below the fire to conceal the ashes, was blacked too. At that stage the range appeared to have been dulled, but after much time spent in brushing up the black lead with two different brushes and in giving a final rubbing over with a black velvet pad, it gleamed and shone until one's reflection could really be seen in it. The hinges of the oven door, the edges of boiler and shelf, and the fender top were of bright steel. Its silvery smoothness had a mirror-like shine that was maintained by weekly rubbings with a powdered substance known as bathbrick. This was applied to all the steel parts of the range with a damp cloth and polished off with a dry one. The fender was a traditional household possession of those days. It covered the whole length of the hearth-plate, which was laid over the large hearthstone on the floor immediately in front of the fire. The hearth-plate was of strong, enamelled tin and easily washed. The purpose of the fender was for keeping things warm. Being about a foot high from the floor, its top received warmth from the fire. Before dinner was served, the clean plates were put on the fender to warm for a while, and hot food taken from the oven was rested there too. On Fridays Grace completed her fireside work by lifting away both fender and hearth-plate to give the stone beneath a good scrub. The whole range gave her feelings of pride and pleasant gratification when she had given it its Friday shine. She was well satisfied that the lengthy time spent on aching knees while doing the range was justified by the good result achieved.

The kitchen had a thorough clean on Friday besides the one after Monday's wash. Though there was a black range in the kitchen it was never used, because it did not function properly for some reason or other and, in any case, Grace did not really need it. All the same she polished it up with black lead now and then to keep it presentable. The stone sink and adjoining slab were well scrubbed on cleaning day, a solid block of donkey stone being rubbed over them during the process. This got rid of grease and dirty marks on the stone. It was inevitable that some soot appeared at times on the kitchen sink, because the big black iron saucepan in which potatoes were daily boiled was brought from the house fire to the kitchen so that its water could be drained down the sink. Although a special piece of wood was put in the sink bottom, for the pan to stand on while the potatoes were mashed, bits of soot often dropped from the sides of the pan. After the dinner-time washing up, when the pan was empty, any more loose soot was swept off into the coal bucket and the pan put on the kitchen hearth till next day. There was no furniture in the kitchen apart from one simple wooden rectangular table set against the wall opposite the sink. Covered with white oilcloth, it was convenient for holding the milk jugs and crockery that were put there during washing-up. The mangle occupied most of the side opposite the fireplace. Adjoining the fireplace on one side was the set-pot, and on the other a built-in cupboard. This held such things as candles, soap, washing powder, starch, blue bags, shoe polish and brushes to name but a few. The paraffin can had its place in the space beneath the sink. Standing on the floor near the set-pot was the 'pig bucket'. All vegetable peelings were put into this bucket, as well as scrapings from the dinner dishes and empty-ings from the teapot. When Alf was about to feed the pigs he would fetch the bucket and empty its contents into the mix he had prepared for them. The big coal bucket known as the 'skep' and another coal bucket were also kept in the kitchen. Their place was in the corner between the outer door and that leading into the house, this position being most convenient where carrying distance was concerned.

The stone floor had one or two hessian sacks laid upon it and usu-ally part of a pegged rug that was too old and worn to remain in the house, and so had been relegated to the kitchen. On Fridays these were shaken out in the yard and left on the wall while the floor was scrubbed with hot soda water and simultaneously scoured with yellow-stone to keep it a good clean colour. The pieces of yellow-stone were obtained from a certain quarry about a mile away from home, and the periodic expeditions to renew supplies were regarded as pleasant outings for both adults and children. The floor scrubbing itself was far from being pleasant, the soda in the water wreaking havoc on sensitive hands. In frosty weather both Grace and Mary Emma developed cracks in theirs.

These were quite deep, stiffly painful, and sometimes bled. Yet they accepted this as an inevitable part of housework and never grumbled. The idea of wearing rubber gloves for harsh work did not occur to either of them, because such things were not even considered by working people then.

The pantry and cellar were cleaned on alternate Fridays, being scrubbed in the same way as the kitchen. Both contained 'stones' on which the food and other possessions were kept. These were table-like structures, the tops being made from huge, smooth slabs of stone. The pantry was entered by a door on the left at the bottom of the stairs. Its stone accommodated food that was in daily demand, such as bread, bacon, eggs, butter and cheese. Baking equipment was stored in the pantry too. Round the wall was a shelf which held, among other things, tins containing cakes.

On the cellar stone the bowls of milk were stood while the cream settled on top and the slateful of Tuesday's butter kept cool prior to being used. To some degree the cellar did the job of the modern refrigerator, as jellies would always set when placed on the stone and meat would keep fresh for a considerable time. The main function of the cellar stone, however, was to accommodate the sides of bacon and hams laid in salt after the pig killing. On the cellar shelf were stored jars of jam. The butter churn was placed up there too when not in use. The two wooden washtubs which saw service on Mondays were stood on the cellar floor. Cleaning the pantry involved moving everything from the stone while it was given a good washing over. In the cellar the stone required hard scrubbing to get rid of the salt when meat was taken out. As with the kitchen, the pantry and cellar floors were washed on one's hands and knees and scoured with yellow-stone. During those years at Coates Farm many scrubbing brushes were worn out and replaced.

The 'room' was cleaned every other week, its wooden floor being scrubbed like so many other things. Last, but not least important, the 'closet' across the croft was also scrubbed. The two wooden lids covering the holes were done first, then the seat itself, and finally the floor and passageway outside. The paper used in the closets at Coates during that time was old newspaper. Nobody in that vicinity used anything different, because toilet paper as we now know it was not bought by people who merely had earth closets.

Other weekly jobs carried out on Fridays were the cleaning of windows and the swilling of flags. The sash windows were cleaned with a wash-leather. Doing the outsides of the upstairs windows necessitated sitting on the window ledge outside the bedroom. The position seemed quite precarious to an onlooker, because the cleaner could have fallen backwards onto the hard flagstones if she had lost her one-hand hold on the window. Grace's confidence that the job could be done without accidents was fully justified. 'Sitting-out' was a quicker method than fetching and fixing up a ladder when washing the outsides of upstairs windows. The flags in front of the house were swilled with water from the rain-tub outside the little gate between flags and yard. Except in very dry weather there was always some water in the tub which was placed against the house wall for the purpose of catching rainwater from the roof. Grace would have considered it a waste if she had drawn water from the kitchen tap for the swilling when that in the rain-tub sufficed.

Cutlery was cleaned fortnightly over newspaper spread on the house table. This 'sitting-down job' was regarded as an easy, relaxing job simply because it did not require much physical energy, being performed while one was sitting. All the same, it occupied a lot of time. The cutlery in use then was strong and durable, lasting literally a lifetime, but because it was not of stainless material regular cleaning was necessary. To renew their brightness, knife blades were rubbed with emery paper, forks and spoons with a substance called 'Silvo'. This grey liquid from a tin was applied with one soft rag and polished off with another. Then everything was rubbed with yet a third cloth to get rid of any remaining traces of polish. Another tin marked 'Brasso' contained a similar liquid to the Silvo, though its colour was rather different, being more of a dirty yellow-brown. This was used for bringing up the shine on brass doorknobs, the strip of brass around the fireguard top and the water tap in the kitchen, and perhaps most important of all, it shone up the brass hanging-lamp.

The weekly bathing took place on Friday evenings. The set-pot was filled and the fire lit beneath. There were two zinc baths, a small one for the younger children and the big one for older children and adults. Bathing was done in front of the house fire. Grace allowed clean bath water for every individual, patiently ladling out the used water into a bucket and carrying it up into the kitchen to empty it down the sink. The set-pot had to be replenished as the bathing progressed and more clean water was taken out. Ernest would say to his wife, 'You should let 'em all get bathed in t'same water, as we had to do. There were six of us and I was last because I was oldest, but it hasn't done me any harm.' Grace was more than a little surprised on first hearing this. Ernest was usually particular about cleanliness, and as for his mother using only one lot of water for them all, she could hardly believe that was true of the fastidious Selina. She sensed he was half joking in exaggerating the facts about his childhood bath-nights.

Grace planned the main house cleaning for Saturday mornings. Firstly the chairs were dusted and taken into the 'room'. Next, the three pegged rugs were rolled up and put on the wall outside. Then the two long, heavy strips of matting which almost covered the floor were taken up and put on the wall with the rugs. The stone-flagged floor was always swept then, because some dust riddled through the matting. The corners and sides of the room where matting did not reach were covered with linoleum. Sawdust was put in certain places between the linoleum and the stone to absorb damp, and was renewed from time to time. The linoleum was washed on Saturdays and made to shine with Mansion polish. The stone flags were scrubbed every two or three weeks. Shaking the long pieces of matting needed the combined strength of Grace and Mary Emma. Standing in the yard with the length of matting between them, they took a corner in each hand. By repeatedly tossing the piece up and down and shaking it from side to side they eventually eliminated the dirt. Such vigorous exercise called for strong arms and a firm grip, because the matting was heavy to lift and hard to hold. By the time both pieces had been dealt with, carried back into the house and relaid on the floor, the rug shaking which followed seemed easy by comparison. The chairs were returned from the room and the rest of the dusting done.

Apart from the table and chairs, the house furniture included a large cupboard which contained the crockery and packaged food such as sugar, tea, cocoa, oatmeal and rice. There was always treacle on the shelf too, as that was a commodity much used for putting on porridge and pancakes and on bread as a change from jam or dripping. On one of the lower shelves within easy reach was the big brown, oval salt dish. The smaller salt cellar which was put on the table at meal times was filled from this big dish. It was practicable to have a larger supply at hand, because much salt was used daily in the household cooking and for butchering requirements. The salt was bought in rectangular blocks about two and a half feet long and ten inches square at the ends, and the block in current use was kept in the cupboard too. When the brown dish was nearly empty the long salt block was taken out onto the house table and a big enough pile of salt grated from it to fill the dish. Other pieces of furniture contained in the house were a sofa placed near the main window which looked onto the road, and a dark varnished dresser along the wall opposite the fire. In its drawers were towels, tea cloths and much of the children's clothing. There were times during that decade of the thirties when the pram was positioned in the corner where the small window gave view to the fields at the back of the house. Because of constant effort by Grace and her helper, the house was always a cosy, homely room where plenty of activity went on. That it was well kept was evident from its Saturday clean.

When the children were old enough they would sometimes be given the job of toasting the pile of bread needed for the hash dinner. Holding each slice to the fire-bars and turning it to toast the other side was quite hot work, even though a long toasting fork was used. Yet the smell of that toasting bread heralded the appetising meal soon to be enjoyed, and the sight of the completed pile, keeping warm on the fender, was ample reward to the toaster. What a pleasure it was for children and adults alike to sit together round the table, seeing everything back in place clean and shining after the morning's upheaval, and how they relished their Saturday dinner of toast and hash.

On most Saturday afternoons Grace performed a duty which, though it brought her sorrow, was compelling nevertheless. Taking a bus to Penistone she would visit Frank's grave and place on it fresh flowers. When Phyllis was about eight she accompanied her mother on those visits to the cemetery, and liked to fetch water for the flowers from a little well in the bottom corner near the drive. Quite often they would meet with an elderly woman who always appeared pale and sad. As she talked she would sometimes start to cry. Phyllis noticed then that her mother became unhappy too. She wished they hadn't met the lady, and was pleased when it was time to leave her. When she asked her mother afterwards who she was and why she was so sad, Grace said the lady's name was Mrs Vaughton. She had been crying because she was thinking of her two sons who were killed in the war.

The main Sunday duty, as far as Grace was concerned, was to see that her children went to Sunday School properly dressed. The girls invariably wore hats on that day, as otherwise their attire would have been thought of as incomplete. After they returned from the morning session, she had them take off their best clothes and put on others in which they could play until dinner was ready. After the meal was eaten she helped them to change back again into the Sunday clothes for the afternoon session. Returning home for the second time they donned the play clothes once again, keeping them on then until bedtime. Grace's children did not complain about having to get changed twice, nor did they regard as hardship the twice walking up and down Bower Hill. Just as Grace herself had done as a child, they accepted without question that it was what one did on Sundays. Like her they

---

enjoyed their days at Sunday School, as it continued to be very well run by conscientious superintendents and teachers such as Joel Marsh, Tom Haigh, Austin Wordsworth, and Ida Cherry. Apart from what her children learned at Sunday School, Grace said that going there 'kept them from being at a loose end'. They had all Saturday to play around home, and it was good for them to have a different sense of purpose on the Lord's day.

Besides all the various daily and weekly occupations at Coates during those years, there were also the seasonal activities. In spring, when there was a surplus of eggs on the farm, Grace made a pickling solution in a little tin bath that she kept in the cubby hole under the stairs. The solution was made from a substance called 'water glass' which, when mixed with water, would preserve the eggs for several months. The eggs were added at different times while they were plentiful, being lowered gently into the pickle so that no cracks occurred. In the following autumn and winter, when the hens almost stopped laying, eggs were taken out of the bath as required. Whilst in the solution they had become covered with a white coating, but this was soon washed off under the tap and the eggs, still good, were ready for immediate use. The cubby hole under the stairs, incidentally, was commonly referred to by the family in Yorkshire dialect form as 't'egg 'oil'.

When young nettles made their appearance around the farm, Mary Emma and the older children were dispatched with scissors and bucket to fill the latter for the making of nettle beer. Grace boiled and simmered the nettles with lemon for some time before straining them onto sugar and cream of tartar. When the liquid was cool she added yeast to set the beer 'working'. When that stage was finished it was put into stone bottles and corked. Nettle beer was a refreshing drink to anyone doing an energetic job on a warm day, and particularly appreciated by men at toil in the hayfield.

At Coates, the spring-cleaning was carried out along the same lines as at Willow Lane. Ceilings were brushed over with whitewash and rooms re-papered in turn, one or two being done each year. Paintwork was washed and furniture polished. While the stair carpet was taken up for a thorough clean, the brass rods that held it in place were given a new shine with Brasso on the house table. In kitchen, pantry and cellar the walls, as well as ceiling, were all given a new coat of limewash for the sake of hygiene, as was the closet across the croft. Nothing had to be missed, whatever the circumstances. There was one occasion when one of the children was unwell on the day she planned to spring-clean the house. As the child demanded most of her attention during the day, the work had fallen somewhat behind schedule. In order to catch up on this Grace stayed up all night to finish the job. She was just washing the floor on completion as Mary Emma reported for the new day's duties.

In summer she made lots of jam in the brass preserving pan that had belonged to her great-grandmother, Betty Pickles. She obtained most of the fruit from people in the locality who grew it in their gardens, or from Ernest's customers who could supply it. The raspberry, strawberry with gooseberry, and plum jams that resulted were all much enjoyed during the months that followed. Lemon curd was made when lemons were cheap. Equally delicious was the blackberry and apple jam made from blackberries that she, Mary Emma and the children picked themselves on expeditions down Bird Lane, and from bushes that grew along field-sides. Besides the jam, she made blackberry jelly, which needed rather more time and patience, as it involved straining out all the seeds. She also made wines: rhubarb, elderberry and orange.

A certain day in the summer was taken up with 'bedding washing'. The ideal day would be warm and sunny but with some breeze because, under such conditions, the woollen blankets dried more quickly and remained fluffy. As with all the other washing, the bedding was done in the wooden tubs and put through the mangle. It could not have been done at the Monday wash, however, because of the amount to be done, apart from special drying weather being necessary.

Ernest always kept a pig to be killed for their own use, as had been the custom at his former home. Grace was kept busy after the killing in helping her husband to make up the 'fries' for neighbours. Cutting up the fat for lard was a long job too. After spending much time on cutting it into small pieces, she put the fat in her pudding tin and placed it in a hot oven. The crackling sound that soon followed signified that the melted lard was ready for pouring off. Grace took out the tin and, after pouring off the first lot, pressed the pieces of fat with a fork and put the tin back again to enable the rest of the lard to seep out. She made sure that it was all extracted before putting the shrunken solid bits into another dish. These were later eaten as 'scraps'. This 'rendering' process, as it was called, occupied a whole evening, since the fat from a pig filled several pudding tins. While it was going on, and particularly at those times when the oven door was opened for the fat to be poured, a sickly smell pervaded the whole house. It was not a pleasant smell unless one happened to like fat, as Ernest Bramall did. When the rendering was at last completed, Grace had several earthenware jars full of pure white lard to show for her labours.

This did make lovely pastry, besides being used in other cooking. With some of the pork from the pig killing she made pork pies, a skill at which she excelled.

There was extra work to be done in the preparations for Christmas. Cakes and puddings were made at home of course, and sometimes Grace made her own mincemeat too. Making Christmas fare was a far more lengthy occupation then than it is today. Raisins were not 'stone-less' when bought, so the pips had to be taken out individually by hand. Currants too needed careful examination, because they were not pre-washed. The chopped, mixed peel which is now obtained ready for use straight from a carton was neither chopped nor mixed fifty years ago. It was bought in sugar-preserved pieces which had to be painstakingly chopped fine at home. Suet for the puddings was not available in shredded, packaged form but obtained from the butcher in a lump that had to be shredded on a hand grater. Such preparation of ingredients was done in the evening, since it could be done while one was sitting to the table. The actual mixing and baking of cakes, and boiling of puddings, was carried out a day or two afterwards. Making the mincemeat took up much time, as all the various ingredients were hand-turned through the same mincer as was used for the potted meat making.

An occasional occupation on winter nights was rug pegging. When one of the three rugs in the house began to show signs of wear, Grace would borrow the wooden loom from her sister Blanche, whose family also pegged their own rugs. The loom had been made by their brother, Stanley. It stood upright on the floor and the harding material was fixed onto rollers. A row of staples on top of the loom served as a guide for keeping the pegging straight and even. Cloth clippings measuring about four inches by one were secured into the material, a row at a time, by a sharp-pointed pegger. As each row was completed, cogs were turned to move the rollers so that the pegged part gradually became wound round the bottom roller. Old coats, trousers, cloth skirts and woollen dresses were cut up for clippings when rug pegging was imminent. It was not every winter that a rug was pegged, because they lasted several years despite constant wear. A new rug was always given pride of place on the hearth in front of the fire. The previous hearth rug would be moved to the bottom of the kitchen step or in front of the sofa, while the old, worn-out rug that was being replaced was relegated to kitchen or pantry.

Shopping was not a big problem at Coates Farm. One or two visits a year to Barnsley sufficed for buying of clothes, shoes usually being bought at the nearer small town of Penistone. Many of the household requirements were brought to the farm by hawkers. Some commodities were fetched from Mrs Wray's shop at Four Lane Ends, but Ernest brought most of the groceries from Penistone in the course of his meat rounds. He thought it good policy to trade with the shopkeepers who gave him their meat custom. There was of course no need to shop for the important items of milk, eggs, bread and butter, and meat in its various forms, because these were all produced at home.

The weekly routines at Coates did not afford any time or opportunity for the tea and coffee 'breaks' folk indulge in today. Grace and Mary Emma were thankful to have three good meals a day, that being more than some working-class people got in the early thirties. They did not look for anything inbetween. Neither of them was to be seen sitting down during the day, except for meals, unless their hands were occupied with some task at the table. The children would have feared something was sadly wrong with their mother had she not been busily engaged. They would have been greatly surprised to have seen her reading a book or even a newspaper during the day.

So was Grace's busy life of energetic activity continued through those years when her children were young. To them she was the focal point of the whole house and, indeed, of their whole lives; everything else seeming to revolve around her. She was always there when they returned from school, and always took time to ask about their lessons and listen to what they had to tell her. Grace looked after her children well without too much indulgence. They in turn knew they could not expect attention when she was occupied with necessary duties. At such times they got on with their own devices, secure in the knowledge that she was around.

CHAPTER 16

Happenings in the Thirties

BETWEEN 1924 AND 1931 Grace had six children, four of whom survived. In July of 1930, when Betty was just over a year old, she went into hospital at Sheffield where a premature baby girl was still-born. Her stay in the Jessop Hospital, and subsequent convalescence at Norton, was the first time in her life that Grace had slept away from home. When she eventually returned to Coates after her 'holi-day', as she afterwards called it, her joy at being home was further increased on receiving a bunch of flowers that Phyllis's teacher, Mrs Clayton, had very thoughtfully sent up for her from school.

In the November of 1931 another boy was born, to be called John. He was a very big baby weighing ten pounds. His birth was the most difficult of all Grace's children, so much so that Dr Masser decided he would have to administer chloroform to ease the situation. To his dismay, and probably more so to that of his patient, he discovered that the bottle had lost its cork and the chloroform it had contained was spilt. In consequence, Grace suffered greatly while John was being born, but when the ordeal was over she displayed that remarkable resilience which was so characteristic. Dr Masser, much relieved that mother and child were well in spite of everything, complimented Grace on the fine healthy boy she had produced, remarking with a smile, 'I won't say this is going to be the last baby to be born into this family.' Her reply, understandably, was to the effect that she hoped it was. Yet though she had reached the age of thirty-eight when John was born, the doctor's prediction was later to be proved true.

Despite the trials in her life and pressure of work which, by today's standards, would be regarded as nothing short of drudgery, Grace counted herself amongst the more fortunate working women of that time. At least she and her household never went hungry, which was more than could be said of many families in the area. When the Peni-stone steelworks of Cammell-Laird suddenly closed down in 1930 there was much unemployment as a result. It would seem that at least some of the men received little or no warning of what was about to happen. The only intimation Mr Davies of Dean Head, Oxspring, had was when he was actually on his way to the Sunday night shift. Reaching the point from where he could see the works' chimneys, he was greatly surprised to see they were not smoking. By their stillness those tall, silent chimneys told him and many others of his workmates that their jobs no longer existed. For several years after the closure of Cammell-Laird's, Penistone was a distressed area.

Grace's sister, Blanche Purseglove, was one of those who found it hard to make ends meet because her husband had worked at 't'Nibble'. Though some monetary relief in the form of 'dole' was given to men out of work, this only provided for a mere subsistence living. When the Means Test was in operation, Frank Purseglove had his dole money knocked down to sixpence a week because his daughter was earning a wage. It was expected then that money earned by sons and daughters would be paid over to parents as contribution to the general family upkeep.

All the Purseglove girls had done well at school, and in particular had shown considerable artistic ability. Flora and Mary Emma, when in their teens, were so keen to foster this talent that they attended evening classes in art at Penistone St John's school. There they passed examinations which enabled them to continue with further study at the Harvey Institute in Barnsley. Flora was by that time working at Brownhill's silk mill in Denby Dale, a distance of six miles or so by bicycle. Her working hours were from a quarter-past seven in the morning to a quarter-past five in the evening, so on the nights of the evening classes she rode her bicycle all the way from Denby Dale to Barnsley after finishing work at the mill. So great was her enjoyment of drawing and painting that she willingly sacrificed a proper meal at the end of a hard day's work in order to reach her classes on time, managing instead with a little packed-up food. Flora followed that routine twice a week for three years. She completed the course with flying colours, obtaining first-class certificates in fashion drawing and a distinction in design. She was then recommended by her teacher to go on a full-time art course in Sheffield with the view of making it her career, but owing to the home circumstances this was impossible. She could not give up her work at the mill because her money was needed to help support the family.

Young people were pleased to get almost any kind of job at that time, irrespective of whether the type of work appealed to them. To turn down jobs because they were felt to be unsuitable led to one's dole money being discontinued. Quite often the unemployed were directed into work a long distance from home, which meant their living away. Some mothers were reluctant to allow their daughters to take doubtful jobs in strange places, but the 'no dole' rule still applied if the work was refused.

There was one young man, however, who did go out of the district to work and was able to raise a laugh on his return. Vincent Murphy of Old Mill Lane, Thurgoland, was sent to a job in Oxford. When he alighted from his train at the station there he found himself mingling with students who were returning to the University after being on holiday. Vincent was rather taken aback when a young lad, obviously eager to earn himself a penny or two from the afflu-ent crowd, confronted him with, 'Carry your bag, sir?' Realising with surprise that the lad thought him to be one of the students, Vincent clutched the bag containing his few possessions tightly to him as he mut-tered a hurried refusal. At this the

'Carry your bag, Sir?'

would-be porter, feeling frustration and knowing he had nothing to lose, made scathing remark to one of his young mates. Indicating Vin-cent he exclaimed, in a tone of derision, 'Father hasn't given him any spending money this term.' If the words were meant to be cutting they did not upset the penniless 'student' in the least. On the con-trary, Vincent Murphy was amused and happy to know that, for a few brief moments in his humble life, he had possessed the exalted image of an Oxford University student.

Some of the Oxspring and Penistone girls found jobs in the woollen mills at Denby Dale in the Huddersfield direction, which necessi-tated early rising to allow for the travel. The work in those mills was hard, much of it being dirty and boring. Other people in the Peni-stone area worked in a local rug mill where, in return for hand-pegging a cloth rug measuring two yards by one, a girl received half-a-crown (12½p today). Considering she had to cut her own clippings too, it meant working very quickly to earn even a minimal wage. It is said that one unscrupulous employer even tried to curtail the earnings of girls who were speedy and hard-working. If he thought they were get-ting too much money by finishing their rugs quickly, he would set them to do some that required a difficult pattern working in. This had the effect of slowing down the pegging and deliberately reducing the wages, for the piecework rate of half-a-crown a rug still applied whatever the pattern involved.

A change that occasioned great local interest around Four Lane Ends at the beginning of the decade was the making of the Penistone Bypass road. It was realised that a straighter, wider road was needed to provide for traffic of the future. The old roads of course had not been made with motor vehicles in mind; those through Penistone would soon become congested as traffic increased, because they were narrow in places, with many bends and corners. The decision was taken to improve the road between Thurgoland and Ingbirchworth so that vehicles travelling to Huddersfield and other points north from Sheffield, Rotherham and places south could avoid passing through Penistone. The road to be altered passed through Four Lane Ends and included the stretches of Copster and Jockey which had been so well traversed by Grace in her earlier days when she took her young brothers for outings in the bassinet, and on Sunday evening walks to church.

Work commenced on the new bypass on the 25th of October 1930, but progressed only slowly in comparison with the modern rate of road making. For that period in time, however, the Penistone Bypass seemed quite a remarkable achievement. On Copster the existing road was widened at the Thurgoland end, but an entirely new section was then taken straight across farmland to rejoin the first road where that became straighter again near Grants Farm. The narrow, twisty part of the old road was thus allowed to fall into disuse apart from walkers who preferred a quieter way and learner drivers who, long afterwards, considered it an ideal stretch for their initial steering practice. The remaining part of the old road was widened and, in the process, the top was blasted off the steep Copster hill near the little house which had been the home of Grace's Herbert grandparents and had since belonged to her father. James Spenceley did not live there, however, but remained at Tunnel Top. The top of the hill above Four Lane Ends was taken off so as to lessen the gradient down to the crossroads. The Jockey road was widened and a new section cut out of farmland between Jockey House and Tunnel Top, thus bypassing Willow Lane Farm. The old part of the road that still bends round in front of that familiar place is almost as quiet now as it was in the pre-motor car age, used only by visitors to the farm itself.

The new bypass was surfaced with tarmacadam, as many roads in other places already had been following the advent of the motor vehicles. There was a causeway for pedestrians alongside the new road, with railings to separate it from the grass beyond. With the building of Penistone Bypass, the character of Four Lane Ends began to show signs of change. No longer could people stand in the middle of the road while they chatted, nor could children play on it with safety when vehicles came along in increasing numbers and at ever-increasing speeds. There was rather more traffic using the Barnsley road through the crossroads too since the Yorkshire Traction bus company had begun operating buses to Penistone.

The building of the new road was a necessity, as succeeding years have proved. At the time it also served another purpose by helping to alleviate some of the unemployment in the district. A number of Cammell-Laird's former employees were given work on the road. While there were not enough jobs for everyone, the situation was eased a little, especially as a system of work sharing was put into operation. A man could work on the road for ten weeks and then draw dole money for a similar period. This system enabled more men to take a turn at working, which was thought to be better than some of them being continuously unemployed.

While changes were taking place around them, an important one took place at Coates Farm in 1932. Eager to keep abreast with his time, Ernest Bramall decided he would become 'motorised' too. In that year he exchanged his horse and cart for a brand new Morris van. It was obtained from Penn's garage, which was established at Penistone's Bridge End. The van was brown in colour and its arrival caused much excitement in the house. To actually have a motor vehicle on the place seemed at first incredible. After some brief instructions from the garage people, Ernest was soon driving the van confidently. Grace watched in admiration as he drove it through the gate and along the lane with its first load of meat. Apart from Bert Milnes, who farmed at Far Coates and had a motor for his milk round, theirs was the only other vehicle in the area around Four Lane Ends, though there were several tradesmen in and around Penistone who, by that time, were exchanging their horses and carts for vans, just as they were doing. That was all in the line of business of course. No working-class man in Oxspring possessed a car merely to carry him to work in 1932, or still less for the purpose of pleasurable outings. Knowing it was primarily to further his business efficiency that her husband had bought a van did not lessen Grace's pride in any way. She was happy to see that his years of hard work were paying dividends, and felt that her own efforts in supporting him and by exercising thrift in the house were being rewarded.

Having the van to take him around more quickly did not prompt him to shorten his working hours. Instead he expanded his business by taking on more customers, so was still out late on Fridays and Saturdays as before. Ernest Bramall was a popular, well-respected butcher who was long remembered in the Penistone and Hoylandswaine areas. He was noted for his cleanliness, good sales manner and fair dealings. At Christmas it was his habit to give each customer a calendar with a letter pocket. The calendar of course displayed his name and advertised his trade as family butcher.

To increase his business efficiency still further, Ernest soon acquired another innovation. In the clammin' 'oil was installed what, at first sight, appeared to be a huge cupboard. It was actually nothing less than a real refrigerator. In the absence of electricity at Coates, the ice was fetched in the van from Barnsley. It came in large blocks wrapped around with sacking. These were carried into the building and deposited on the floor. Ernest or Alf then smashed up the blocks into smaller pieces which could be shovelled into a bucket. A ladder was propped against the 'fridge' and the ice carried, a bucketful at a time, up the ladder, to be fed into the refrigerator from the top.

In 1933 new regulations regarding the slaughtering of animals were enforced. Up to that date it had been quite legal for any person to kill them, whether or not they had the ability to do the job properly. It was a well-known fact that animals often suffered cruelty at the hands of inexperienced or clumsy slaughtermen. The new law stipulated that no one would be permitted to do any future killing unless he held a slaughterman's licence. Ernest Bramall received his from the Penistone Council in the December of that year. That licence, bearing his signature, has been retained in his family for the past half-century. It states that Ernest was a person who was considered fit to be engaged in the business of slaughtering. Rules were printed on the licence of points to be observed so as to minimise the chance of cruelty being caused. It was stressed that a beast's head had to be kept immobile while it was being stunned, but this was something which Ernest had always done and was nothing new to him. It was also ruled that no animal had to witness the killing of another.

Growing concern for the animals' welfare was shown by the introduction of another law not long afterwards. This made compulsory the use of a humane killer in all slaughtering. The new implement took the form of a gun which instantly rendered an animal unconscious before it was killed. Apart from eliminating the animal's pain, it was easier for the butcher to use, particularly when slaughtering large beasts, as it was more accurate and required less physical effort on his part. Further use of the poleaxe for knocking down cattle was forbidden, so that heavy implement which Ernest and his forebears had wielded through four generations fell at last into obsolescence.

During the year when her husband obtained his slaughtering licence, Grace decided she would obtain new teeth. Her natural teeth had been troubling her for some time. In common with many busy mothers of that time, she had never made visits to the dentist unless they were aching so badly as to need pulling out. Having six children within a short space of time and attending to their needs, while sometimes neglecting her own diet, could well have contributed to the deteriorating state of her teeth. In 1933, therefore, Grace paid two visits to the Penistone dentist, Arthur Fieldsend, to have all her remaining teeth extracted. Arthur Fieldsend had a room for his dentistry at the back of the chemist's shop in the High Street, so anyone needing treatment had first to walk through the shop before arriving at the dentist's chair. Grace had local anaesthetic by 'the needle', which was the usual method employed in teeth extraction then. Though she was basically a tough little person, the experience evidently left her looking rather pale. On emerging from the shop they met an acquaintance by name of Atkinson who, noticing her lack of colour, exclaimed with urgency in his voice, 'Tak' 'er 'ooam Ernest lad, be quick an' tak' 'er 'ooam,' as if half expecting her to faint on the spot.

Obtaining her new teeth coincided with the visit to Penistone of the Prince of Wales, who later became King Edward the Eighth and Duke of Windsor. After leaving the dentist's on that December day, Grace walked down to the Occupational Centre in Sheffield Road to join the crowd that had congregated there to see him. Children from local schools had been allowed a vantage point on the high bank across the road near to the old entrance of the former steelworks. Grace's elder daughter was among the little contingent from Oxspring school and felt flat disappointment because the prince did not measure up to her preconceived image of him. He was just too ordinary-looking, and not at all like the princes she had seen in books. Nevertheless, it was a memorable day for Penistone district. The fact that the heir to the throne had visited the small town and listened to its people's problems did much to raise morale.

The Prince of Wales was at that time touring areas of depression in various parts of the country, and Penistone was included. It had not then recovered from the effects of the Cammell-Laird closure. Though some men found jobs in the Stocksbridge steelworks of Samuel Fox, there was still unemployment. The packed-up lunches that many children took to school consisted only of bread smeared over with lard or sprinkled with sugar. Women who could not afford to buy good meat would welcome the chance of getting from the butcher a sheep's head. This could be stewed and, though it was mostly bone, with the addition of a few vegetables it resulted in tasty broth. In that period of depression many children had only one pair of shoes. When these were sent to the cobbler's for repair the child had to stay away from school until they were mended or perhaps go in a pair that an older brother or sister had outgrown; in such cases the shoes were likely to be ill-fitting. This poor state of affairs continued for another year or so. Then, in 1935, things began to improve when the Huddersfield firm of David Brown purchased part of the site of the old steelworks and commenced new industry.

One day in 1934, when their eldest child was ten, Grace was agreeably surprised to learn that her husband had bought a piano. He had obtained it second-hand for four pounds but there was absolutely nothing wrong with it, and it was a good-looking piece of furniture too. He told Grace that Phyllis should have lessons on how to play the piano. 'It will stand her in good stead when she becomes a teacher,' he predicted. The words showed a perfect example of accurate foresight on his part because, though he did not live long enough to see them fulfilled, they proved to be true nevertheless. The piano was installed in the 'room'. This was still unheated and the floor uncovered, but these shortcomings did not detract from the pleasure occasioned by the actual possession of a piano. The question of who was to be music teacher did not arise, because Ernest had shrewdly thought of a way by which the piano lessons could be had as a means of settlement for a long-standing business debt. Before explaining how this came about it should be said that Ernest was meticulous in keeping accounts of his customers' payments. He had a hard-backed cash-book in which he entered all items to be paid for. The midweek orders were booked down and payment received together with that for the weekend meat on Friday or Saturday. Names and prices were crossed off when the week's meat had been duly paid for.

In common with most tradesmen he allowed a little credit, but there were one or two women whose attempts at avoiding paying for their meat might have gone on indefinitely had he done nothing about it. One good lady invariably called down to him from upstairs when he knocked on her door, 'Put it on the table Ernest. I'm just having a bath. I'll pay you next week.' Needless to say, she would be 'having a bath' the following week too. Even when Ernest varied his time of calling, this preoccupation strangely, or perhaps not so strangely, still coincided with his visit. After a time Ernest's book showed that she

Grace, Ernest, and their family in 1934

was owing quite a lot of money. This caused him some frustration, because the lady was not exactly a person of small means. She lived in a nice house with material comforts, dressed well, and presented an appearance of general wellbeing. Unlike some of his poorer customers who made do with a sheep's head, she had usually requested the better cuts of meat which, of course, were more expensive and quickly increased the debt. Ernest realised he must stop leaving meat at her house, at least until he recovered the money owing to him. Fortunately he saw an opportunity of doing just that when he learned that his customer's daughter had qualified as a piano teacher. He soon came to an amicable agreement with his debtor whereby weekly piano lessons would be given to his daughter instead of the money payments which he knew would never be forthcoming. The arrangement worked very well. The customer's daughter was a cheerful young woman, patient, kind, and a good teacher of the piano. The butcher's daughter liked her pleasant personality and enjoyed being one of her pupils. Apart from the music, the fact that lessons were taken in a nicely-carpeted sitting room seemed quite a novelty. It was not until many years later that she understood the real reason why she never had to give her teacher a shilling as the other pupils did. At the time she was satisfied to be told, 'Your father's paying for you', which, of course, was not untrue.

About that same time Grace, her husband and four children had a family picture taken by the studio photographer. It was the first occasion since the eldest child was a baby that time was made for such an event. It also proved to be the last occasion. The picture shows Ernest still a handsome, dark-haired man, though somewhat heavier than formerly. Grace thought his increased weight was due to the fact that he was doing less walking since acquiring the van. She herself had become a little thinner of face but looked healthy, happy, and serenely contented. At forty-one her dark brown hair showed no sign of grey. It was thick and long when she let it fall down her back prior to washing or brushing it. The style of dressing her hair was simple. She made it into one long plait which she then twisted round into a coil, to be secured at the back of her head with hairpins. That method kept her hair neat and tidy all day, so it required no further attention while she was working. Grace never patronised any hairdressing establishment in her whole life, but kept her hair clean and shining by her own efforts. Though she retained long hair to the end of her life, she had her two daughters' cut short after the prevailing fashion. The family picture shows both girls had straight hair with forehead fringes, whereas the two-year-old John, seated on his mother's knee, had fair curls. Norman, in his seventh year, was a sturdy boy whose attire included a smart suit and shining boots. All four children healthily reflected their mother's care.

Two sad family events happened in that year of 1934. At Willow Lane Ernest's mother died after a cut to her foot caused septicaemia. Until then Selina had remained active despite her seventy-three years. Contact had been maintained between the people at Coates and their Willow Lane relatives, and they all knew that Selina would be greatly missed. She had been such an essential part of the Willow Lane scene for so long. Yet they had to admit that seventy-three was a good age.

The other happening brought grief in full measure to Grace's sister Mary, for she suffered the loss of her eight-year-old daughter Jean. When Mary married her husband, Eric Marsh, they had lived in Penistone for a few years but had then moved away on account of Eric's work. They were living at Middlesbrough when Jean died, but the little girl was brought back to Penistone to be buried at Netherfield. Grace's reaction on first hearing the sad news of her niece was to exclaim, 'Poor Mary.' From her own experience of losing a small child she knew what anguish her sister would be feeling. Jean had been a bright, happy and intelligent little girl. Her mother, understandably, was heartbroken. The illness that had caused Jean's death was chorea and rheumatic fever. Mary had one younger child, a boy named Jack.

Towards the end of the year Grace had to go to hospital again, or rather it was into a nursing home she went at her husband's insistence. He wanted her to have the best treatment possible and had been told on good authority that she would get it at Sister Mawhood's. Grace's trouble on that occasion was strangulated hernia, or to put it simply, she had rupture of the intestine. This could have been long-standing since she had lifted and carried too-heavy weights all her life, but it flared up quite suddenly one Friday night. It was the children's bath night. Grace had been having abdominal pains before she lit the set-pot fire, but had tried to ignore them. She bathed the young-est children and put them to bed, but was then unable to do more. By the time her husband returned from his hawking round, it was obvious that the doctor was urgently needed. On diagnosing the trouble he immediately ordered her to Sheffield, saying an operation would be necessary to avoid danger to her life. Events moved quickly.

The operation, under chloroform, was performed without delay and Grace began to recover. Her days of recuperation in the nursing home really did seem like a holiday to her, so well was she looked after. One thing happened while she was there which, to her at the time, seemed quite wonderful. She, the other patients, and nursing staff were all able to listen on the radio, or wireless as it was called then, to the first Royal Wedding ever to be broadcast. That was the wedding of King George the Fifth's son, the Duke of Kent, to Princess Marina of Greece. There was no wireless at Coates Farm, so Grace was the only member of the family to actually hear those royal voices as they made their marriage vows.

It is not known whether their lack of a wireless on that important occasion prompted Ernest to buy one or whether Phyllis's entreaties had anything to do with it. She had informed her father that friends at school had wireless sets in their homes and enjoyed listening to 'Children's Hour'. Whatever the reason, a wireless soon made its appear-ance at Coates Farm; moreover, a special shelf was put up to accom-modate it in the corner between the fireplace and small window. While Ernest Bramall was not a man to copy other people merely for the sake of it, he was not slow to follow modern trends if he considered them important. Where the wireless was concerned he evidently decided that possession of one would be beneficial to his family, including himself. During his remaining years he was always keen to hear the news broadcasts which brought far-away London and even places abroad into their sphere of life. Though he had always read his newspapers, the wireless seemed to convey information more intimately, drawing places and events more closely together. Both he and Grace enjoyed listening to lighter programmes too, particularly music if it was tuneful.

On one Saturday afternoon in the spring of 1935, when the wireless was still a novelty to them, Grace and her family listened eagerly to the commentary of the Football Association Cup Final. Their local team, Sheffield Wednesday, was one of the finalists, and great was the joy when that team won. The last minutes of the game were tremendously exciting as the teams were drawing two goals each until five minutes before the end of the match. During those minutes two more goals were scored for Sheffield Wednesday by the same player, Ellis Rimmer, who was thus the hero of the day, having enabled his team to gain the decisive four–two victory. Much as Ernest would have liked to hear that broadcast, it was something he had to forego because, the day being Saturday, he was on his hawking round.

At the end of the year, however, Ernest did sit down with the rest of his household as they listened, spellbound, to King George the Fifth's Christmas Day broadcast to his people. They all thought it fascinating to hear the king speaking to everyone through this wonderful invention of wireless. No king in England had ever done so before George the Fifth.

The wireless at Coates worked from batteries which, for some reason, most people referred to as 'accumulators'. There were two of these on the wireless shelf, one being in use at a time. When the battery needed recharging one of the children would take it down to Jim Wood's garage at Oxspring and bring it back during the course of journeys from school. Jim was a popular figure in Oxspring for many years, operating his small business from wooden premises opposite the Toll Bar. He was always ready to oblige people by filling their 'cumulators', and patient with the children to whom he dispensed 'haporths' and 'pennorths' of sweets from his little shop at one end of the garage.

Both Grace and her husband were pleased when, during that year, their eldest child became a pupil of Penistone Grammar School, after gaining a County Minor Scholarship. Unlike some parents, they thought it a good thing that girls should be given a chance of higher education and a career other than a domestic one. The two eldest children of Ernest's sister Gladys were already in attendance at the Grammar School, as was the son of Grace's brother, Willie Spenceley. All three had gained scholarships to enable them to attend.

While the presence of the wireless was making life more up-to-date in the house by the mid thirties, two new items were added in the kitchen. One of these was the 'Jiffy' washing machine. It was a squarish container which stood on short metal legs. When filled with soapy water and the clothes put in, its lid was fastened down. The agitator, which worked out the dirt from the clothes, was fixed to the underside of the lid and connected to the handle on the outside. By moving this handle rapidly from side to side across the top of the Jiffy's lid the contents of the washer were agitated with swishing action. Though the Jiffy was described as a machine, the handle had to be operated manually, so it did not exactly save time. The advantage of the washer was that it could be worked from a standing position, whereas washing in the tub necessitated much back bending. It had rubber rollers too, so the dirty water could be squeezed out more effectively before clothes were passed to the 'seconding' tub. Though she had acquired a more modern invention, Grace did not immediately dispense with her tub. She could not trust the Jiffy to reach her high standard of cleanliness all on its own, and used it merely to replace the 'firsting' tub. It was a decided improvement though, generally speaking. Besides being easier to work it was more compact and less likely to result in a wet floor as washing by tub, rubbing board and 'peggy' sometimes did. It was easier to empty too. From the tub most of the water had to be taken out by lading can and the tub lifted up to pour out the rest, but water from the Jiffy ran straight away through a rubber pipe into a bucket when washing was finished.

The other innovation which became a fixture in the kitchen for the next few years was the milk separator. This was comprised of many metal parts including numerous small 'cups' that fitted in certain order onto a metal base. There were two spouts of different size, the smaller one being for the cream to trickle through after its separation from the skim. This flowed from the larger spout when the machine was in motion. A large metal bowl to accommodate the new milk was fixed at the top of all the other parts. This had a small hole in the bottom into which a bung was fitted. The separator at Coates was on an iron stand bolted into the stone floor. When assembled for use it stood about four feet high, being conveniently placed between kitchen table and cellar door. Having a machine to separate cream from the rest of the milk obviated all the work of skimming large bowls and carrying them up and down the cellar steps, but cream was still taken down there to await the churning day.

The separator was in use twice a day, morning and evening. When milk was brought up warm and fresh from the mistal, it was poured through the sile into the bowl at the top. The separator was worked by a handle at the side. This had to be turned in clockwise motion, at a regular, even speed that was neither too fast nor too slow. After a little practice the turner knew from the whirring sound created if the correct rhythm was being upheld. If the machine was being turned at a speed that was anything less than correct when Ernest was around, his voice would soon be heard. 'You're turning too fast, slow it down a bit,' or 'Waken up, you're going to sleep o'er t'job' were comments one was likely to receive. Needless to say, his remarks had an instant effect on the handle turner, who quickly jerked his or her mind back to the job in hand. As the handle turned, the milk slowly seeped through the intricacies of the revolving cups. The bung in the middle of the bowl, when twisted slightly on commencing to separate, allowed only a small passage of milk. As the level of milk in the bowl at the top gradually lowered, cream trickled slowly from the small spout into a basin while the skimmed milk flowed at a quicker rate into a clean bucket standing on the floor beneath the larger spout. The handle was kept turning for fifteen or twenty minutes, depending on the amount of milk to go through. It was an occupation usually delegated to the older children before they set out for school in the morning, and again when they were home in the evening.

Though the separator was rather more effective than hand-skimming, it could not entirely be called a labour-saving installation. Apart from all the handle turning, much time was spent in washing it. Every morning it had to be taken apart, the various pieces rinsed free of milk in cold water, then given a good wash in hot. Finally they were scalded by boiling water from the kettle. In the evening it had to be rinsed out again. Before the second separating it had of course to be reassembled. The calves and pigs probably benefited from the new method since they received the skimmed milk fresh each day whereas previously it was two or three days old.

Although a van had been bought primarily to serve the butchering business, there were times during the thirties when Ernest put it to other uses for his family's benefit. On two or three occasions each year he drove them over to Cawthorne Lanes to visit his sister Gladys, her husband Fred and their five children on their small farm. Those were pleasurable outings for all concerned, though the children had to sit inside the back of the van on boards which had no back rests. They could see little of where they were going as the van had only two small rectangular windows in the back doors. Yet the fact they were riding in their own vehicle was delight in itself. Grace's children experienced as much joy then at the prospect of a trip to Cawthorne Lanes as children of the latest generation do now when about to take a faraway holiday. That van was surely boarded with as much enthusiasm as are some of today's jet planes. Enjoyable outings also took place to birthday parties at Willow Lane. These occurred quite frequently since Willis and Jessie Bramall had six children in all. Similar visits were paid to Berry Moor farm at the bottom of Coates Lane where Ernest's sister Hilda lived with her husband Joe Elsworth and four children. Grace and her children would walk to these nearer relatives for tea, but sometimes her husband would join them later and accompany them home. Grace in her turn made many birthday parties at Coates to which the relatives and other friends were invited. The pleasures of those joyful days were long remembered by her children.

Most years Grace and Ernest took their family to the annual Penistone Feast at the end of June and to the Agricultural Show which, in those days, was held on the third Thursday in August. For them the latter event was one of the main highlights of the year. The excitement really began in the morning when some of the neighbouring farmers who were showing their horses walked them past Coates Farm on the way to Penistone. From the house window Grace, who had very good eyes, was quick to see who was coming along. 'There's your Uncle Joe with his horse and foal,' she would call to the children, or, 'Thompsons are just coming on with their horses.' George Thompson was the farmer from Hadley House down Coates Lane. Perhaps she would comment, 'That looks like Houghlands who've come up Bird Lane. Laura said they might be showing their foal.' Grace's observations had the electrifying effect of sending the children scurrying along to the end of the lane to get a close-up view of those magnificent animals, the shire horses, as on huge feet they clopped patiently past, their proud owners walking steadily beside them. The immaculate grooming of the animals, their plaited manes and tails bedecked with ribbon, was evidence that the men had risen very early from their beds that morning.

When Grace's family arrived at the show in the early afternoon, the children had to exercise patience for a while. Their eagerness to watch the horse-riding events had to be kept under temporary restraint because Ernest's first steps inside the showground invariably led his contingent in the direction of the fat cattle. His family stood around with indifferent expressions while he enthusiastically prodded and patted each beast. As he did so, other men who were obviously of the butchering and farming fraternities, and to whom he was well known, would ask intermittent questions such as, 'Wot's to think on 'er Ernest?', or 'Do yer reckon that 'ud do fo' you Ernest?' From Ernest's replies could be inferred that he was seeing those poor creatures as joints of meat in a butcher's shop. Though her husband was not one of the official judges, Grace could see by the serious looks of the cattle connoisseurs that his opinions were highly valued. When the children were eventually taken to see the horse riding they appreciated it all the more for having had to wait for it.

Outings when all the family went together were few. Neither Grace nor Ernest believed they should both be away from the house for too long. Neighbours sometimes came for meat at odd times, and the butcher liked to be there to oblige. If he was out Grace would go across to the shop to serve them.

One day, however, just before the van was bought, they did have a day together at Scarborough, but it was not exactly a pleasurable one for Grace. Her husband had ordered Penney's taxi from Springvale to take them all the way, no doubt thinking it would be more comfortable and convenient than the train, but Phyllis was sick several times during that journey. On arrival at Scarborough, Grace's first job was to clean out the taxi. The same thing happened on the return journey. Fortunately it was only during her early years that their daughter was made ill by motor riding. As she grew older it no longer affected her.

One of the first outings in the van was to some pleasure gardens at Honley. They had tea there and, among other things, Ernest hired a rowing boat on the lake. Phyllis was rather apprehensive about her father's ability as an oarsman as she had never before seen him in that capacity, but he proved to be quite capable nevertheless.

The only other family outings that can be recalled were those to the Christmas pantomimes in Sheffield, but they, like the birthday parties and other treats, gave lasting enjoyment.

Ernest liked the theatre and it was his custom on Monday evenings to go to the Variety Performance at Barnsley's Theatre Royal. The fact that he went on Mondays could have been because of a need to escape the scene of the butcher's shop. Having spent the morning among the stench of killing and the afternoon among cattle in the market he no doubt felt the desire for a little brightness afterwards. Grace would not accompany him on those evenings. Even though Mary Emma was willing to put the young ones to bed, Grace felt that to be her own duty. All the same she was quite content to see her husband don his navy-blue suit and bowler hat as a change from his butchering clothes. As she waved happily to him from the kitchen window as he passed on his way out, he raised his best walking stick to her in return and smiled broadly in acknowledgement. It gave her pleasure to see him thus. She knew he had had few opportunities in his life to enjoy its lighter side and was glad he seized them when he could. When their elder daughter reached the age of eleven or twelve Ernest often allowed her to share his delight of the theatre by taking her to the Monday night performances.

To everyone's surprise, Grace did take a proper holiday in 1936. She went to the seaside at Blackpool. Whether it was her own idea or whether it was at her husband's instigation is not certain. It seems likely that Ernest was in favour of it, at least, because the piece of paper still remains on which the train times and connections are written in his hand. The journey between Penistone and Blackpool involved a change at Manchester. It was the first time any of the party had slept in a seaside boarding house, so the whole thing was quite an adventure. Grace took Mary Emma with her because her niece would not have had a holiday otherwise. Moreover, she would help to look after the four children. The boys had never been away from home before, and the only times Grace had slept in another bed were during her stays in hospital. The girls had slept for a few days at their 'Auntie' Madge's house at Wakefield, and Phyllis had once stayed for a week at Cawthorne Lanes with her Auntie Gladys, but the Blackpool venture was the first family holiday they had together. Even then Ernest could not go with them, because of the business. Admittedly the holiday was short, being of only three days' duration, including the travelling days. They went on a Sunday and returned the Tuesday following. Everyone made the best of their time however, and were well provided with food by a very plump lady called Mrs Aplin. John's favourite occupation while in the boarding house was flushing the toilet, even when it did not need flushing. Seeing the water gush forth was a real novelty to the four year old who had never encountered a water closet before. In the end Grace had to curtail his activity by telling him firmly how wrong it was to waste water, or anything else for that matter.

At a different time Ernest took a similar Sunday-to-Tuesday break at Blackpool on his own. It was the only holiday he ever had. Generally speaking, it was only on Sundays that he could get a little daytime relaxation from the week's duties. Most Sunday mornings he went up to Tunnel Top to see his Uncle Bill and Aunt Polly, and to have a talk about farming matters with his cousin Walter. He usually took one of the children with him on those visits as his Aunt Polly liked to see them. She had tragically lost her only daughter some years earlier. Bertha, who had seemed to be a strong, healthy young woman, had died in childbirth at twenty-four, just a few weeks before Grace had her first child. After his Uncle Bill died in 1936, Ernest continued his Sunday morning visits to his Aunt Polly who, despite her troubles, was always ready to welcome them with smiling face. Polly had not kept up with the times as far as clothes were concerned, but continued to cover her short, dumpy little figure with a long black dress and an apron that almost reached the floor. Her outward appearance had not greatly changed since that unforgettable time she had invaded the taproom at Fours in a futile attempt to extricate her husband. When Ernest had visited the folk at Tunnel Top he would call in at Willow Lane on his way back to see his relatives there, timing his return to Coates to coincide with the roast beef and Yorkshire pudding being ready for eating.

Grace always liked to keep an eye on her children when they were young. She liked to know where they were, whom they were with, and what they were doing. When they were not at school they mostly amused themselves by playing in the yard and fields around the farm. During the thirties Ernest had the flagstones outside the house replaced by concrete because they were very old, worn and uneven. The smooth new concrete was an ideal surface on which to play ball, skipping, hopscotch, and whip and top. On light summer evenings the children would play happily outside until bedtime. There were of course frequent walks down Bird Lane during the longer days of spring and summer. At the end of May or beginning of June, Grace and Mary Emma took them on another delightful, though longer, walk through Storthes Woods which lay some distance beyond Far Coates. Grace's sister Blanche and her youngest daughter Myrtle joined them on those occasions, also Hannah Dawson and her two children from next door. Hannah had stayed in the same house after her marriage, her father Arthur Illingsworth still living with them. The way to Storthes Woods was along Maggett Lane or down Battye Lane, depending on which end of the woods one wanted to reach. The return home would then be by the alternative route. The purpose of the woodland walk was to view the delightful expanse of bluebells which stretched endlessly through the trees, giving off that sweet scent that is the bluebells' own.

An even longer walk that some of the party took during the summer was to the small village of Midhope at the edge of the moors a few miles to the south-west. Blanche could not accompany the others on those outings because of her weak heart. The walking distance amounted to seven or eight miles and involved steep hills both ways. It was a tiring walk for the younger children and for the adults who had to push the chair containing the youngest child, but everyone enjoyed those expeditions to Midhope. Walking into new territory, as it were, was an adventure in itself, and they were all interested in looking inside the quaint little church there, with its ancient, boxed-in pews. One year they were well on their way home when it was realised that one of the children's coats had been left behind in the church, so everyone trooped back again to recover it. Their journey that day was lengthened by another two or three miles; needless to say, not one of the children required any rocking before being put to bed when they finally reached home.

Haytime was always enjoyed by Grace's children. Though their acreage was only small in comparison with Willow Lane and Far Coates farms, it seemed a big event because other people were involved too. Ernest did not have his own equipment for haymaking, as the few acres did not warrant it. The grass was cut by Houghlands' sons who brought their mowing machine from Bird Lane. Grace let her family watch from the gate as the horses pulled the mower into the field, but she never allowed them to be in a field where that machine was working. When the hay had been turned, dried and made into cocks, Ernest's brother Willis would come from Willow Lane to help with the leading, bringing his horses and dray. The children were pleased to be allowed to ride on the empty dray as it was pulled up to the hayfield, but on arrival in the field were not allowed to be idle. Ernest promptly presented hand-rakes to those he thought big enough to use them, with instructions to follow the forkers as they lifted the cocks onto the dray. It was inevitable that small amounts of hay should drop from the men's forks and that a little was left on the ground after each cock was forked on. The children's duty was to rake up all the pieces that had been left and add them to another cock due to be forked. Ernest's sharp eyes made sure that the allotted task was properly carried out. His occasional call of, 'Look there, you've missed a bit', was sufficient to send one of them hurrying back to rake up the piece which had escaped the child's, though not the father's, eye. When the load was complete they walked behind it back to the farm to watch it being forked off through the 'pickin' 'oil' window into the laithe. One man tossed the huge forkfuls through while the other two stacked the hay in place inside. Just how that opening in the stone wall acquired its dialect name is not certain, but it has never been called by anything else. When the dray had been emptied the children were eager to scramble onto it again as the men were ready to go for the next load. The hay leading usually took place in the evening when Ernest had finished his day's butchering and his brother could spare time from his own work. Grace saw to it then that the strenuous efforts of the day were rewarded by a tasty, cooked supper in the house, to which the haymakers did full justice while resting their aching muscles at the same time.

Life at Coates was never dull, even in winter. In that age before the rectangular boxes made their appearance in people's homes, families took pleasure from each other's company and made their own entertainment. On winter evenings board games were played on the house table. Ludo, snakes and ladders, and draughts were probably the most popular at Coates. Ernest and Alf were both good at draughts and would often have a few games together after the tea table was cleared and before Alf went home. Ernest would then play for a while with the older children before going down to the 'Fours' for a drink and a game of dominoes with the local men. He liked to be back home for nine o'clock, even so, to read the papers and hear the news on the wireless. Another of his relaxations was to study the atlas. He was very well informed on world geography and, had he been given the chance, would have liked to see more of the world for himself. 'South Africa: that's the country I'd like to go to,' he informed his wife one evening as he perused the atlas. Ernest, alas, never got the opportunity to see any country other than his own. He never even saw his own capital city. The fulfilment of his ambitions to travel had to be left to his children and grandchildren.

As a change from playing in their own home on winter evenings, Grace sometimes allowed them to go in turn round to her sister's house. Blanche seldom went very far from Coates on account of her health, but she was always good to the children and made them feel welcome. Consequently, they liked their Aunt Blanche and enjoyed going to her house. There, besides playing ludo and the other board games, they were initiated into card playing. Of all the various card games played, perhaps the most popular one was 'Newmarket', since that was actually played for ha'penny stakes. The fact that all money was returned to its original owners at the end of the evening did not lessen the enjoyment of the game. Another attraction which their aunt's house held for them was the piano. Blanche would often exercise her talent by playing songs to which they all sang, and other pieces which did not have words but were good to listen to, all the same.

There were two important national events during that decade which were of great interest to everyone. They were the Silver Jubilee of King George the Fifth and Queen Mary in 1935 and the Coronation of King George the Sixth and Queen Elizabeth in 1937. On both occasions tea was provided for all the villagers in the local schools, followed by sports and games outside. As was her custom whenever a tea was held in Oxspring School, Grace supplied the potted meat for everyone's sandwiches free of charge. She had earned for herself a good reputation over the years for that commodity, and Bramall's potted meat was much sought after. It formed the staple ingredient for all the Sunday School tea sandwiches for many years.

Grace's shopping trips to Barnsley during that period occurred only two or three times a year in spite of the improved bus services. One expedition was made some weeks before Whitsuntide to buy the new clothes that were needed. Grace would buy material for the girls' best dresses which would be worn at that special time and afterwards on Sundays and going-out occasions. The material would be taken to a dressmaker in Springvale who was called, appropriately enough, Mary Hemmings. Mary was quite lame but a good dressmaker. She made up the clothes to Grace's satisfaction from styles chosen from her pattern book. Mary had to make provision in her sewing for the dresses to be let out the year after, and was instructed by Grace to put deep hems round the bottom so they could be lengthened as the girls grew. This was because the dresses had to serve two years as best and a while longer for more regular wear. The girls' coats and hats and boys' suits were also renewed on alternate years only. Grace and her husband made their best clothes last several years, keeping them well brushed and cared for in between use.

The other main shopping excursion to Barnsley was just before Christmas. Grace and Mary Emma, sometimes accompanied by Myrtle, would take the children to see Santa Claus who was installed for a period in the reputable store of Butterfield's. They would then look around the various toys, games and books, so Grace could decide on what gifts to buy to supplement the ones already ordered through a local Christmas Club. As she could only afford time for the one shopping trip she had to be methodical and quick about it. Her system was to allow the children to look at the things on display which she thought suitable, then ask them what they would most like Santa Claus to bring. After telling them they might just get something of the kind if they were lucky, she urged them to go with Mary Emma to another part of the shop, ostensibly to look at something else, while she stayed behind to buy the hoped-for gifts.

September 1937 brought another happy event to Grace's life. Her family was further increased by the birth of her last child, thus proving true Doctor Masser's prediction of six years before. The latest arrival was another fine boy whom she named James Philip. The former name was after her father, though Philip was the one to be generally used. Grace was forty-four when her youngest son was born. She was still very active, energetic and alert. The rest of her family shared her delight at having a new baby brother.

Though her children were basically healthy, they did seem to catch most of the common childhood illnesses. Four of them were ill in bed at the same time when the mumps was prevalent. When anyone was confined to bed during cold weather, the necessity of putting fires in the bedroom meant extra work of carrying coal upstairs and taking down ashes. In common with most other children they suffered their share of cuts and grazes. The immediate treatment for such minor injuries then was to dab on iodine from a little bottle. Its application stained the skin a deep yellow and caused quite an acute stinging, but was looked on as a safeguard against infection. Even so, there were times when a wound 'went the wrong way', meaning it became inflamed and festering. The remedy then was to apply a piece of lint that had been dipped in boiling water and fasten it to the wound with a bandage. The heat was intended to draw out the infection. While the method was generally effective, it was important for the lint to be put on very hot, otherwise it did no good. Grace never wished to hurt her children if it could be avoided, even when in the process of trying to cure their ills. When applications of hot lint were necessary she took the trouble, therefore, to carry the equipment upstairs and put on the hot fomentation while the recipient was fast asleep. Though this sometimes caused a little subconscious flinching, the feeling of more intense pain was spared.

There were callers at Coates whose visits added variety to the routine of everyday life. In connection with the butchering business, the 'skin and bone man' came to take away those leftover products from the slaughtered animals which could be put to further use as leather, glue and fertilisers. Periodically the 'greaseproof paper man' called to replenish the stocks of that commodity so essential to the meat rounds. The thick, heavy packages were carried upstairs for storage in the small spare room until needed. On Mondays the children always looked forward to the visit of Mr Fred Haigh, the 'paraffin man', who came from Thurgoland. This was not because they were particularly interested in the paraffin he sold. The reason for his popularity was that, besides the lamp fuel, he had penny bars of Nestle's milk chocolate for sale too, all in their bright red wrappers. Grace allowed them each a bar of the chocolate. On Thursdays the greengrocer made his call. Mr Hobson, the first greengrocer, was succeeded after a time by Mr Gill. His horse-drawn cart carrying the fruit and vegetables came from Hoylandswaine and usually reached Coates after the children had returned from school. They accompanied her outside to the cart, their interest centred on a small, lidded box which Mr Gill kept beside his weighing scales. When he raised the wooden lid there was revealed a variety of attractive looking sweets that could be purchased for pennies and ha'pennies. Grace allowed the children only a ha'penny each to spend from Mr Gill's box; while she was buying her vegetables they had to make big decisions as to what to buy with their ha'pennies. At less frequent intervals a scissor-grinder travelled around Four Lane Ends and Coates. Grace or Mary Emma would take out any scissors that needed sharpening and he would do them while they waited.

There was another caller whose visits to begin with were not exactly welcomed. This man was known simply as 'the Jew'. It was not that Grace had anything against Jews in general. In fact her Doctor Masser was Jewish, and a very fine doctor he was. The salesman, however, was a persistent type who could be a nuisance when one was busy. He was a broad, fat man with a very big nose and wide, smiling mouth. At least, it was always smiling on his arrival at the door though not necessarily on his departure. The Jew had a bulging suitcase which he slapped down heavily onto the kitchen floor and quickly proceeded to open. Ignoring Grace's protests that she wasn't needing anything that day he remained undaunted. Still smiling, he began to lift up items of drapery from the case and enthused on how low the prices were considering the high quality of his goods. When an adamant refusal to buy was staunchly maintained, the smile on his face would fade, to be replaced by an expression of assumed pain and disgruntled frustration. The suitcase would be slowly closed, heaved laboriously from the kitchen floor and carried back along the lane with such dejection as if all the worries of the world were contained in it. When the customer did show an interest in something she really needed, the first price asked for was never the one finally paid over. It was common knowledge amongst all the local women that no one ever paid the Jew what he originally asked for. In fact he himself would have been surprised had anyone done so. The method to adopt was to 'banter him down' till the price was right, or even a little lower if one was in good bantering form. Sometimes the seller would close his case in apparent despair when agreement could not be reached and start to leave but, having actually crossed the yard, he would return and tell his customer she could have the article for the price she had named although she was robbing him. Grace, who never in her life robbed anyone, was often amused at the Jew's antics. She and her niece soon began to regard his visits as a bit of entertainment, apart from the challenge they presented over the prices. When a sale was amicably completed he would show pleasure by chatting to them a little about his wife and daughters. As they came to know him better they had to admit there was something likeable about the man. They felt sorry for him in a way, because that suitcase seemed so heavy as to sometimes cause him to pant. Grace's sister and her next door neighbour Hannah were very skilful in the business of bantering. Blanche usually came across to the farm after the Jew's visits to exchange news of what had been bought and how much each had managed to banter down. The only drawback in entertaining that particular caller was the time factor. It was all very well if one had ten minutes or longer to spare, but he could be something of a nuisance when one had urgent work to do. At such times he had to be prevented from banging down his suit-case, for once that was on the floor it wasn't easily moved.

One particular day Grace was giving the 'room' an extra good clean and didn't want to leave off until it was finished. They were half-expecting their caller with his pack, so before going into the other room Grace told her niece, 'If t'Jew happens to come today see if you can get rid of him. We can't be bothered with him when we're busy.' 'What shall I say to him?' questioned Mary Emma. This called for a little thought, since her aunt would not tell a deliberate falsehood. The Christian principles that Sunday School and her parents' teaching had laid down for her when young remained with her throughout her life. After a moment's deliberation a solution presented itself, however. 'Just tell him I'm not here, which will be true because I shall be in there,' Grace exclaimed triumphantly, indicating the other room where she was going to be working. Some time later she was on hands and knees cleaning the room floor, her mind entirely on the job at hand, when she heard Mary Emma's voice speaking to someone in the kitchen. The door was slightly ajar and catching the words 'gone to Penistone', Grace thought it was someone seeking her husband, as he had in fact gone there. Pushing the door wide open she called across the house to her niece, 'Who is it, Mary Emma?' As she did so,

the Jew's grinning face looked back at her from the kitchen. 'Ah, I see you!' he called exultantly, taking in the situation and no doubt realising that a deliberate attempt had been made to avoid him. Mary Emma was overcome with embarrassment and shame at being found out in a lie. She was a basically truthful girl but loyal to her aunt too. At the Jew's insistence of wanting to know Grace's exact whereabouts she had felt compelled to provide her with a definite destination to make her reply sound more convincing. Thinking quickly, on the spur of the moment, Penistone seemed the ideal excuse for

'Who is it, Mary Emma?'

the imaginary absence. Though the message that his presence was unwelcome was plain, it was not sufficient to deter the caller, who had probably become hardened to similar rebuffs during his years as a salesman. He appeared neither hurt nor offended but regarded the two blushing faces before him with great good humour, his own broad countenance wreathed in smiles as he proceeded to undo his pack. While that particular visit did cause them much embarrassment at the time, it was one that Grace and Mary Emma recalled with amusement later on as they saw the funny side of the situation.

On Christmas mornings the first caller at Coates Farm was Jack Langley, a boy from Four Lane Ends. Grace always welcomed Jack as the 'letter-in' of their Christmas at the farm. He was the most suitable boy in the immediate locality for that important job, having the dark hair required and a clear voice with which to sing 'While Shepherds' and announce good wishes for the festive season. Jack always arrived early, usually while the children were still in bed examining their gifts from Santa Claus. After his singing he was invited into the house and, being the first person to cross over the threshold, was rewarded with a silver sixpence and a mince pie. For Grace and her family, Jack's voice was an essential part of their Christmas happiness during those years. Other singers came too, a little later. Some of them were girls. They were all welcomed and given threepence each and a mince pie. One year a girl arrived before Jack but she had to wait in the yard until the boy had been to perform the letting-in. On New Year's mornings the ceremony was repeated. In fact it was regarded that letting in the New Year properly was even more important than letting in Christmas. Grace still held the old traditional belief that, unless a dark-haired male from outside one's own family was first to cross the threshold on New Year's morning, bad luck was likely to ensue throughout the year. Such superstitions, passed down from one generation to another, were only slow to die in country households like theirs.

Generally speaking, those years of the thirties were securely happy ones for Grace, despite the hard daily toil and struggle to look after her family. Her husband was with them, working hard to provide the things he could best afford and which, in his opinion, mattered most. She was so engrossed in their own little community and its everyday doings that, unlike her husband, she did not at first pay too much attention to the international news which came over their wireless. Wars in Spain and Abyssinia seemed far away and did not affect them. Yet, by the time the wireless was four years old, she, Mary Emma and the oldest children were listening to it along with Ernest and Alf.

They listened with some apprehension as the name of Adolf Hitler was spoken with increasing frequency. It was rumoured there might even be another war because Hitler, the German leader, had taken land from other countries and was wanting still more. Grace, recalling vividly how her brother and his friends had cheerfully gone off to the Great War in 1914, exclaimed in disbelief, 'They said that was a war to end wars. Surely there won't be another one.'

The year of 1939 began happily enough for the people at Coates, yet that spring and summer were to be the last in the old familiar order of things. It was not merely because the unlooked-for war with Germany was actually declared in that year. Though 1939 could be regarded as the end of an era by the nation as a whole in view of the many changes that would follow, it also marked the sad ending of a chapter in Grace's personal life. Those months that saw the beginning of a second war were the last in which she proudly helped her husband prepare for his hawking rounds, the last in which she polished up his black boots and leggings, and tied the smoothly starched and ironed white apron strings behind his back. Before another summer came to Coates, Ernest's well-loved figure would no longer be seen hurrying across the yard between house and shop. No more would he enquire after the children's progress at school, play them a friendly game of draughts, and switch on the nine o'clock news. To his family's sorrow he would have left Coates Farm.

CHAPTER 17

Years of the Second World War

FOR THIRTY-ONE YEARS Ernest Bramall had not failed to deliver his customers' meat on Fridays and Saturdays. During the winters he had sometimes suffered from heavy colds but had stoically carried on working even though his wife begged him to stay at home. Alf, in his twenties, had been with them since leaving school and was well trained in the business, but Ernest still felt he had to do the main rounds himself. He often worked when he was unfit. There was the time too, when he slipped on the ice while delivering meat to customers on Penistone's Station Row. Falling heavily to the ground, his shoulder was dislocated. Doctor Masser, who was quickly summoned to the spot, needed all his strength and skill to get the shoulder back in place. Ernest, fully conscious, suffered agonisingly while it was being done. Yet, when the doctor's work was finished, he carried on as usual to complete his round.

He had always thought of himself as a strong, tough man who could shrug off ailments. The fact that he had indeed been physically strong and healthy caused him some frustration when signs appeared to indicate he was no longer so. The trouble began with a tight feeling in his chest which was diagnosed as heart and circulatory disorder. The doctor told Ernest bluntly that he couldn't cure him, but that if he rested and took things easily he could live a long time. He also ordered him to eat less meat. Ernest was more than a little dismayed at the news. Grace, offering her consolation, told him it was all the rigours and hardship of the years that were wearing him out. She maintained it was the effects of thirty years' work without rest that was catching up on him, and he should do as the doctor said by taking things easy. This he found difficult to do, it being totally against his habit to be idle. After a while, however, his wife's persuasion, added to his own tiredness and shortness of breath, compelled him to rest to some degree.

The twelve-year-old Norman assisted Alf on the Saturday round and did farm work mornings and evenings, but when Alf took a holiday Ernest was forced, with great effort, to resume work again because no one else knew the rounds.

The weight he had gained during the last years was said to be detrimental to his condition. When he lost three stones in as many months, the doctor claimed it was all to the good, but Grace was apprehensive at its happening so quickly, especially since he looked ill and seemed so much weaker. As 1939 ended and 1940 began the doctor's reports were not optimistic, but even then Grace did not lose hope that her husband might eventually recover. He was up and around much of the time, though any undue exertion did affect his breathing. He continued to administer his business for a time after he was forced to relinquish the physical work involved, and continued to interest himself in reading and listening to the wireless. The main news during those winter weeks was of the war between Russia and Finland, which ended in March.

Then, at the beginning of April, came the shattering blow that dashed Grace's hopes. Her husband suffered a stroke that took the use of his right side. Only then did she accept the doctor's words and forewarn her children that they would soon be fatherless. She had previously kept the serious nature of his condition from them, but realised that the knowledge could no longer be withheld. Seeing her husband in almost helpless state, and knowing he was being taken from them, was a hard burden for Grace to bear. Some of her relatives and neighbours offered support by staying with the patient during the nights, so as to allow her to get a little sleep. Willis and Jessie came down in turn from Willow Lane, and Ernest's sister Hilda from the Coates Lane farm of Berry Moor. Though Grace slept little during those nights, their presence gave a good measure of comfort. Throughout the daytime the faithful Mary Emma took over more of the household tasks to enable her aunt to spend more time with her dying husband. The children were at school, of course, except for Philip. At two and a half he was too young to understand fully what was happening, and would cheerfully trudge upstairs to offer his father grapes.

On one of those days of heavy oppression Ernest, knowing his end was not far off, had requests to make to his children. He asked the eldest ones to look after their mother and told eight-year-old John to be a good boy. John was the most mischievous one of the family, who occasionally got into boyish trouble. At another time, when Grace alone was with him, he had a message for her too. 'I've always thought the world of you,' were the golden words she treasured to her own life's end.

Ernest lived for two weeks after the stroke, conscious and coherent for most of the time, but outside events no longer held interest for him. As Hitler's armies were surging into Denmark and Norway during those early April days of 1940, he was steadily slipping away from life. As the sixteenth day of the month dawned, so did Ernest's life come to a close as he passed away peacefully in sleep. His wife and brother were both at his bedside, having kept an all-night vigil. The first thing of which Grace became aware at that moment of her loss was that it was snowing. As she looked up from the bed and across to the window, she felt bemused to see it flurrying against the panes in a brief, yet sudden, shower.

Later that morning the deaf but kindly Mrs Thompson, from the far end cottage, came across to the farm to give silent though efficient help. As she moved quietly about in the hushed, upstairs room, Grace was grateful for the gentle, caring manner she showed in doing what was needed. Four days later Ernest made his last, slow journey to Penistone to be buried with his little son Frank in the family grave at Stottercliffe cemetery. He was forty-eight when he died, but the doctor had told his wife that he had arteries like a man of seventy. Yet he had never looked old. His black hair showed no sign of grey and his teeth were still good even though he had never visited a dentist.

Grace did most of her weeping in private. Exercising her strength of will, she put on a brave face in front of the children. She reckoned that losing their father was enough, without her upsetting them further, so she tried to appear cheerful no matter what her inner feelings were. She determined to take her husband's place as far as was humanly possible, doing duty of both mother and father. The task she faced was a tremendous one. To bring up five children whose ages ranged from two to fifteen was not easy in itself. Added to that, the butchering business had to be carried on. Not for one moment did she entertain the idea of selling it. Ernest had spent a lifetime's work in building it into a thriving concern; it could almost be said that he had killed himself in the process. She would not lightly give it up. Although her sons were only young then, the day would surely come when one or more of them might be glad to take it over and follow in their father's footsteps in becoming butchers. That would be up to them, of course, but at least it was her duty to see they were given the chance. So, while still grieving inwardly, she forced herself to direct her energies to the work immediately at hand. Her general aim was to see that things at Coates Farm continued running as Ernest would have wished. He had always been methodical in the affairs of his business and, during the year of his illness, had given her more insight into the running of it. Because of their years of hard work and careful spending, the business was on a sound financial footing. Grace possessed enough intelligence and common sense to realise that it would only continue so as long as she carried on being careful and methodical, bearing in mind the words she often quoted, 'Fools and their money are soon parted.'

When her husband had been too ill to do the slaughtering, his brother Willis had rallied round to assist Alf, despite the pressures of his own work at Willow Lane. Ernest had still forced himself to Penistone's Monday market to buy the animals they required. As the war continued and meat rationing was enforced, slaughtering one's own animals was prohibited by law. Buying and selling in the cattle market ceased, so in one sense the butchering at Coates was made easier. Instead of the ritual of killing, sawing and cutting in the smelly, steamily unpleasant atmosphere of the shop, the meat was fetched, already killed, from Sheffield. It was ironic that the new controls were introduced just too late to allow Ernest the rest he needed. He actually attended the very last market before the controls were enforced in the following week, which was only a short time before his death. Grace often reflected that, had the war with its rationing come six months earlier, her husband might still be with them. At least he would have had chance to rest at home on Monday afternoons instead of dragging himself out to stand in a cold cattle market when he was unfit.

Under the new order of things the butcher's difficulty lay in sharing out the meat so that all the customers were fairly treated. The quantity allowed under the rationing system was far less than most people had been in the habit of buying. The large joints of beef which bigger families consumed on Sundays along with their Yorkshire pudding had to be considerably reduced in size. Farming families, and others engaged in heavy manual work, had been among the best meat customers, and having to curtail their orders so drastically was difficult for the butcher. Men doing heavy manual work were allowed a bigger ration of meat than those with lighter or sedentary jobs, but it still fell far short of what they had previously eaten. Though the farmers could kill a pig of their own now and then, they missed the amount of beef to which they had been accustomed. From that time those large, oval and oblong meat dishes which had graced the dinner tables of many ordinary working families ceased to be in use. The years of war, its aftermath, and the changing way of life it brought about, caused those old meat dishes to become obsolete, to be viewed by a newer generation as museum pieces. Generally speaking, Ernest's customers had become better off by the end of the thirties. The district as a whole had recovered from the earlier depression as industrial jobs became plentiful at the new David Brown works in Penistone and Samuel Fox's steelworks in Stocksbridge. Consequently most people were able to afford more and better-quality meat, and the restrictions hit them hard to begin with.

In common with other butchers, Alf found it difficult to satisfy all the various customers. Not only were they restricted in quantity of meat, but also in choice. Out of the weekly allocation some people had, of necessity, to take the less palatable pieces which might otherwise have gone into the potted meat. It was a delicate job to ensure that these did not go too often into the same households, and that all customers got a fair turn at being able to choose what they wanted. Despite the shortage, there were still some very rough bits which would sell only as potted meat. Grace therefore continued to make it on Thursdays as before, though perhaps in less quantity.

The war years brought paperwork which had never been encountered before. Every household had to choose one particular butcher with whom to register. The meat counterfoils in each ration book belonging to the house had to be handed to the butcher, who then had to compile a register of all his customers. Information as to numbers of people registered, specifying children, adults, and manual workers, had to be forwarded to the appropriate authority so that the butcher's allocation could be assessed. At Coates the job of sorting out all the counterfoils into alphabetical order and compiling the register fell to Phyllis. It was something she enjoyed doing, and saved her mother the time. Grace had plenty of other things to attend to. There were forms to fill in concerning the meat received and sold. The coupons collected weekly by Alf on the rounds had to be checked and forwarded to the Food Office. Apart from coping with details of new administration, she made sure that the meat was delivered from a scrupulously clean van, and laundered Alf's smock and apron just as she had done her husband's. She always cared that the business should maintain the same high standards and good name it had had in Ernest's time.

Having no killing to do, and less meat to deal with, meant that Alf could manage fairly well with Norman's help. Though that boy was only twelve, he did not complain about having to work at weekends and evenings when his contemporaries were playing games of football and cricket. It was fortunate that he grew to like the work. On Saturday mornings Phyllis took out meat orders to houses in two outlying areas where to go by van would have been uneconomical. The walk across fields and lanes was a pleasant enough way to pass an hour or so, which was about the time it took. The fact that less meat was sold than formerly also meant there was less profit to be had. Grace had to continue to be careful in providing for the household. She received no widow's pension nor any other pension. Though Ernest had, with foresight, joined a scheme some time before to make provision for financial assistance, he had died too soon. Had he lived for a few more weeks he would have been in the scheme long enough for his widow to receive benefit. As it was, Grace struggled on bravely, showing sturdy independence by refusing to ask for anyone's help unless it was really necessary. The two or three years that followed her husband's death were, however, far from being happy ones. She had often to exercise great patience and tact in warding off the worries and feelings of insecurity she experienced through those difficult times. The fact that she held on tenaciously to the business for the sake of her children was at no little sacrifice.

In 1940 Grace's family, in common with all others, was accustomed to blacking out the windows at night in case enemy planes came over. Wardens walked around people's homes at regular intervals to check that the blackout curtains were adequate. If the merest chink of light showed outside the matter had to be speedily rectified. The gas masks which the children carried to school each day soon became as much a part of their equipment as their satchels and lunch bags. Philip, being only two, was not issued with the same type of mask as the other members of his family. His gas mask looked far more interesting and attractive because it had the shape of a Mickey Mouse. The older children regularly wore their gas masks during practice drills at school but, thankfully, were never called on to put them to a real test. Besides the gas masks and ration books everyone was furnished with an identity card which showed the holder's name, address, date of birth and identification number.

The war certainly did seem much nearer as that year progressed. If there were some who had doubted Hitler's power to begin with, they were quickly made aware of it by June, when he over-ran most of Western Europe and forced the British withdrawal from France. Everyone who went to the cinema came to recognise the 'bulldog' figure of Winston Churchill and his inevitable cigar as he appeared continuously on the newsreels. Though Grace did not frequent the cinema, she became acquainted with his picture through the newspapers and his voice over the wireless as he made his inspiring broadcasts. Hitler, of course, was a familiar figure too, recognised by even the smallest child. The young ones were quick to believe, in those days, that everything German was bad. When boys engaged in mock battles it was usually the 'Germans' who finished up 'dead' on the floor while the British stood victoriously over them. They were encouraged in their beliefs by the boys' comic papers of the day which always portrayed German soldiers as cruel and arrogant, though often somewhat stupid too.

The first time that actual violence of the war came close to Coates Farm was on the 12th of December 1940. On that Thursday evening the German bombers attacked Sheffield, some twelve miles away. Grace's eldest daughter was at an evening sewing class in Oxspring school when the air raid siren began its eerie wailing. The class was immediately called to a close and its members urged to hurry quickly home. Phyllis and her friends ran most of the way up Bower Hill. When they reached Four Lane Ends they could see that the sky over Sheffield was brightly lit by the fires resulting from incendiary bombs that had already been dropped. Grace was relieved to see her daughter back in the house with the rest of the family. Hardly had she joined them when they heard the loud, crumping noises of the heavy explosive bombs that were being unleashed on the city. In the farmhouse the feelings of fear were intense at the realisation of what was happening. Although they knew that Sheffield was the target, it was quite possible that a stray bomb could land on their house if the aiming wasn't accurate. Grace said they had better all sit down quietly until it was over, since they could do nothing about it. Her apparent calmness caused them to do just that. They kept to their seats, almost too petrified to speak, for what seemed ages, while the explosions continued to wreak their relentless destruction. To that family at Coates the shattering bangs sounded much closer than they really were. At one stage the house windows shook and rattled as if they would break. When the bombers finally dispersed and Grace's family resumed normal activities, their thoughts turned to the people who lived in or nearer to Sheffield.

Next day they learned of the devastation caused by the bombs. One of the worst-hit places was the Moor, one of the main thoroughfares in the city centre. Most of the big departmental stores alongside the Moor were razed to the ground. Some folk reckoned that the long street had, from the air, been mistaken for the river, and large shops for the steelworks situated at each side. This could have been the case since, three nights later, the bombers returned to attack the steelworks.

Phyllis was again in Oxspring school with her friend Joan Fieldsend, attending the Sunday evening service, when the up-and-down tones of the siren dismally gave out warning of another impending attack. Once again the girls hurried up Bower Hill to sit with their families until the long, loud note of the 'all clear' reassured them that danger was past. Only on those two occasions did the Germans bomb Sheffield. There were other nights, however, when the ominous drone of massed aircraft seemed to come almost directly over Coates Farm. The tension felt by the people below was only relaxed when the noise receded, telling them the planes were going elsewhere, most likely to Liverpool. The time that elapsed before they were heard again on their homeward flight suggested such a distance had been covered, and reports received later confirmed that the assumptions had been correct.

With food restrictions in force, changes had to be made on the small farm at Coates as well as on larger farms. Butter could only be made for the family's own use, so less churning was done. Grace reared young calves then, so when there was a surplus of milk it was fed to them. At other times she mixed up powdered milk for their feeds. Usually she enjoyed tending the calves, but on one occasion received a nasty kick full in the face from one of them. The calf had a sore on its hind leg and, as she was bathing it, it suddenly struck out without warning. Blood poured from her nose, though luckily it was not broken.

In spring the chicken coops were set up in the croft as they had been before the war. There were six or seven, each containing a broody hen sitting on a dozen eggs. For three weeks the hens sat, only coming off the eggs briefly for food and water. When the chicks eventually hatched and grew, they helped to maintain the laying flock. Production of eggs was therefore kept up at the farm, but there were new regulations to be adhered to. The eggs could no longer be sold to private customers; instead, they had all to be sent to a packing station for further distribution, apart from those retained for family use.

The commodity that Grace missed most under the rationing system was sugar. She had always been in the habit of baking pies, cakes and other confectionery that used a considerable amount, not to mention the summer jam making which needed even more. The small quantity of sugar allowed on ration was insufficient for her to produce all the excellent fare they had previously enjoyed. Like everyone else, her family had to adapt to rather more austere living and be thankful that their situation was no worse. Though the rationing deprived them of many enjoyable things, no one was ever at the point of starvation. The food was adequate on the whole and people remained generally healthy, some even more so than before the war. Greater use was made of natural foods that were available, such as vegetables and fruit from gardens and hedgerows. Surplus fruit was bottled so that it could be eaten out of season. At Coates the blackberries were never allowed to go to waste, even though there was less sugar with which to sweeten them. One way of saving a little sugar for other purposes was to stop using it in drinks. Many people, including Grace's family, adopted this method, using instead the saccharin tablets that were available or merely taking their drinks unsweetened.

Less food was coming from abroad because there were fewer ships to transport it, some being deployed to carry armaments instead. Ships that did carry food were sometimes attacked, resulting in the cargo being lost. Maximum effort had therefore to be made to produce more food at home. Farmers were urged to plough up more land in order to grow bigger crops of corn and potatoes. Even the smaller farms such as Near Coates were approached by someone from the War Agricultural Executive asking for land to be ploughed. As an incentive to encourage farmers to grow more food, substantial payments were offered. For growing potatoes, ten pounds an acre could be had. While this did seem a generous sum, Grace knew that, on their few acres, ploughing up land would not bring much financial gain in spite of the monetary grant. She hadn't even a plough to begin with. Near Coates was essentially a grassland farm, geared to the needs of the butchering business, and arable crops had never entered into the scheme of things. She had none of the equipment necessary for the planting and harvesting of corn and potatoes, and knew that the cost of paying neighbours for the loan of theirs would cancel out most of the profits. Nevertheless she was anxious to do her share towards the war effort and agreed to have a few acres ploughed. Potatoes were grown, and enough corn to warrant a half-day's threshing.

On the bigger farms that already had the machinery and horses to pull it, the farmers were quite pleased with the ten pounds offered for each acre of potatoes grown. Yet, some time later, when the food crisis was past, the situation was reversed. Instead of receiving payment, the farmers had to make payment to the Potato Board for the privilege of growing potatoes. One Oxspring farmer wryly remarked, 'Aye, they reckoned to be gi'in' us summat and naah they're taken' it all back ageean.'

At the time of crisis when the extra ploughing-up was in full swing, farmers had to notify the authorities as to the size of their potato acreage so that the grant to which they were entitled could be assessed and duly paid. In case any of them was tempted to add on a half-acre or so, a man appointed for the purpose went round checking up on the areas. The method of measuring was simple. In striding out the length and breadth of the potato piece a stride was recognised as equivalent measure to a yard. At least one local farmer erred to some degree when declaring the area of his potato piece; whether or not he did so intentionally is not known. The official who came to check his statement was a big, well-made man. After striding easily around the field and making quick calculations, he insisted that the area of potatoes grown was actually smaller than the farmer had reckoned. The payment to be received would therefore be less than he had at first expected. Naturally the farmer felt a little aggrieved. When he told his neighbours about it soon afterwards he said defensively, 'It were yon chap made it out to be less than wor it is 'cos he took such long strides.'

The gardens belonging to Coates cottages all produced as many potatoes and other vegetables as possible in those days of 'Dig for Victory'. Arthur Illingsworth in the middle cottage was particularly energetic where his garden was concerned, though he was in his seventies. He had been a keen gardener even before the food crisis, and enjoyed being out of doors. Still alert and active, both physically and mentally, his face was fresh and healthy-looking, and his one good eye was keenly blue. Mr Illingsworth had a greenhouse in which he grew tomatoes and, during those years, sold produce to passers-by from a small hut he erected at the side of his garden nearest the road. The clatter of his clogs was a familiar sound to all at Coates as they clapped on the flagstones when he returned to the house for meals after working in the garden. Sometimes his daughter Hannah's voice was heard too, good-naturedly admonishing him with 'Don't bring any muck in t'house father.' Hannah was a fastidious person who had plenty of dirt to contend with, since her husband worked in the pit and miners returned home then covered in dust and grime. In spite of this and the fact that they had only cold water on tap, the Illingsworth house was scrupulously clean. Arthur had worked in the pit too until he retired, although he had lost an eye in the course of his work and wore a glass one in its place. In his young days, work at the coal face had been extremely hard. He was not entirely teasing when, with an eye on his son-in-law, he made the remark, 'Colliers today don't know they're born. They don't know what it is to work wi' a pick an' shovel in t'two-foot-six like we had to do.' A gleeful little chuckle escaped him as he finished the information and his knowing expression took on a certain smugness, as if he alone held the secrets of a collier's life in those earlier days. The words, spoken with some conviction, conveyed to his listeners that he felt a sense of pride in having belonged to an élite band of men who did real men's work in their day. Arthur Illingsworth continued to be active in his garden for many years after the war, living to a good old age.

During the war, foods such as oranges and bananas were in very scarce supply. Bananas were only rarely seen; when they were, they could only be obtained for the young children by showing their own ration books. When a limited quantity of oranges occasionally found its way into the market, the usual procedure was for two oranges to be sold to anyone buying a bagful of cabbage first. Queuing became the order of the day at such times, and people became accustomed to it. They soon learned to expect having to queue for certain things if they wanted them badly enough. In the towns a limited amount of confectionery for sale attracted long queues. Women had to join the queue early and wait for a long time to stand a chance of getting any. Even then, it could not be guaranteed that there would still be a cake or pie left by the time one's turn came. They would have found it quicker and less tiring to stay at home and make their own confectionery if only they had had the sugar with which to sweeten it. There were disappointments of course when, after queuing for a long time, the food ran out before everyone had got a share. Yet people got used to such disappointments just as they got used to having to stand on overcrowded buses and trains. Generally speaking, the local folk did not grumble about these inconveniences. They realised that there were people in other places who were suffering far worse. If anyone did begin to moan they were usually checked by somebody else's cheerful reminder of, 'Don't you know there's a war on?'

Quite early in the war the 'safe', rural areas of the country were accepting child evacuees from London and the more vulnerable parts of southern England. Oxspring, Penistone, and all the surrounding country districts came into the 'safe' category, and families played their part in looking after children who had been forced to leave their own homes and parents behind. The houses at Coates, however, had no spare room to accommodate evacuees. Grace's family occupied all the beds they possessed, as did the Pursegloves and Illingsworths too. The Thompsons had space, but Mrs Thompson's deafness would have been too much of a handicap where being responsible for children was concerned. At Tunnel Top two brothers were given a good wartime home on Walter Bramall's farm. They were twins named Tony and Donald Doody, aged about nine, who came from Shoreham in Kent.

Walter and his wife Lucy had no children of their own, and took a great liking to the boys. They were a bright, lively pair who soon made friends with the local children, in particular with Willis Bramall's son, George. Living on neighbouring farms, they made the journeys to and from school together and were in close association at other times. Grace's son John, who was also about the same age, became friendly with them too. The twins adapted well to life on the farm, so much so that, when the war was over, Donald elected to stay on at Tunnel Top instead of returning to Shoreham with his brother. He accepted Walter Bramall's offer of regular farm work on leaving school and remained with them for some years, looking on the cheerful, kindly Lucy almost as a second mother. Contact was always well maintained with his own mother, however. Mrs Doody paid visits to them at Tunnel Top and welcomed Lucy and Walter to her home.

At Four Lane Ends Mrs Wray, who kept the small corner shop, took in evacuees too, one of them being a chubby, ginger-haired little boy of about four, called Pat Ives. It was typical of that good woman that she was willing to accept other people's children into her home. Her family was grown up and had their own homes but, besides her elderly husband, she had a semi-invalid lodger in her household and two child relatives for whom she cared, since they were motherless. The addition of an evacuee did not cause her any harassment. Mrs Wray invariably appeared calm and pleasant when she served her customers in the shop, despite her many family commitments. It sometimes happened that one of the young ones had urgent need of her while she was in the shop. Where the situation was such that she could not immediately attend to the child's wants, she showed patience rather than annoyance. If she was in the process of dispensing treacle, for example, the calls of 'Auntie Phoebe' were met with 'Just a minute, dear, I won't be long.' Mrs Wray sold her treacle from huge glass jars which she held in both hands while tilting the required amount into the customer's jar. Once she had started pouring that sticky commodity she had to continue no matter what were the demands from the living room. They had to wait until, with deft expertise born of long experience, Mrs Wray uptilted the heavy jar again, twisting it around at the same time so the flow of treacle ended inside the jar and not outside.

One year, the day of the Sunday School Sing was exceptionally hot. By the time the children had sung their hymns in Oxspring village and toiled up Bower Hill in overpowering heat, some of the younger ones and those of lesser stamina would have found it difficult to stand and sing at Four Lane Ends for another half-hour as was the custom had it not been for Mrs Wray. She had anticipated the children's thirst and tiredness, so made copious quantities of cooling drinks from the lemon crystals she sold in her shop. When the scholars reached Four Lane Ends she dispensed the refreshing lemonade amongst them and, so revived, they were enabled to continue singing with renewed enthusiasm.

When Flora Purseglove fell off her bike, as she tried to take the corner too quickly after coming downhill from the Jockey, it was into Mrs Wray's house that she was led. The good woman attended to her cuts and bruises, and let her rest a while until she was fit to go home. Mrs Wray was quite a big woman whose motherly, bespectacled figure, unhurried presence, and willingness to partake of a little conversation while she was serving customers, were well liked by the people around Four Lane Ends. Grace Bramall once said of her, 'If anybody deserves a place in Heaven, it's Mrs Wray. Nothing's ever too much trouble for her.' At the same time there were other folk saying the same thing about Grace. She and Mrs Wray had much in common. Though they were both busy enough with work of their own, they often made time to help others too, which indicates that there may be truth in the old saying, 'If you need something doing, ask one of those who've got most to do.'

The year after her husband died, Grace's brother George appeared in the yard one day, holding by the hand his small, three-year-old daughter who looked rather forlorn. 'I've brought our Marie for thee to look after,' he announced without any preamble. 'We're just abaht bet up yonder.' George Spenceley was an able, industrious man in his own sphere of work, but was not skilled in domestic matters. 'Up yonder' referred to High Lea, his farm just off the Penistone Bypass road a half-mile further along from Tunnel Top. The long hours he had to put in on the farm did not allow him any time to help his wife, even had he so wished. On the contrary, it was Elsie who often interrupted her housework to assist him outside. She had a seventeen-year-old girl from Thurgoland who lived in with them and helped with their four young children. Her name was Elsie too. She was a willing, cheerful girl who, despite the continual hard work, enjoyed being with the Spenceleys. Normally they managed quite well and things at High Lea ran smoothly, but when the two Elsies both became incapacitated at the same time, George was somewhat bewildered. His wife had leg trouble which necessitated her resting it. To ensure that she did this, the doctor had ordered her to bed for a time. The young Elsie's trouble began in the leg too, but proved to be more serious. She had later to go into hospital where, despite an operation, she was not cured.

The Spenceleys were greatly saddened when she died before reaching her twenties, not only because they had lost a good worker but also because they felt she had been one of their family. This ultimate outcome of tragedy was not of course foreseen on the day George brought his daughter to Coates. He told Grace that he could cope with the two boys who were of school age, but Marie was an active child who was at an age when she could get into danger unless she was constantly supervised. It was more than he was able to do besides all his farm work.

With her brother in such obvious dilemma and her sister-in-law, for whom she had a great liking, helpless in bed, Grace would not have refused him what he asked, even though he brought the child without giving her any forewarning. Little Marie stayed with her aunt willingly, while a relieved George hurried back to his farming duties at High Lea. When John came home from school that afternoon he wanted to know who the small girl was. Until then he was not really acquainted with that particular cousin, so his mother decided to try out his reaction to a little teasing on her part. To his question Grace replied seriously, 'It's a little evacuee they've brought us.' It was immediately obvious that John did not relish the prospect of an evacuee in his house. In some agitation he urged his mother to, 'Tell 'em to fetch her back again.' When Grace explained who Marie really was and why she was staying with them, John accepted the situation without more ado.

At one time Grace helped a poor family who lived in Bower Hill by baking pies for them from gooseberries growing in their garden. The mother of the family had died and there was no one else to make them pies, cakes, or much of anything else for that matter. She sometimes took other food, too, and clothes for the children. About the same period she had friends whose son had to spend a long time in a sanatorium at Blackpool. Every week, when they went to visit him, they took with them a Victoria sandwich cake that Grace had made specially for him. Whether or not the sandwich assisted in his recovery we do not know, but happily the youth did get well eventually and has lived a normal life ever since.

Then there was the old lady who kept dogs. She was not a native of Four Lane Ends, or even of Yorkshire, but had come in from elsewhere. No one ever knew from just where because she was something of a mystery woman who did not tell anything. She came daily to Coates Farm for milk, but never revealed details of her previous whereabouts to Grace, though she spoke sociably enough. Her manner of speaking suggested that she had had a good upbringing and probably seen better days. What always remained a mystery was how and why she had allowed herself to fall into a state of personal neglect. She was so dirty that folk did not want to go near her. Her only friends seemed to be the small black Scottish terriers she kept. Despite the appalling squalor of her house, Grace went into help when she was ill and in need of someone's attention. After living at Four Lane Ends for a few more years she decided to move on. No one ever knew to which place she went exactly, though she did tell the people at Coates Farm that it was somewhere in Sussex. Grace assisted her with the packing prior to departure, since the woman had implied the job was too overwhelming to tackle alone. Having helped her, Grace could understand why. Her house was in such chaotic state that the sorting out and organising of packing taxed even Grace's mental and physical energies.

Rattling along to Holmfirth

During the war years, wallpaper was in such short supply as to be almost unobtainable. At Coates they had been in the habit of renewing the wallpaper regularly, doing a room each year in its turn, so that nothing ever looked too old or shabby. Because of the scarcity, the room whose turn it was to receive attention had not been done at the usual time. When she felt the work was becoming too long overdue Grace determined that, war or no war, she would try to obtain some wallpaper if at all possible. After making exhaustive enquiries she at last heard of a little shop at Holmfirth that had somehow acquired a limited amount of that precious commodity. Losing no time at all she and Mary Emma went into action. Though the small town of Holmfirth was well outside her usual area of shopping, being about eight miles away on the far side of Penistone, they made the journey which involved travel by two different buses. At Penistone they changed from the Yorkshire Traction onto a Baddeley Brother's bus, which plied between that town and Holmfirth. In those days the Baddeley buses had the local reputation of being very uncomfortable. It was said that their name was quite appropriate because, as one man put it, 'If you weren't badly when you got on that bus you'd be sure to feel badly when you got off it.' In fairness to those early buses it should be said that the route to Holmfirth was not in keeping with a smooth ride whatever the vehicle. The fact that Baddeley's bus rattled along, shaking and jolting its passengers in the process, was not entirely the fault of the bus. There were many ups and downs, twists and bends in the road to Holmfirth and its surface was far from being smooth. The rattling of the bus could have also been partly due to its travelling half-empty. Being further away and more 'off the beat' than Barnsley, people around Penistone tended to go to Barnsley rather than to Holmfirth. Grace had always thought of Holmfirth as a remote, almost inaccessible place to reach, but the knowledge that wallpaper might be there when Barnsley had none suddenly gave the further place a higher status in her eyes. She was more than willing to endure the discomforts of Baddeley's or any other bus which would take her there. Being eager to accomplish her mission, she disregarded the inconveniences of the journey. In the event she and Mary Emma did achieve- their goal. The shop in Holmfirth still had what they wanted. Travelling back to Penistone they probably never noticed the shaking of the bus as, armed with sufficient rolls of that precious wallpaper, their thoughts were on how nice that certain room would look when the paper was put to use.

When people found it impossible to obtain wallpaper in spite of prolonged searching, they resorted to another method of refurbishing their rooms. The general trend was to 'stipple' the walls. Instead of taking off the existing wallpaper, it was brushed over with a coloured wash onto which an all-over pattern was pressed or dabbed by means of a sponge. The method was simple and easy to carry out. Though only regarded as an enforced substitute for the traditional practice of re-papering, stippling did result in clean, attractive-looking walls. It was a method adopted by many folk during the war years. At Tunnel Top the old, but still active, James Spenceley stippled one of his rooms quite unaided, and even Grace had to admit that it looked very well.

Mary Emma and Alf, whose working lives from leaving school had been spent at Coates Farm, had started going out together some years before the war. In 1941 they were married. Mary Emma did not have a long white wedding dress. In that time of austerity clothes were rationed as well as food, and the number of clothing coupons allowed restricted one's buying even if money didn't. There were very few brides then who did wear the traditional long dress. Mary Emma looked very nice, all the same, in a shorter dress of powder blue, which could be worn afterwards for 'dressed-up' occasions. 'After their marriage she and Alf lived, to begin with, in one of the terraced houses at the far end of Bird Lane, not far from the Pinfold. Having worked with her aunt Grace for thirteen years, Mary Emma relinquished her duties at Coates Farm. Alf continued to do the butchering for another two years. He then took the tenancy of a small farm on the Copster road and devoted all his time to it. Grace's eldest son, Norman, continued the business at Coates. He was sixteen, just as his father had been when he took over from his father. The big difference was that Norman's father was not there to advise him; he was helped by his mother instead. Soon afterwards they engaged a young Four Lane Ends boy who was leaving school to do some of the farm jobs and assist in the meat deliveries. To Norman fell the problem of cutting up and sharing out the rations to the customers.

In the summer of 1942 Grace had to go into hospital again. The trouble was similar to that which had occurred eight years earlier. She had another rupture which needed an operation. Unlike the first time, she decided not to spend money on nursing home care. Having the family's upbringing to consider, she felt it would soon be needed for their benefit. It would have been a different matter if Ernest were alive to support them. Part of her savings was set aside to pay for her eldest daughter's college course, as there were no student grants then. In encouraging Phyllis to train for the teaching profession, she was fulfilling one of her husband's wishes, but it did mean sacrificing other things. Grace was always willing to forgo personal comfort for the sake of her children, so instead of going into a nursing home she decided on the Royal Infirmary in Sheffield, where the cost was considerably less. She had the operation a few weeks before Phyllis began her college training. The girls kept house during the two weeks when their mother was in hospital, though they did not make any bread or potted meat. In the infirmary, life was rather cheerless under wartime conditions. Though her operation was successfully carried out, Grace suffered discomfort from a sore back which she attributed to having to lie for a long time on a hard mattress. The nursing staff was rather depleted just then, so the patients could only receive minimal attention. At night the ward seemed airless and oppressive, the high windows being shut and covered over with the heavy blackout curtains demanded by law. That stay in hospital was far from being like a holiday, and Grace was only too pleased to be back at Coates Farm.

During the years of the war, extra coal was obtained from open-cast workings. In fields down Coates Lane and Bird Lane outcropping took place, which indirectly enabled Grace to earn a little extra money for herself. One day an executive from the workings arrived at the farmhouse door to enquire if there was anywhere around Four Lane Ends where he could buy a mid-day meal. He was a Manchester man who had obtained lodgings in Barnsley while he was working on the outcrop site, but wanted a hot dinner if possible near to the workings. He asked Grace if she knew of anyone who might be able to oblige him. Grace did not, but immediately volunteered to cook his dinners herself. That was only the beginning. Soon she was making meals for other officials too who were engaged in the coal outcrop's administration. For half-a-crown she provided a substantial three-course dinner. The men were highly appreciative of her excellent cooking, so much so that, when they wanted to celebrate a special occasion some time later, they asked if she would make them an evening dinner at the farm. The celebration was to include other business associates and their wives too, so making quite a large party. Yet, nothing daunted, Grace acceded to the request and accommodated them all in the house. To her previous query as to what they would like to eat, one of them had replied, 'Oh, please make us some of your meat and potato pie, with that nice crispy crust.' She had gained an especially good reputation for that particular dish and was happy to oblige. It gave her satisfaction to see how her meals were enjoyed and to know that the money earned by her efforts would be put to good use. Providing the meals meant that she and her family often forfeited their own meat rations, since the allocation seldom exceeded the basic quantity allowed for the customers. Fortunately they still kept a pig for themselves and had enough eggs and milk, so they did not suffer unduly.

In common with other places up and down the country, a certain amount of black-market trading went on in their area during that time of food control. Shop keepers and meat hawkers alike knew their main aim was to satisfy the customers. If they didn't, those customers would quickly change their patronage to a retailer who did. Loss of trade could lead to one's being forced out of business altogether. So rules had to be broken in order to cling onto one's livelihood. It sometimes happened that a butcher's allocation of meat actually fell short of the amount to which he was entitled. In such case he would have found it impossible to supply all his customers with even their bare rations, had he not accepted a little unauthorised meat from a dealer, or resorted to killing an animal himself on the quiet.

To help their meat situation at Coates, Grace bought a second-hand sausage machine. It was manually operated, of course. She obtained a recipe and the necessary ingredients with which to make sausage. They included soya meal and rusks to mix in with the meat available and 'rops', which were the cleaned intestines of animals and would become the sausage skins. The rops were fitted over a spout on the machine and became filled as the handle was turned. The sausage was a popular addition to the potted meat and probably helped in the promotion of good custom. Another factor that was contributory to the healthy continuity of the business was the loyalty of their regular, long-standing customers. Families who had traded with Ernest and Dyson through two generations and received good service throughout the years were content to trade with Ernest's son too, since they continued to be served with courtesy and consideration. They knew the young butcher was keen to give satisfaction in spite of the rationing difficulties and having to carry on without a father.

Amid the many changes and innovations brought about by the war, one thing that excited great curiosity and some amusement at Four Lane Ends was the appearance of American jeeps with their coloured occupants speeding through the crossroads. Most local people had never, until then, encountered at first hand anyone with black or brown skins so, to begin with, those servicemen from across the Atlantic were objects of wonder, especially to the children. As time went on and they were frequently seen, not only as they hurtled along in their jeeps but also in Penistone pubs, they were accepted as part of the wartime scene. A large number of these coloured Americans was housed in a camp at Scout Dyke, just outside Penistone on the Huddersfield road, so the bypass route including the Jockey, Four Lane Ends and Copster was used by them a good deal when travelling to and from their billet.

The function of these overseas servicemen was to take over work already begun by the Royal Air Force. That was to transport loads of bombs to and from the dumps which were sited in the remoter areas of the parish. Unlike the R.A.F., the Americans were mechanised in their methods of stacking up the piles of bombs. Whereas the former had lifted and passed up the bombs by hand, the latter used ladders with roller rungs which did the lifting for them in half the time. This was typical of the Americans, who regarded speed as an essential part of life.

The speed of their jeeps certainly caused the Four Lane Ends people to

'Wanna lift, Pop?'

stare in amazement. Never before had they witnessed vehicles going so fast through the crossroads. Grace and her family were highly amused one day when her father actually had a ride in one of those jeeps. He came into their house laughing but still half-bewildered as he related to them his experience. It appeared that he had walked to Thurgoland that afternoon from his house at Tunnel Top, in order to tend the graves. As he was walking back along the Copster road the sudden loud noise of a vehicle screeching to an abrupt halt alongside caused him to turn his head in that direction. Two grinning black faces looked at him from the jeep, one of them enquiring genially, 'Wanna lift Pop?' As he spoke he opened the door invitingly and made room for him to sit beside them Although James Spenceley was in his middle seventies, the spirit of adventure was not dead within him for, after only slight hesitation, he accepted their offer of a lift and climbed into the jeep. Hardly had the door closed than they were off in such haste that caused James to clutch his cap as his head jerked suddenly backwards. It seemed to him they flew rather than drove along the Copster road. In no time at all the brakes were squealing to a stop by Travellers Inn, where James had asked to be put out. The men got out with him and, giving the vehicle a brief inspection, one remarked to the other, 'Gee, she's red hot.' Relating this to his daughter, James commented that it was not surprising if it kept up such a pace all day. What a contrast such mode of transport presented to the old waggonette in which he had travelled that same road more than forty years earlier.

Besides gaining a reputation for fast driving their jeeps, those Americans were considered by many folk in and around Penistone to be fast in off-duty activities too. They frequented the Rose and Crown Inn mostly, where they quickly made acquaintance with some of the local unmarried girls, not to mention a few who were married but whose husbands were away in the forces.

For security reasons the areas in which the bomb dumps were sited were closed to the general public at that time. Local farmers, and anyone else who needed to use those small country roads near the bombsites, could obtain passes which enabled them to go through the area. Guards were posted by the Americans to ensure that no unauthorised person entered the forbidden territory. There was one incident, however, that caused a few laughs at their expense. A Hunshelf farmer by name of Gerald Battye, having spent an evening at Greenmoor's Rock Inn, was returning to his farm on the Stocksbridge side of the hill. He did not possess a pass, because he lived out of the area. That evening he had been unable to get a lift home so, being compelled to walk, decided to take the shortest way to his house, which happened to be through the guarded area of the bomb dumps. Whether his sojourn at the Rock had rendered him oblivious to the fact that he hadn't a pass, or whether he was consciously flouting the law for the sake of convenience, is not certain. In either event his reaction to the challenge was commendable. When he found himself confronted by a big, dark-faced figure with a gun at the ready, demanding to see his pass, Gerald fumbled in his pocket. Drawing out a piece of paper which was actually one of Goldthorpe's corn bills, he waved it at the guard nonchalantly, who, without even inspecting it, muttered quickly, 'Okay, okay,' and hurriedly motioned him to proceed. Such was the security. If Gerald had been a master spy those guards would have been none the wiser.

One security measure that was generally adopted all over the country was the removal of signposts showing place names. This happened quite early in the war when threat of enemy invasion was considered a possibility. Even after the Battle of Britain, when that danger had receded, the signs were still absent for the duration. This never adversely affected the local communities, since people did not travel away from home in their own cars merely for pleasure. In any case, the rationing of petrol was barely enough to allow vehicles to be run for business purposes, so the absence of directions to far away places caused no hardship.

On that wartime scene one thing that struck a lighter note, at least as far as the people at Coates were concerned, was the evening broadcasting from Germany by William Joyce who, when the war was over, was executed for treason. Generally known as Lord Haw-Haw, the man's aim was to frighten the British and undermine their morale by false propaganda. Through exaggeration, distortion of facts, and sheer fabrication, he emphasised the superiority and strength of the Germans, implying that the British forces would soon be annihilated and their country conquered. The broadcasts always began with the words, 'Germany calling, Germany calling . . .,' but if those serious tones were meant to strike fear into the minds of the listeners, they had the opposite effect. Listening to 'Haw-Haw' was accepted as a bit of light entertainment, for people judged the propaganda to be mostly lies. They thought the man must be stupid or naïve if he expected anyone to believe all he told them. At least, that was the opinion of Grace, her friends, neighbours and acquaintances around Four Lane Ends.

The wireless did much to brighten the evenings at that time with lively programmes such as 'I.T.M.A.' ('It's That Man Again'), 'In Town Tonight', 'The Old Town Hall' and 'Ray's a Laugh' among others. The voice of Vera Lynn belonged not only to Vera but to the whole nation as she helped to raise morale among the forces and folk at home alike.

Two of her most popular songs began with the words:

There'll be bluebirds over the white cliffs of Dover . . .

and

When the lights go on again all over the world . . .

Vera sang them with such sincere feeling that reassured her listeners and convinced them that the words would eventually prove to be true.

Stanley Illingworth
(Killed in Normandy 1944)

Yet, before that longed-for state of peace was finally attained, the cruel, ruthless side of the war showed itself in stark reality to the Four Lane Ends community when they heard the sad news that one of their boys would not be returning home. Stanley Illingsworth's family lived in the older of the two Pickliffes houses just off the Copster road, and were relatives of the Illingsworths in the middle cottage at Coates. Stanley was a dark-haired, slightly-built young man with a quiet, likeable personality. He had looked very smart in his soldier's uniform. As a member of the Durham Light Infantry he was with the Allied Expeditionary Forces in north-west Europe in 1944 and was killed in Normandy on the 14th of June, just eleven days short of his twenty-first birthday. When the wallet from his pocket was later returned to Stanley's mother, it was seen that a bullet had entered it and made holes in the two photographs it contained. One of these was of his girlfriend and the other of his cousin. A small, stainless-steel mirror behind the photographs had stopped the bullet from going right through. Stanley's mother, being one of Grace's personal friends, told her of how she had received the wallet; Grace tried to offer consolation as best she could.

Another local man who lost his life by enemy action during the war was George Wartigg from Bird Lane.

Bill Marsh of Bower Hill, Oxspring, had been a fit, healthy young man when he became a paratrooper earlier in the war. He wore the red beret proudly over his shock of auburn hair. While taking part in the airborne landings at Arnhem in 1944 he was taken prisoner. Because of ensuing experiences, his health was undermined so that, though he survived the war, Bill never again reached his former standard of fitness.

CHAPTER 18

Last Years at Coates Farm

WHEN THE WAR finally came to an end in 1945 the general feeling at Coates was one of relief and thankfulness that the fighting and killing had stopped. It was good to know that the menacing drone of enemy aircraft would no more be heard above them in the night sky, and that young men they knew would at last be free to come home. Throughout the war everyone had been aware that there were such places as prison and concentration camps, but it was only later, when people saw on the cinema screen the pathetic figures of gaunt, starving creatures recently liberated from those camps, that they understood the full horror of it all. Grace's family realised that, despite the rationing and austerity they experienced at home for six years and more, it was as nothing in comparison to what many others had suffered. They at Coates had certainly been amongst the more fortunate ones.

The rationing of food still continued. It was only slowly, over a period of several more years, that food, clothing and other goods were obtainable in larger quantities and with greater variety. For quite some time furniture, bedding, and many household items to be seen in the shops bore the 'utility' mark which signified they had been manufactured with economy of labour and materials. Yet, though the style of 'utility goods' was of necessity plain and simple, those articles were on the whole very durable and lasted far longer than many things made in later years. Meat was kept on ration until 1954. The difficulties experienced by butchers during the war still prevailed as they tried to satisfy their customers' wants. Black-market trading was rife and continued to be a thriving business for some of those who indulged in it.

By the end of the war, Grace's children were almost all grown up, except for the youngest, who was in his eighth year. Life at Coates carried on basically as before but with the inevitable changes that time brings about. Grace's second son, John, had the same love of farming and butchering as most of his Bramall forebears but, owing to the raising of the school-leaving age, had to remain at school until he was fifteen. At the age of eleven he had appeared to show no desire to attend the Grammar School, and refused to take the County Minor Scholarship examination even though his teacher declared he stood an excellent chance of passing. Grace was in favour of his trying for a place at Grammar School too, but John was adamant in saying he wanted to leave school as soon as he could. Whether this attitude to education was purely his own, or whether there were underlying influences that stemmed from his father's death, will never be known. The fact remained that John was thirteen when the war ended and already initiated into his future career. Though he enjoyed a game of football, and was reckoned to be a good player, he had to withdraw from the team on Saturdays because the meat hawking took priority on that day.

The house at Tunnel Top which had once been filled by the large Spenceley family had become strangely quiet, with Grace's father living there on his own, apart from at weekends when his son Frank came up from Sheffield. James Spenceley remained hale and hearty despite his age, looking after himself and tending his garden. Grace, Blanche and their daughters went to clean for him occasionally, but for the most part he was still actively independent. When one of his grandsons married, James, though nearing eighty, was one of the smartest men at the wedding, his immaculately-kept suit showing to advantage his tall, still upright and imposing figure. At the reception his enjoyment of the music and dancing was evident. His face showed delight as he joined in the waltzing, as if recapturing some of the youthful pleasure experienced at Mrs Neville's balls so long a time before. His grand-daughter Flora was not a little amazed at his vigour when he led her enthusiastically, yet in perfect rhythm, through the steps of a schottische.

James had an operation for a cataract in his eye when he was eighty, but made a good recovery. He was always able to read his newspaper with understanding, and kept his faculties until the day he died. His last years, however, were spent in the end cottage at Coates that had been previously occupied by the Thompsons. When Ned and Annie died, Grace and her sister persuaded their father to move into the vacant house in order to be near them. Tunnel Top was too lonely a place for him to be living there all by himself, they insisted, and James had to agree. At Coates he still retained his independence by having a house of his own, but could take meals and talk with his daughters when he so wished. There was also his next-door neighbour, Arthur Illingsworth, with whom he could chat about gardening, a subject of mutual interest.

It was Grace's father who, one morning at the end of 1947, climbed over the wall that divided the cottagers' yard from the farm lane to impart to her the sad news that Blanche had died very suddenly. It was a bad shock for them all, as there had been no warning. Though she had never enjoyed good health, there had been nothing to indicate that her condition had worsened. Blanche's youngest daughter, Myrtle, was perhaps the one to be most affected by her mother's death, since she herself had been in ill-health for several years.

Only a few weeks later, in the February of 1948, another sudden death occurred in the Spenceley family. George Herbert, the elder son of Grace's brother, Herbert, was accidentally killed at the age of thirty-four, being crushed by an excavator which he was teaching another man to drive. The accident happened on the road near Four Lane Ends, a place familiar to Grace and her relatives through so many years. It seemed ironic that her nephew as a soldier should come unscathed through six years of war, including the bitter fighting of the North African campaign, only to lose his life not long afterwards in a peacetime occupation so near his home. Sadly, Grace's brother Herbert was by that time an inmate of Storthes Hall, the mental hospital at Kirkburton where her Aunt Blanche had died. He had been taken there before the war because of his epilepsy. Herbert was not a mental case, but his wife had said she was unable to look after him on account of the fits. Grace worried over her brother being in an institution for the mentally ill, since he was quite a sane man and upset at being in such a place. In those days Storthes Hall was commonly spoken of as 't' 'sylum' and its inmates regarded as creatures to be shunned by the rest of society. Even the name had a forbidding sound, as it stood for a place which most people chose to ignore. Grace visited her brother at regular intervals, sometimes accompanied by one of her daughters, but having to leave him there at the end of the visit was hard for them both. There was nothing she could do, however, to allow him to return home. Had there been a way to help him she would certainly have taken it. As it was, Herbert had to learn of his son's death whilst already in unhappy state himself.

Later in that year happier events occurred to brighten Grace's life. She was gladdened to learn that her youngest son had won a County Minor Scholarship which enabled him to attend Penistone Grammar School. Philip could not remember his father, as he was only two and a half when Ernest died. Grace had brought him through those early years unaided, and it was natural that she should feel proud of his achievement. She had always encouraged him in his school work and shown interest in his progress, despite the pressures of all her other commitments.

Another pleasurable happening was the wedding of her brother Frank. He was the last of the large Spenceley family to marry. Whilst working on the railway in Sheffield during the war he met Dora who, like other women at that time, was doing a man's job as station porter. Dora was small, neat and trim, with a good sense of humour. Grace took a liking to her from the start. Frank and Dora made their home in Sheffield, but visited their relatives at Coates from time to time.

Then, at the end of 1948, Grace's eldest daughter got married to a farmer living in Hunshelf not far away. Needless to say, when there was decorating to be done in the old farmhouse, Grace was always ready to assist. Having had long experience in putting on wallpaper, it was she who took the lead in those operations, showing her daughter how it should be done. The rooms in that house were high, so the job of wallpapering involved much climbing on and off tables and ladders, yet Grace with characteristic energy did this as a matter of course. She was then in her fifty-sixth year.

Grace's youngest brother, Stanley, was tall and well built like his father. As a boy he had been strong, always appearing ready to partake in any rough and tumble that was going. After first working at Cammell-Laird's he had entered the Police Force, but unfortunately had to retire when he suffered from duodenal ulcers. This was a big disappointment for Stanley, who had enjoyed his work in the Force. He later became a boilermaker at the Stocksbridge works of Samuel Fox. The ulcers continued to trouble him from time to time, so that he often lost work due to prolonged stays in hospital and several operations. Stanley and his wife Carrie lived at Oxspring then, in a house near the Waggon and Horses Inn. They had no children of their own, but were always happy to make Grace's family welcome when they chose to call. In 1949, however, they carried out their long-considered plans to emigrate. Carrie already had a sister and niece in Australia, and she and Stanley went to live near them in Sydney. Later on they all moved to Melbourne, where they remained. Grace was sorry about their decision to emigrate, expressing her fears that they would not see one another again. Her assumptions were later proved to be correct. The night in February when the couple called in at Coates Farm to say their goodbyes was the last time Grace ever saw her brother and his wife. Strangely enough, Stanley's health improved in Australia. He was able to carry on working for most of the time until he reached retirement age. Both he and Carrie lived to their seventies, though they only paid one visit to England and that was in the year they died.

Grace did not dwell too long over the disappointment at seeing her brother go. After all, it was his decision to leave. In any case, she had other things to interest her. At the end of that year she experienced for the first time the joy of becoming a grandmother, when her daughter had a little girl. When, after a few weeks, the baby was very ill with pneumonia, Grace stayed up all night to minister to her, along with Mrs Davies who was a valued friend of her daughter. Luckily the child recovered after hospital treatment and grew up healthily.

On a June evening in 1951 Grace's father had tea with them at the farm, after which he took his usual walk to the beginning of the lane leading on to Far Coates. There was a seat conveniently placed near the junction of the lane with the road, and it was his habit to sit there to read his newspaper and watch the traffic passing between Coates Lane and Four Lane Ends. There were considerably more cars and lorries by that time than in the pre-war years. From his seat James could also look down on his old home, Travellers Inn, and see the Copster road leading to Thurgoland. Sometimes old Jim Matthewman, who was father to Alf, would walk along the lane from his home at Far Coates to sit on the seat too. He had done so on that particular evening. A third man who joined them was James's son-in-law, Frank Purseglove. After staying out for some time to enjoy the fresh air and conversation with the other two, the eighty-five-year-old James declared it was time for him to go home. He knew Grace would be going across to his cottage to make him the 'Bengers Food' he took before retiring for the night. On the short walk home, however, James fell at the edge of the kerb, bumping the back of his head, and had to be carried to his house. He was barely conscious, and died a few hours later. It was thought he had tripped over his stick while moving aside on the pavement to allow another man to pass him as they met. James Spenceley was very much missed at Coates and around Four Lane Ends. He had been highly respected, not only by his family, but also by the local community. He was always held in particular esteem by Winterbottom's, his former employers, at whose mill he had worked as a wiredrawer until he was seventy.

The year after her father died, Grace witnessed the innovation that heralded a major change in lifestyle for all the years ahead. The 6th of February 1952 was the day on which the king, George the Sixth, died. On that same day, workmen appeared in the yard at Coates Farm, their ultimate objective being to bring electrical power to the premises. As was to be expected, the work took a long time to complete, and there was much upheaval in the house during the process. It was fortunate for Grace that her younger daughter was living at home and willing to help with everything. Since leaving school at fourteen, Betty had worked locally and given her mother invaluable assistance at the same time. Catering, washing and cleaning for the family of five provided plenty of work when carried out by the old methods. The advent of electricity, however, was the beginning of a new order of things.

When the day of the big switch-on finally arrived, the situation at first seemed unreal. Grace had, of course, been in other houses and shops in town which already had electricity, so was not unacquainted with its power. It was the fact of actually having it in her own house that was so wonderful. Being able to light up a room at the touch of a switch instead of having to fill a lamp with paraffin, clean the wick and wash the glass was appreciated as a luxury. In due course, a Hoover cleaner was bought to obviate crawling around the floor on hands and knees with a brush and shovel. Even so, the fastidious Grace would take up the matting each week as before. She insisted that, while the Hoover did pick up efficiently from the surface of the matting, the dust which riddled through to the stone floor beneath must needs be swept up by the old method. Where carpets were concerned, however, she was delighted to find the new appliance was a real boon. The 'room' had, by that time, been furnished for several years. In fact, before Ernest died he had sanctioned the installation of a new tiled fireplace. He agreed that as the children grew up and no longer needed the room as a play area they would appreciate it more as a best sitting room. He had no objection to buying some good furniture when they were old enough to take care of it. So, some time after the new fireplace made its appearance, Grace had bought a carpet square to cover the white wooden floorboards. The corners of the room and sides where the carpet did not reach were covered with linoleum on which she could use Mansion polish to keep a good shine. She then bought a three-piece suite comprising two armchairs and a two-seater settee for twenty-one pounds ten shillings, drawing the amount of money from her Co-operative savings account. Cleaning the sitting room carpet with the electric Hoover seemed child's play after scrubbing bare floorboards on hands and knees for so many years. The upstairs cleaning was also much facilitated by use of the modern appliance.

The kitchen floor Grace continued to scrub, as the stone flags remained only partially covered during the rest of her years at the farm. Her scrubbing brush was still used in pantry and cellar too for cleaning the stone tables and floors, and, of course, for keeping up the high standard of cleanliness in the closet across the croft. Not until Grace left Coates Farm did that little place cease to be used, when the combined luxuries of bath, washbasin and toilet were installed to make a real bathroom from what had been her pantry. Knowing that she would probably be leaving the farm after a few more years, Grace did not consider it wise to spend hard-earned money on making major improvements to someone else's property. The landlord did not offer to provide those modern amenities that are now classed as essentials rather than luxuries, and at that time he was under no compulsion to do so.

Grace had never been trained to expect that life should be made easy all of a sudden, or to think that she had an unconditional right to the good things of life. From her earliest years she had learned to resign herself to doing without what could not be afforded and be thankful for the blessings that did happen to come her way. While continuing without complaint to fill and empty by bucket the old tin bath, and make those necessary journeys across yard and croft, she rejoiced in her latest blessing of electricity. She was not slow to seize the opportunities it laid open to her. The flat irons, which had to be heated in front of the fire bars and laboriously changed as they grew cold, were put to the back of the cupboard when the purchase of an electric iron proved that the job could be done more quickly and easily by that appliance. An electric kettle boiled water in a fraction of the time it took the iron kettle on the fire, so the early morning cup of tea could be had in a matter of minutes. Grace had sometimes used a Primus stove for boiling a kettle or pan in the absence of a fire or when the fire was slow in burning. She had found it to be a useful bit of equipment in the pre-electricity days. Even so, making one's cup of tea by means of the Primus was not exactly quick and effortless, since there were preliminaries to be attended to before heat was obtained. The stove had first to be filled with paraffin, methylated spirits had to be poured carefully into a little groove and lit, and, at the point when this was burnt away, the operator had to pump up the stove. This had the desired effect of producing the necessary ring of flame provided the pumping process had been started at the precise time. If one was a moment too soon or a moment too late at that vital stage of the operation, the flame did not materialise and the whole ritual of pouring and lighting a fresh lot of meths had to be repeated. Sometimes the tiny holes that allowed the passage of the jets of flame became blocked and had to be cleaned out with a metal pricker made specially for that purpose. Whilst requiring these certain attentions, it could be said in its favour that the stove gave a good, even heat once it was alight and in order. Grace had become accustomed to its vagaries during the time she used it and regarded it as an indispensable item of her kitchen equipment before electric power was brought to the farm. She still kept the Primus after getting electricity because she found it convenient for cooking chips and for frying and boiling occasionally, but where tea making was concerned she agreed that the electric kettle couldn't be beaten.

Some time later a small Belling cooker was bought, comprising an oven and one solid plate. Both Grace and her daughter considered it adequate for their needs. The coal oven in the house would still be used in cold weather when the fire was big, as it would be wasteful not to utilise the fuel for cooking too. The Belling was set up in the kitchen and its oven used for baking when a large fire was not needed in the house. The solid plate replaced the Primus stove to a great extent, though the latter was retained in case of emergencies.

Grace soon realised how much easier and more comfortable life could be with the aid of modern electrical equipment. Yet she did not immediately buy a new washer. Carrying on for a while with her Jiffy and tub, it needed her daughter Betty's persuasion to decide her to purchase what, in her opinion, was such a great luxury. When the Hotpoint washer, with its automatic rubber rollers, was put to use, she did not regret the decision, though she still used the set-pot for boiling clothes, lighting the fire as before.

All the new electrical goods were paid for in full at the time of purchase. One of the rules by which Grace had always disciplined herself and her family was that nothing should be bought unless it could first be paid for. This applied to furniture, clothing, and all household requisites, including electrical appliances, no matter whether they were large or small. Never in her whole life did she obtain anything for the house by hire-purchase. During her early years she had often been told, 'You must cut your coat according to your cloth.' To her way of thinking the words made good sense. She sometimes repeated the saying to her children as they were growing up, when ruling that they must only buy what they had the means to pay for. That way made sure they were never in debt.

Whilst Grace and her daughter were feeling the benefits of their new household items and, in a sense, catching up with the countless number of town dwellers already in a modern world, her sons were also savouring the delights of electricity. When lights were switched on in farm buildings and butchering premises, the old storm-lantern was put away along with the candlesticks. As finances allowed, an electric refrigerator ensured there was no more need for ice breaking on the 'clammin' 'oil' floor or mounting ladders to take up the ice by bucket. Later on, when slaughtering was again permitted on the premises, an electrical hoist was used to raise the huge beef carcasses from off the floor. This cut out the hard, physical work that winding them up by manual pulley had involved. Realising this as she watched its power with some awe, noting how effortlessly the job was done, Grace remarked wistfully to her sons that it was a pity their father hadn't known the easier method. No doubt she had a vivid picture in her mind of Ernest exerting his failing strength by heaving on the chain blocks.

When meat rationing at last came to an end in 1954, and restrictions were lifted, Grace's sons, working together, made the business flourish. Watching them proudly as they successfully expanded their trade, she saw how like their father they were becoming, not only in appearance but in methodical manner and shrewdness of dealing. As their father had done before the war, so did the brothers buy again for themselves the animals they needed, slaughter them on the Coates Farm premises and hawk the meat as before. Being aware of the advantages afforded them by electrical power, they soon were dealing with a greater number of animals, so that hoist and fridge were in constant use. A bigger van was bought to accommodate the increasing quantity of meat sold. Not long afterwards two vans were in operation. Looking on with satisfaction at her sons' obvious enjoyment of their work, Grace thought that the earlier struggles and sacrifices made during her husband's illness and in the unhappy time after his death had not been in vain. The aim of keeping the business together as a profitable living for her sons had been achieved. She knew too that Ernest would be well content if he could know his life's work was being continued and still prospering in their capable hands.

As in other periods of time, the years of the fifties brought changes within the family structure. Grace's eldest son was married in 1953 and took a house in Barnsley, travelling to Coates each day to do his butchering. In that same year she gained two more grandchildren when Phyllis had a second daughter and Norman had a son. 1953 ended sadly for everyone at Coates. Grace's niece, Myrtle, the youngest of her sister Blanche's four daughters, died on New Year's Eve. She was only thirty-six but had been in poor health for about twelve years. A quiet, gentle person, who never harmed anyone, Myrtle had been well loved by her Aunt Grace and cousins at the farm. She had made Christmas

cards and small gifts for them only the week before she died, a kind
gesture that was typical of her thoughtful, generous nature. No one
had really expected Myrtle to recover from the long-standing illness
affecting her lungs, but that did not lessen the feelings of sorrow when
she finally left them.

When, in the following year, Grace's second son married, he went
to live in the house at Pickliffes, off the Copster road, which had previously belonged to her old friend Betty Fieldsend and her husband
Randolph. Since their death the house was up for sale and John eventually bought it. Pickliffes was conveniently situated near to Coates,
so his continuing participation in the business presented no problems. The fact that there were a few acres of land attached to his new
home was an asset.

In 1955 the youngest son left home too, though not on a permanent
basis. At eighteen, Philip won a Major Scholarship which enabled
him to study languages at Oxford University. He was six feet tall by
that time and a physically strong young man. Though academic, he
was also fond of sport, particularly cricket, in which he excelled as a
bowler. During holidays he gave useful, practical help on his brother-
in-law's farm. When it came to lifting hay bales or forking sheaves of
corn, he was more than equal to any of the regular workers. Unlike
his two older brothers, Philip was generally regarded as being more
of a Spenceley than a Bramall. He bore a strong resemblance to pictures of his grandfather James when he was a young man. Apart from
the apparent likeness of face and figure, Grace maintained that many
of her father's characteristics and mannerisms had also been inherited by her youngest son. During his three years as an Oxford student
he spent most of the holiday periods living at Coates and working on
the Hunshelf farm. When he was away the household at Coates Farm
was reduced to only two people.

Just before the war there had been nine of them seated round the
table at tea-time. Reflecting on the changes that had taken place, she
thought how brief the seventeen years of her marriage had seemed.
They had been so full of bustling activity, with each moment of the
day bringing its allotted task, that she and Ernest had had little time
for outings, or sometimes even for talking together. He had once
remarked, during one of the difficult times, 'Don't worry, it won't
always be dark at seven,' implying things would be easier when the
children grew up. Yet it had not been decreed that Ernest should enjoy
a later leisure time in her company or that they should grow old together.
She had accepted his death as the will of God and knew there were

many other women who were widowed too because of the war, but, being only human, she had often wished he were there to talk to, especially when decisions had to be made concerning the children or the business. Without him she had strived alone to do her best for both. Her relatives and friends often marvelled at the wonderful way she had coped on her own when left with a business and five children to bring up. To the usual query of, 'However did you manage, Grace?' her reply was, 'It's as they say—the Lord prepares t'back for t'burden.'

With her family grown up and generally independent, Grace found she had at last some time to spare for herself. She was able to make a bus trip to Barnsley most weeks to look at the shops. Occasionally she went to Sheffield. Apart from looking at the shops there she sometimes took a tram to Beauchief to visit her friend, Mrs Hawnt. She had become acquainted with that lady in 1942 when they were next-bed neighbours in the Royal Infirmary. A friendship had ensued which was well maintained as long as they both lived, Mrs Hawnt making regular appearances at Coates until she became too infirm.

Among the outings Grace enjoyed most were the visits to Wakefield by train to have tea and talk with her cousin Madge. They had always kept in touch of course, even in the busiest years, but the visits then had been less frequent. Madge had kept house for a cousin for many years, but lived alone after he died. She never married. There had been Tom Ainsty with whom she was friendly as a young woman, but Tom had been killed in the first Great War and there was never anyone else for her. After her cousin died Madge, cheerful as always, refused to be idle. She worked in a local hospital until turned seventy, and devoted much of her spare time to helping charities, particularly those concerning spastic children. Knitting was an occupation at which she excelled, and over the years she donated many of her articles to worthy causes. She always welcomed the visits of her cousin Grace, when they could reminisce about their younger days together at Four Lane Ends. Among other things remembered they laughingly recalled the incident where Madge had been locked out of the house by their strict grandfather Herbert and threatened with his stick. It had seemed a serious, frightening episode at the time, but after fifty more years of living, during which greater troubles had been encountered, they could think of that happening in a more amusing light.

There were other trips which took Grace further afield during those post-war years. A Penistone woman organised annual excursions to places that included Sandringham and London, and invited her to join them. Grace welcomed the opportunity to meet other people and see different places, especially the capital city. She knew her husband would have enjoyed such trips if he had had the chance, but Ernest had never been south of Sheffield. When nephews and nieces were getting married about that time, she invariably received a wedding invitation though some of the other aunts did not. This was probably because she had always found time to take an interest in them as children.

When her son-in-law Charles bought an Austin car, he was pleased for her to accompany them on Sunday evening drives over the moors and surrounding countryside. Grace enjoyed those rides in the car. When Charles and her daughter pulled up to have a drink at an inn on the way home, she willingly stayed in the car with her two grand-daughters while the others went inside. Although she had been brought up in a public house she had never been used to drinking in one, and said she would feel out of place among all the men if she went in. Conceding that times had changed since her days at Travellers Inn, she did not mind her daughter going inside provided she didn't stay too long. Though she refused to go inside the inn, Grace accepted a drink in the car nevertheless. Charles supplied her with a port and lemon or two, her favourite drink, which she sipped appreciatively as she talked to her grand-daughters. The girls loved to have her for company, because she told them stories and sang with them until their parents reappeared. Her son John bought a little square Standard Eight car which could only be driven slowly. When he took her to Sheffield in it to see her brother Frank and his wife Dora, Grace said she enjoyed the drive because there had been chance to see everything properly owing to the slow speed at which they travelled.

Though she was able to broaden her horizons by seeing new places, she did not devote all of those days to herself entirely. That would have been totally out of character. On Sundays she and her daughter made dinner for Norman and his family. The rest of her family were always welcome to a meal whenever they called. She often made cakes for all her married children's families. At Christmas she gave each of them a home-made pork pie, fruit cake and plum pudding. The Christmas Days of those years were always spent at the farm, when Grace liked to have all her children and grandchildren around her. The number of grandchildren increased to six during the time she was at the farm, when Norman had a second son and John had two daughters. While recognising that her sons were managing the business efficiently and she could afford to relax from it to some extent, she continued to give help if it was needed. Many were the times she scrubbed out the large meat van so that they could press on with other work.

Of course she was always ready and willing to assist in looking after the grandchildren, to whom she was devoted. Sometimes they were left with her at the farm; at other times, particularly if it was a case of baby-sitting while the parents had an evening out, she would look after them in their own homes, putting them to bed as she had done for so many other children throughout her life. When any of them was ill, she was quickly on the scene to see what she could do.

Telling her daughter that the young ones were the third generation of babies she was looking after, she would relate how, as a girl, she had been obliged to tend her young brothers because of her mother's poor health and inability to manage them on her own. The reason why she had never followed the nursing career she fancied was because of home commitments. To her daughter's question of, 'Couldn't they have got someone else to do the housekeeping instead?' she replied, 'Oh, but you see there was our Harry. I wouldn't have left him to be looked after by anybody else. He had been used to me doing for him since he was little and had come to depend on me.' She told of her crippled brother and how she had lifted him about till he was twenty. She said she was pleased she had stayed with him as long as he needed her.

'Why didn't Grandad Spenceley get a wheelchair for you to push Uncle Harry about in, instead of carrying him?' Grace was asked next.

'That was something never thought about in those days,' she answered. 'I reckon if we were in the same predicament today we would have a wheelchair for him.'

One autumn morning, when she was in her sixtieth year, Grace walked the three miles to her son-in-law's farm in Hunshelf to assist in their potato picking. On arrival at the farm she did not go into the house for a preliminary rest and cup of tea, but went directly into the field and began work, assuring her daughter that that was why she had come. Throughout the day she kept abreast of everyone else in the field, actually picking more potatoes than many of the younger workers who had been engaged. Unlike some of them, she did not complain about an aching back or aching legs. Her legs probably did ache before the end of the day because, throughout her adult life, she had badly prominent varicose veins, which were attributed to her being so much on her feet and to having had a lot of children in a short space of time. Since she seldom mentioned the condition, her family tended to forget she had them, and even after the day's potato picking the subject of aching legs did not arise. Charles took her home by car of course and said he would have fetched her too had he known she was coming. Grace assured him that the morning's walk had done her good and, in any case, she would not have considered troubling him to fetch her when he was busy. That was not the only occasion when she went potato picking at Hunshelf, for she helped them several times during subsequent years.

In the autumn of 1950, Penistone Ploughing Association held its annual match at the Hunshelf farm. It was the custom at that time for the host farmer to provide mid-day refreshment for all competitors and their helpers. This usually took the form of meat sandwiches which were taken into the fields, together with drinks of tea, by the farmer's wife. The ploughmen could then eat and drink on the spot and, after the short break, continue ploughing until their allotted pieces of land were worked. On that particular occasion it was Grace who cooked the huge piece of brisket in her coal oven at home. The piece was one she had put in brine some time previously in readiness for such an event. After being slowly stewed in the oven for some hours the meat reached a tender perfection. It was taken out and pressed under weights in a large container until cold and firmly set. When sliced up for the sandwiches, that meat with its delicious flavour was unbeatable. At least, that was the general opinion of the consumers by whom it was very well received.

One day in the mid-fifties her son Norman surprised her with a gift. It was nothing less than that most modern of inventions—a television set. Admittedly it was only small, being a 9" Bush model which he had obtained second-hand from an acquaintance. There was nothing at all wrong with the little set. The reason for its sale was that the owner was buying a larger, more up-to-date model. Although the 'Bush' could only offer the single channel of BBC, Grace felt herself affluent indeed. She might never have indulged in such a luxury at all if left to her own devices, for, at that time, there were a great many people who did not own televisions. Her daughter at Hunshelf was among these, since they did not even get electricity until 1956. When buying the television for his mother, Norman evidently thought she was due for a little relaxed enjoyment in the evenings. To sit at ease while viewing the pictures certainly was a pleasant change from concentrating on mending and darning by lamplight as she had done on countless evenings over the years when her children were young. After some initial feelings of guilt at 'sitting down doing nothing', Grace soon adapted herself to life with television, and readily became acquainted with the programmes. One of her favourites was 'Dixon of Dock Green', shown on Saturday evenings. It told of episodes in the life of a London policeman and starred Jack Warner as PC Dixon.

Whilst she had been reluctant to buy a television for herself, she nevertheless surprised her family, friends and neighbours alike during those years of the fifties when she did make two important purchases. In each case Grace's new acquisition was a row of houses. With the help of the Building Society she bought a row of six terraced dwellings at Darfield, the other side of Barnsley, and the row of four houses known as Sycamore View next to the Waggon and Horses Inn at Oxspring. Considering she had left school at thirteen and had no formal instruction in such financial matters as property buying, it showed her as not lacking in initiative. Her intelligence and common sense of course enabled her to discover beforehand what the property was worth. She did her own bidding at both of the auction sales and it was generally considered that, in each case, she had secured good investments. Her idea behind the property buying was that her children would benefit from it in time to come, as indeed they did.

In the March of 1958, when she reached the age of sixty-five, Grace became what was commonly termed an old-age pensioner, though no one who knew her thought of her as being old. Only a short while before, someone had told members of the family that he had happened to see their mother as she was going home from the Four Lane Ends shop; he had expressed his amazement that 'she was running up t'road like a young 'un.' When she first began to fetch her pension money, she did so with some reluctance. Though she had been putting 'self-employed' stamps on a card for ten years in accordance with the 1948 Pensions Act, it was the first time in her life that she was actually handed money for which she had not visibly worked. Having been always accustomed to earning what she received by her own efforts, the money from the Post Office seemed strangely undeserved.

Despite the changes taking place during the post-war years, Grace had endeavoured to keep alive some of the old traditional customs of the earlier period at Coates. To her, the most important of these was the 'letting-in' of the New Year but, as time passed, this presented a problem. The Four Lane Ends boy who had been pleased to rise early at Christmas and New Year's Day and hurry eagerly to the farm in order to earn a precious sixpence, was a boy no longer. After twenty years there was no one to replace Jack Langley as a letter-in on a permanent basis. At least, there appeared to be no other boy of suitable age with the necessary dark-haired qualification. In any case, the custom of letting-in Christmas and New Year seemed to be generally on the wane in the whole area by the fifties, with very few children getting up early to sing carols at people's doors. It is possible that the newer generation of children did not lack for sixpences, or even shillings then, as had been the case before the war. From the time when Jack had ceased to be available on New Year's morning, Grace had resorted to asking one of the men from the cottages to make first entry into the farm-house. Though the carol singing was dispensed with and only the brief traditional greeting given, at least there remained the satisfaction of knowing that someone outside the family had performed the actual letting-in, which was the vital thing.

This was all very well until on one particular New Year's Eve another problem arose. Grace's daughter Betty had been invited to a party at Denby Dale, along with her friend Winnie Dawson from the middle cottage. They had stayed at the party long enough to 'see the New Year in' as they were dependent on a lift back to Four Lane Ends in the car of a couple who were then going forward to Thurgoland. Betty had been feeling a little uneasy at staying out so late, but since there was no other transport, and everyone else remained at the party until

after midnight, there was nothing she could do about it. On arrival at her door, the situation was as she had feared. The door was locked. She knew her mother would be waiting up as she always did until everyone was in, so made her presence known by knock-ing on the window, at the same time calling out a hurried explanation as to why she was late. Grace did not chas-tise her daughter, knowing that under the circumstances she could not be

The only cat to put in an appearance . . .

blamed, yet the situation did pose a dilemma. Making no move to open the door, she informed her in stringent tones that, as it was already New Year's Day, she mustn't be first to cross the threshold. To do that would be letting in their own New Year and could mean bad luck for the next twelve months. A brief silence followed during which Betty began to wonder whether she might have to spend the night in the barn. It soon became evident however that Grace had done a bit of quick thinking and had found a solution to the problem. She cer-tainly did not   intend to keep her daughter outside all night and, in the absence of a dark-haired man to let in their New Year, she had thought of a dark-haired substitute. 'Go fetch one of those black cats from down t'yard,' she called brightly. 'They're supposed to be lucky, aren't they. If you pop him over the threshold first, you can come in after him. That way we shan't be letting our own New Year in.'

There were usually three or four cats kept on the farm. They inhab-ited the outbuildings mainly and were not normally allowed in the house, but in the arising emergency an exception had to be made.

Complying with her mother's instructions, Betty hurried down to the bottom yard. She was beginning to feel cold and longed to get inside the house. After peering with her torch into various corners of the barn, mistal and henhouse, and making repeated calls of 'Puss', her attempts were not wholly successful. The only cat to put in an appearance was the black and white one, which Grace promptly rejected as being an unsuitable letter-in. The fact that it was partially white disqualified it out of hand, since blackness was the key factor of the whole business. In the event Grace had to modify the usual procedure still further by permitting the use of a different substitute. This took the form of a shiny black lump of coal which a much relieved Betty passed thankfully over the threshold before her as she finally stepped into the warm haven of the house. That method of letting in the New Year was used on subsequent occasions when members of the family went to the dance in Penistone's Town Hall. The New Year's Eve dance was one of the great annual events which was held in the town. It attracted a large gathering of people, not only from the town itself but from the outlying villages too. No one would have considered leaving the dance until long after the twelve resounding chimes from the church clock across the road heralded the start of another year. Grace had no wish to spoil her children's pleasure on those special occasions by urging them to be home early. She did not take the view that, because she had never been allowed to go to dances and stay out late, her children must do likewise. On the contrary she occasionally told them, 'I don't want you to have the kind of young life I had.' This did not mean that she condoned regular late nights, but a New Year's Eve dance only happened once a year and she was pleased for them to enjoy it. The piece of coal did duty as letter-in for a few more years, but before Grace finally left Coates Farm she allowed even that small bit of ceremony to lapse. The superstitions which had been instilled into her during early life died hard. Yet she gradually changed her thinking about the importance of the New Year's Eve custom, as shown by the remark made to her daughter. 'We've had our share of bad luck even in years that were properly let in, so I don't see that it makes much difference.'

The autumn of 1958 brought one of the happiest and proudest days in Grace's whole life. On the last day of October she journeyed to Oxford, accompanied by her two daughters, to see her youngest son being awarded a Bachelor of Arts honours degree. They travelled from Penistone by train on that Friday evening and Philip met them at Oxford station. He had booked some comfortable bed and breakfast accommodation for that and the following night. Next morning he showed them something of the town and the various colleges that make up Oxford University. They were much impressed by the age of some of those buildings and speculated as to what the scholars were like who, three or four centuries earlier, had studied there within the ancient walls. In the afternoon was the important ceremony when, with all due solemnity, the degrees were conferred. As she excitedly took her place in the Sheldonian Theatre then sat, happily relaxed, listening to the voices of the professors, Grace no doubt reflected on how the lives of ordinary working folk had changed for the better. It did not matter that she could not understand the Latin in which the ceremony was conducted. The fact that her son had been able to achieve a place amongst those learned ones was quite enough for her. It was good that better educational opportunities allowed the younger generation to follow careers that were to their liking. She thought of how her own aspirations to a career had been swiftly checked, and how her father, who had shown great promise as a scholar, had to leave school at eleven to become an errand boy. Philip was so like him. The one big difference was that her son was able to fulfil his potential as a scholar whereas her father had no such chance. Had he lived two generations later, James might have been there amongst the graduates that day. Things being as they were, he had made the best of what had been offered him.

When the ceremony was over they went for a stroll in Christ Church Meadows. It seemed the perfect ending to a wonderful afternoon. As if in keeping with the pleasures of the day, the sun shone warmly down to brighten and enhance the profusion of autumn colour around them. The trees on either side of the walkway still retained many of their leaves on that first day of November, but enough had already fallen to cover the ground thickly beneath their feet for the whole length of the walk. While they were in the Meadows, Betty took photographs of her brother in his black ceremonial gown with white fur-lined hood. One of Grace showed her small figure neatly smart in best brown costume and little pale blue hat made up of numerous tiny feathers. Smoothly overlapping one another, the feathers gave the hat a soft, velvety sheen. Back at Philip's lodgings, his landlady provided a good meal and put out glasses for them to have a celebratory drink. Grace and her daughters returned home next day after an unforgettable weekend. Philip stayed at Oxford for another year to do postgraduate teacher training.

The following summer marked the end of another chapter in Grace's life. In a sense it was the longest, for she had been at Coates Farm for thirty-three years, the longest time spent in any one house during her life. She had no strong desire to leave the house in which, at that point in time, she had spent exactly half her life. Memories of the years with Ernest still bound her to that house. It was the place where she had brought up her family and successfully launched them into the adult world. Though the years at Coates had brought sorrow as well as joy, she had long felt herself inseparable from the place. When the time came to leave, it was with mixed feelings that she did so. All things considered, from a practical, common-sense point of view it was for the best, and this she realised.

Since turning the business over to her sons, it was only fitting and more convenient that her eldest should live at the farm with his family, rather than travel from Barnsley each day. Another point to take into consideration was that, as she grew older, a smaller, easily-run house would suit her better. A satisfactory solution as to where she should go soon presented itself. The end cottage nearest the farm became vacant and everyone, including Grace herself, thought it ideal that she should rent it. By living there she would still remain at 'top o' t'Coits' and be near to the farm. She could still see her sons and their families frequently and continue to watch the progress they were making in the butchering business. So, in the summer of 1959, Grace moved across to the cottages, into the house which was to be her last home.

CHAPTER 19

Coates Cottages

WHEN ASKED BY a local man if she was happy at the prospect of living at Coates Cottages, Grace replied, 'I would rather have been going back to t'Travellers.' No doubt nostalgic memories of her younger days at the inn remained in spite of the hardships encountered there.

The move from farm to cottage coincided with her youngest son's return from Oxford. Philip had completed his educational qualifications successfully and been offered a position as language master at Barnsley's Holgate Grammar School. He was to travel daily, which meant Grace would have his company most evenings. Knowing this, on the first of August her daughter, who was interested in working with children, took up a residential post in child care at Scholes, near Holmfirth. She would of course still visit Coates frequently on off-duty days.

After being involved with the bustle of the meat business for so long and accustomed to her sons walking in and out of the farmhouse at regular intervals, Grace found her days at the cottage quiet by comparison. Generally speaking though, she adapted well to her new situation and settled down happily. When the subject of possible loneliness was once broached to her, a member of the family jokingly offered a solution. Knowing that Grace had a good sense of humour and would take his suggestion in the light-hearted spirit in which it was meant, he said teasingly, 'You'll have to find yourself a rich old fellow. There are plenty of women older than you who get married again.' As half-expected, Grace's answer caused mirth all round. 'What!' she exploded laughingly. 'You wouldn't see me darken that church door again, not even if his neck were hung round wi' sovereigns.' This apt way of expressing her sentiments was received with much amusement, but the words had been spoken with such conviction that they left no doubt of the truth. Grace had definitely no wish to remarry.

One thing she missed in her cottage house was the morning sun. At the farm her bedroom and the main living room beneath had windows facing east so, when there was sun at all, it was seen to advantage and gave a bright start to the day. By contrast, her cottage and the one adjoining had their main rooms, windows and front doors facing north. The cottage at the other end of the block was the only one of the three to have an eastern frontage.

The front door of Grace's house was two steps up from the roadside pavement and led straight into the 'house' or living room. Improvements had been made to the premises since the time twelve years earlier when her sister Blanche had died there. Hot water was on tap, and one half of the big back bedroom had been converted into a bathroom and toilet. Grace could therefore savour again the delight she had briefly known during her days at Willow Lane, that of using a bath which filled and emptied itself with water that required no heating on her part. The earth closet fell almost into disuse, receiving only ashes from the fire. The stone stair steps, down which she and her small niece had hurtled many years before, had been since covered over with wood. In the living room the old black fire range had been replaced by one that was more labour-saving. Though this too had a side oven, which was heated by the coal fire, very little effort was needed to keep it clean. The tiled and enamelled surfaces required only a quick wash over, which took far less time and energy than did the hard brushing to achieve a shine on black lead. The sitting room boasted a modern tiled fireplace too. At the back of the house a porch had been added to the kitchen for greater warmth and protection from winds and weather. In her sister's time working in the kitchen had been cold in the winter months since there was no heating and the back door opened directly into the yard outside.

Electricity had of course been installed in the cottages seven years earlier at the same time as it reached Coates Farm. Though Grace had a small pantry for food storage, after a while she acquired an electric refrigerator because there was no cellar or 'keeping' place in the cottage. At the farm she had had the use of the butcher's fridge across the yard as well as the cool cellar in the house. She had often found the cellar suited her needs as efficiently as a fridge. Meat remained fresh for a considerable time down there, and jellies did not take long to set on the stone, table-like slab. Grace had no need, therefore, for a fridge until she moved house. The one bought then was an 'English Electric'. It is still in use and giving good service.

The cottage was quite adequate for the family of three, having that number of bedrooms in addition to the bathroom. Downstairs were the three main places of living room, sitting room, and kitchen.

During her second year at Coates Cottage, Grace joined a group of elderly Thurgoland people for a week's holiday at Margate. It was the first full week's seaside holiday she ever had, as the venture to Black-pool more than twenty years previously had only been for three days' duration, inclusive of travel. She enjoyed the week at Margate but, on returning home at the end of it, was shocked to learn that her sister-in-law Hilda had been killed. Ernest's youngest sister had been acci-dently knocked down by a motorbike and sidecar near her home on Dodworth road at Barnsley. She and her husband, Joe Elsworth, had taken a house there when he retired from farming and handed down the business to his sons.

In the following year Grace took a similar holiday. When she returned it was to discover that her own sister Mary, then living near Sunder-land, had had a stroke and was not likely to recover. Grace made the journey by train to see her, but though Mary was able to speak a little and showed signs of recognising her sister, she died soon afterwards. Grace declared she would take no more such holidays since they had twice ended in sorrow. Both Hilda and Mary had been members of her close family circle and, in their youth, friends to each other, being of the same age and living near together at High Oxspring.

There was, however, a pleasurable event which took place in 1961. Grace was chosen by the Oxspring community to perform the impor-tant task of opening their gala and crowning the Gala Queen. She regarded this as an honour accorded to her, particularly as the girl to become 'queen' was her great-niece Pamela Spenceley, daughter of her brother Willie's son, Edwin. Everyone reckoned Grace to be an ideal person to open the Gala. She had lived almost the whole of her life in or near to Oxspring. She had attended the school there on weekdays and Sundays, and in later life had always been helpful and generous in contributing towards needy causes. Being such a well-known and respected figure of the Oxspring scene, she was generally considered to be deserving of the honour.

The event went very well. Before she crowned the queen and declared the Gala open, Grace made a short preliminary speech to the assem-bled crowd. She expressed her thanks for having been invited, and said it gave her much pleasure to be there to perform the opening cer-emony. Telling of her long and close association with Oxspring, she spoke of her schooldays there and life in the village as she knew it when young. Commenting on the changes that had taken place since that time, she felt that most of them were for the better. The poverty she had witnessed as a child had fortunately disappeared, and there were more opportunities in life than formerly, which was a very good thing. Grace enjoyed her day at the Gala and looked back on it after-wards as a memorable occasion in her life.

In the November of 1961 she became a member of the Thurgoland Church Mothers' Union, and participated whole-heartedly in its activities for the next few years. She had had neither time nor opportunity when her children were young to commit herself to regular involvement with the organisation; she had not even gone to church on a regular basis, much as she would have liked to. In those days an insistence that 'Religion's as you live' had to suffice. Grace certainly tried to live up to the Christian ideals throughout her life, whether or not she was attending church at the time. Remarks she made to her children such as 'Two wrongs don't make a right', and 'If you can't do a good turn, don't do a bad one' were remembered by them as sayings which she put into practice. The well-known rhyme of

Good, better, best.
May we never rest
Till our good is better,
And our better, best.

was one that she always tried to follow when living her life, and often quoted to her children in the hope they would do likewise. All the same, she welcomed the chance to renew her church association when it came. On retiring into the cottage, and consequently having fewer commitments, she resumed the Sunday attendances at church as she had done before her marriage. She made many friends amongst the Mothers' Union members and enjoyed helping in the social and fund-raising events they held from time to time.

In 1962 Grace and her younger daughter paid another visit to Oxford, their purpose being to see Philip receive his Master of Arts degree. As on the previous occasion, it was a proud day for Grace. Philip wore his ceremonial black gown but, instead of the white fur trimming, the hood which draped behind his shoulders had a lining of crimson satin. This signified his advancement to the higher degree. Grace had ensured that her own appearance would not fall short on the grand occasion. She was neatly costumed as before but, in addition, wore round her shoulders a fur stole which had been pressed upon her by her daughter-in-law. She had been rather reluctant to borrow it as she had never adopted the habit of using other people's things, especially clothes. After the ceremony Betty took a photograph of her mother and brother. It shows Grace's fur-clad figure appearing quite small as she stood happily beside her tall young son in his gown and mortar-board hat.

During the early years of the sixties she still gave valuable help to her family, even after she passed the age of seventy. She enjoyed talking with her grandchildren and displayed the same patience to them

Grace and Philip at Oxford

as she had done towards their parents. Many were the meals she made for her grandchildren when they called on her, and often were the occasions when she took them for walks down Bird Lane. At times when she visited the homes of her married children she was never idle but would attack any dirty pots that happened to be on the sink, wash children's socks, help with meal preparation, and generally seize on any job that needed doing. To make things clean and tidy was second nature to Grace. When she finally did sit herself down, it was usually with some item of mending in her hands. She acquired two more grandchildren during those years. Her son John, who already had two girls, added a boy to his family in 1961. Her eldest daughter at the Hunshelf farm had a third daughter three years later. On the morning she came home from hospital with the new baby, it was to a spotlessly clean and shining house, to a cheerfully warm living room with brightly burning coal fire, and the delicious smell of an appetising, freshly-cooked dinner. Grace had ensured, by her efforts in taking care of the practical requirements, that the best possible welcome would be accorded them.

The television continued to give pleasure in the evenings. In December 1963 the small 9" Bush set was exchanged for a larger black and white model priced at £63. Together with the aerial the actual cost was £64 13s 9d. The new set was a decided improvement on the first one, for it had the Independent Television Channel as well as the BBC. Grace soon became addicted to watching 'Coronation Street', which remained her favourite programme for a long time.

An occupation from which she derived pleasure and satisfaction in her later years was gardening. One Sunday afternoon her son-in-law came down from Hunshelf and helped Philip to clear the piece of waste ground between her house and the farm lane. This 'top garden' had, many years before, been a rough, stony playground for the Purseglove children. By dint of some effort the two men transformed it into a lawn with centrepiece and surrounding border for flowers. Once it was in order Grace spent much time in tending the plants and generally keeping the garden looking nice. On hot summer afternoons she allowed herself a little time in a deck chair on the lawn where, relaxed, she could view the results of her efforts.

She remained in her usual good health until the end of 1965. Just before Christmas she had a slight stroke which only temporarily affected her leg. It did nothing to dampen her spirits and she was soon up and about again.

In 1967 her youngest son got married to a Finnish girl he had met in Hamburg. They were on the same summer course in German at the time, as Liisa also was a teacher of that language. Their first home after marriage was at Silkstone Common, so Grace saw them frequently. She was delighted when, in the next year, they had a son, to be followed two years later by a daughter.

Grace lived long enough to see all but one of her grandchildren. She saw the eldest of them achieve a University degree and start her career. During her lifetime she had witnessed astounding changes in society. At the end of her days there was a higher standard of living throughout the country than she had ever known, or even thought could be possible when she was young. Most of her relatives and acquaintances over a wide area had their own cars, using them for going to work and for pleasurable outings too. All her children, and some of the grandchildren, were amongst the growing number of car drivers. They were also amongst the increasing numbers of English working-class people who were savouring the delights of holidays abroad, making their journeys by ship and aeroplane. Grace was glad to see the younger generation experiencing pleasures she had not encountered. At the same time she often remarked that life was becoming rather too fast, so that people were missing things that had been enjoyed by her contemporaries. She also held the view that, despite an easier, more affluent way of life, there were many people who still appeared to be discontented. For her part, she seemed satisfied to see her family happy, and asked little else for herself. Her daughter, thinking of her welfare, sometimes asked if she would prefer to live in a bungalow in preference to the cottage, but though they actually went to look at a few, Grace maintained she would rather stay at Coates.

When she was seventy-five she suffered another stroke which was more severe than the first. Even so, she recovered sufficiently to get around again and resume her interest in the garden. When indoors she occupied her spare time with embroidery and knitting squares which were afterwards sewn together to make a sizeable blanket. Outings in the car continued to give her pleasure. She accompanied her daughters on shopping trips, visited her cousin Madge at Wakefield, and had enjoyable rides around the countryside. Sometimes they would drive through the village of Cranemoor to take a look at Victoria Tavern, the house which had been Grace's first home. Venturing further afield, she was taken by her daughter for holidays in Wales and on the east coast.

Grace lived to be eighty years old. During the last two years of her life she sometimes became confused with events. Betty then gave up her residential position and took a daily job in order that her mother should have company in the house at nights.

Ever mindful of her welfare, Betty thought she might like to watch a colour television in preference to the black and white one. So in August 1973 a colour set was purchased and installed in the sitting room. As things transpired, Grace did not have long to enjoy it. Three months later, on the day of Princess Anne's wedding, she was ill and confined to her bedroom. She was unable to witness the colourful spectacle of that Royal Wedding on television.

Through the following days, friends and relatives visited her as the serious nature of her condition became known. Mr Thompson, who had been vicar of Thurgoland church when Grace was attending there, came all the way from Huddersfield where he had since taken up work at another church. His wife came with him. On the evening when her niece Mary Emma stood by her bedside, the smile on Grace's face spoke more than words. It conveyed a special warmth to the one who had loyally helped and shared with her those busy and often hard days of the twenties and thirties.

During the last few nights of her life, her daughters took turns at staying up with her in the bedroom, in case she asked for anything. Each of them had one night of strange experience.

After one of Betty's turns of vigil, her sister enquired next morning as to how their mother had been during the night. Betty was smilingly bemused as she related how Grace had been awake most of the time but had appeared happy in an unusual sort of way. She had been talking quite a lot, and though the words were unintelligible they gave the impression that she was addressing them to someone she was seeing and of whom she was very fond. Phyllis was puzzled by the account, but the next night, when it was her turn to stay up and watch, the same thing happened again. Grace woke in the middle of the night and, half sitting up, began to talk quickly. What she said did not make words in the accepted sense, yet the manner of her conversation was the same as it had been during her days at the farm. Her face had an expression of great elation as she talked with brisk animation to someone only she could see. Pausing at intervals as if listening to others, the talking went on for a long time. At one point she reached forward her arm in a gesture that implied she was drawing a child towards her. Then, being aware of the daughter seated by her bedside, she drew her into the conversation too. It seemed from her joyful manner and convincing gestures that she was telling her about the others. The confidential way of speaking, together with a little intimate laughter from time to time, was reminiscent of her conversations of former years. The laughter, intimacy of talk, and obvious elation caused her daughter to join in the laughing too. She thought it a strange situation for them to be sitting up laughing together in the middle of the night when Grace was actually dying, yet she was happy to see her mother so. When morning came and she told her sister, they agreed the two nights had been uncanny. The fact that each had had a similar experience seemed significant. It was as if, through their mother, they had been allowed a tiny glimpse of the great unknown.

Grace left her earthly life peacefully in the early morning of November 23rd, as both her daughters stayed beside her. When, a few days later, she finally moved away from Coates, it was first to a service in Thurgoland church, a place where she had often worshipped and for which she always had affection. The day was bright and clear, with a frosty crispness in the air, as the procession of cars drove slowly along the Copster road. Grace was borne into the church and carried out high on the shoulders of her nephews.

After the service, when the journey to Penistone was resumed, it seemed only fitting that it should be by way of Four Lane Ends and the Jockey road, so passing close by Travellers Inn, Willow Lane and Tunnel Top, those three dwellings in which she had lived much of her life. Travelling down the long hill from Hoylandswaine crossroads to Bridge End, the cortege then made its way to Stottercliffe cemetery where she was laid to rest with her husband and little son Frank.

Back at Coates Farm the family gathered together with their many relatives and friends. They talked of Grace, of a brave life and work well done. As they talked, their feelings were happy rather than sad, for it seemed, in that house, she was amongst them still.

Postscript

TWENTY-ONE MORE years have passed since the end of the story. The only member of James and Elizabeth Spenceley's large family to survive to the present time is Grace's brother George. Since retiring from farming, he and his wife Elsie, both now in their nineties, have lived in their bungalow at Hoylandswaine. The only other Spenceley relative of that generation now living is Frank's widow Dora.

Flora Purseglove, the niece who had to work in a mill at fourteen instead of continuing her studies, did further her education in later life and gained an English 'O'-Level when in her fifties.

Of Grace's children, four only remain, as John died three years after his mother. Many of her relatives of the present generations still live in the Oxspring and Penistone areas, but some are further afield. One grandson visited South Africa in the course of his work, thus achieving something his grandfather Ernest had hankered after but never had a chance to attain. One of the grand-daughters is currently living and working in Australia. Philip's two eldest children have followed him in the educational field by obtaining Oxford University degrees and are embarked on professional careers.

So have horizons widened, and such is the relentless tread of time, that already members of the youngest generation are discussing computers and technology in terms that would seem alien to Grace, their great-grandmother.

To write further of Grace's children and grandchildren, however, not to mention the great-grandchildren, would be another story.

Index